FOR THE TIME BEING

Collected Journalism

DIRK BOGARDE

VIKING

VIKING

Published by the Penguin Group
Penguin Books Ltd, 27 Wrights Lane, London w8 5tz, England
Penguin Putnam Inc., 375 Hudson Street, New York, New York 10014, USA
Penguin Books Australia Ltd, Ringwood, Victoria, Australia
Penguin Books Canada Ltd, 10 Alcorn Avenue, Toronto, Ontario, Canada m4v 3b2
Penguin Books (NZ) Ltd, 182–190 Wairau Road, Auckland 10, New Zealand

Penguin Books Ltd, Registered Offices: Harmondsworth, Middlesex, England

First published 1998
1 3 5 7 9 10 8 6 4 2

Copyright © Motley Films Ltd, 1998

Set in 12/14.5pt Monotype Bembo
Typeset by Rowland Phototypesetting Ltd, Bury St Edmunds, Suffolk
Printed in England by Clays Ltd, St Ives plc

A CIP catalogue record for this book is available from the British Library

ISBN 0–670–88005–1

This book is for
John Coldstream and his wife, Sue,
with my love and gratitude

CONTENTS

LIST OF ILLUSTRATIONS

Endpapers: Christmas in Sussex, *c.* 1931, by Dirk Bogarde (copyright © author's collection)

Frontispiece: Dirk Bogarde, 1993 (copyright © Jane Bown)
Plate section
  1. Aged five (copyright © author's collection)
  2. On leave from the army, 1944 (copyright © author's collection)
  3. With Bertrand Tavernier, 1991 (copyright © Jeanne-Louise Bulliard/Sygma)
  4. At the Olivier Theatre, 1993 (copyright © Julian Calder)
  5. With Charlotte Rampling, 1985 (copyright © author's collection)
  6. With Joseph Losey, 1962 (copyright © Canal + Image U.K. Ltd)
  7. Theo Cowan, 1976 (copyright © Universal Pictorial Press)
  8. With Brigitte Bardot, Pinewood, 1954 (courtesy of CTE (Carlton) Ltd)
  9. With Kathleen Tynan, 1981 (copyright © author's collection)
 10. At Hatchards (copyright © Alan Grisbrook)
 11. With Katharine Whitehorn at St Andrews University, 1985 (copyright © D. C. Thomson & Co.)
 12. Russell Harty, 1986 (copyright © author's collection)
 13. With Luchino Visconti, 1970 (copyright © Mario Tursi)
 14. With Norah Smallwood, 1980 (copyright © author's collection)
 15. With Glenda Jackson, 1981 (copyright © author's collection)
 16. With Candida (copyright © Roddy McDowall)

Text illustrations by Richard Cole

All text illustrations were first published in the *Daily Telegraph*.
Copyright © Richard Cole

INTRODUCTION

On Wednesday, 18 September 1996, I went into hospital for what was considered to be a minor operation. Relatively speaking, I suppose it *was* more or less minor: the removal or bypassing of a main artery in my right leg, which had started to fur up and which for more than a year had caused me agony. I once caught sight of myself in a mirror at Peter Jones, with tears of pain pouring down my face, which was ridiculous. So I arranged to have it dealt with. I was told the whole thing would take between five and ten days.

I packed a small case with toothbrush and razor, watered the house-plants, locked my flat and went out to the hired car. It was mid-afternoon. No one was about: above all, no reporters or photographers, who sometimes used to lurk in these environs. In good spirits, I set off with one of my regular drivers to a hospital which I knew very well, not just as a visitor: I had been a patient there myself. So I was really like a favoured guest returning to a small hotel. The day before, I had delivered the manuscript of my new novel, *Closing Ranks*, to my publishers in Kensington. My editor was on leave, but I thought it was more 'orderly' if the book was out of the way while I was in hospital. We arrived, and I told my driver that I would telephone to let him know when to pick me up – in about a week's time.

I had to fill in the usual hospital forms: name, address, date of birth, etc. and next of kin. This was vexing. I had never really thought about next of kin. I realized that they must be my sister, who is three years younger than I am, and my brother, fourteen years younger. Elizabeth was happily buried away in a cottage in West Sussex, surrounded by grandchildren whom she adored and with a car quite capable of getting her to Worthing for Marks & Spencer; but she had never driven to London, so I didn't see much help coming from that quarter if I suddenly needed it. Gareth was constantly flying to Moscow and LA and any other area of the globe where his attention and expertise were needed. It would therefore be difficult to summon him to arrange coffins or whatever next of kin had to do (I was shortly to find out). So I nominated his eldest son, Brock, whom I liked enormously and who seemed to like me. He lived in Wandsworth with his wife, Kim, and their two young children, and was extremely sensible, level-headed and willing, quite apart from being thoroughly capable. So, with that information handed over, I got into my bed and prepared myself for whatever might be coming.

What came was a posse of nurses and consultants. There were more consultants than I had ever known existed. Cardiologists, neurologists, anaesthetists – the only one lacking was a gynaecologist. I don't remember much about what happened once they had gone. I think I watched a bit of television and went to sleep. I had, incidentally, not told anyone where I was, apart from Elizabeth, who was particularly worried that I had taken with me neither pyjamas nor slippers, as I didn't wear them. She said if I didn't have them I would cause a lot of trouble. I said I would manage, and we left it at that.

The following morning, having had nothing to eat or drink (I was a 'nil-by-mouth' patient), I was carted down to the operating-theatre. The next thing I remember is coming through the blur of anaesthetic and wondering what everybody was doing. I was in the intensive-care unit, surrounded by people who all seemed cheerful enough. The nurses and doctors were pleased: the operation had, I gathered, been a triumph. It had taken four or five hours – so much for 'minor'. I was hauled to my feet and encouraged to give a urine sample; a bit undignified, I thought, but I was soon to learn all about the loss of dignity. I suddenly felt the ground beneath me begin to give way. I shouted out: 'I'm going!' And a man's voice said: 'Going where?' I replied: 'I don't know, but stop me!'

I have always believed that life is a series of corridors, down which you can go at your leisure. Along both sides are doors, open, shut or ajar. All are marked 'opportunities'. You can go through them if you wish, or ignore them. The only door you can *not* avoid is the one at the end, on which is printed the word 'death'. I was being pulled towards it, down my own metaphorical corridor.

I gathered from the nurses some while afterwards that I swore enough for an entire army, using words they had never heard of and words that I had never heard myself. I was being urged to hold on, and I fought and struggled. I only remember calling out: 'I'm not ready, I'm not ready! Not yet!' And that was the end of me.

When I next came to, in the gloom of the intensive-care unit, the shadowy figure of a pretty little nurse was leaning over a huge ledger at a desk lit by a single lamp. I asked where I was. Somewhat startled, she told me, then offered me a drink and a change of pillows. I lay there, bewildered, and when I next opened my eyes it was to see a weary Brock sitting anxiously beside me. I smiled at him. He smiled back, and patted my arm.

For at least a week I was sedated. Only when I emerged from the hazy distance could I talk to Brock. Talk is not quite the right word. I realized that something had gone wrong with my speech and that I was dribbling rather a lot, as he kept wiping my chin with a tissue. By now, although vocally impaired, I was more or less *compos mentis*. I could hear. Everyone on the ward had been worried that I might not be able to swallow, but I could sip water and take my pills. I was surrounded by drips and feeds and oxygen: in fact, I seemed to be wired up to just about every piece of equipment under the sun. I could not understand truly what had happened. Brock said that the operation had been a success, but that I was to lie still and get strong. I began to be fed through small china or plastic cups with spouts on them. Life wore on. I did what Brock told me and gradually grew stronger.

By this time I had been in hospital for two weeks. Brock had, thankfully, taken over my entire life. He had told everyone in the family of my situation and gave them reassurance. He had called my publishers and one or two of my close friends, like Maude (the 'Swiss army knife'). He gave instructions that I was to receive no visitors for the time being, apart from my solicitor, Laurence

Harbottle, with whom I discussed the new problems in my life; it was now quite clear that I would have to put Brock in charge of my fortune, such as it was – to sign cheques, pay my daily lady and generally do for me all the things I could no longer do for myself. Little did I know at the time, thank God, that I would never again be able to do anything for myself.

The only other person who knew was my editor at the *Daily Telegraph*, John Coldstream, for whom I used to write book reviews. He was allowed to come to see me every Sunday, which he did faithfully; he also sent me a postcard almost every day. One thing I had overlooked when I set off so complacently for hospital was to leave a message on the answerphone. People would call from time to time and receive nothing but a constant ringing tone. I can't remember now how this came to my notice, but after about four weeks Brock agreed that we should make a short, discreet statement. We did so, via the *Daily Telegraph* and the Press Association: sharp-eyed readers may have picked it up.

From my bedroom window I could see the roofs of a row of houses, with curtains of varying colours and sizes; the Post Office Tower; and the branches of what looked like a plum tree. It was by now mid-October, the leaves were falling urgently, it was quite cold and I was extremely comfortable. I was allowed to watch television – my only means of seeing what the outside world was like. People began to find out where I was and flooded me with postcards, which Brock stuck all over the walls. One of these he had bought himself, cut into a circular shape and positioned in the place of honour, above my bed. It was of Diana, Princess of Wales. She had arrived unannounced one day, sat down on the edge of the bed, took off her gloves and said she had come to 'pay homage'.

Being by nature a lazy fellow, I found this enforced idleness rather enjoyable. I loved the nurses, and they were equally kindly disposed towards me. The one thing I did not like was being on a 'sloppy diet', which had been essential until it was established whether or not I could swallow. So far, so good. The dribbling gradually stopped and my speech returned more fully. I pleaded for a whisky and was told that once I had taken the nauseating vitamins, or whatever they were, I would be allowed a glass of whisky which I could drink through a straw. This was an agonizing procedure, but I managed. I have not touched a drop of whisky since.

Every week or two, all the consultants met in a small room next to Matron's office to discuss my situation. Brock was asked to attend, and one day I was invited too. I was wheeled down in my chair, to find them all standing around like penguins. I asked about my progress. Each one said I was doing very well, but it was a tortuous business. It would take a long time, and I would have to be patient. I had realized by this stage that my left leg, arm and hand were incapable of movement. It didn't matter so much in bed, but it did everywhere else. I asked how long this would continue and everyone said: 'Oh well, it depends.'

I asked nervously if it meant that I would never be able to walk again and that I would be wheelchair-bound for the rest of my days. They all looked uneasily at each other or at their fingernails. I was told it depended on how determined I was, that it would take time, that you can't rush health. So I became faintly absurd and said I wished somebody would tell me the truth. There was more shifting about, and I could see that Fiona, my adorable nurse, was ashen-faced and willing me to shut up. But I pressed on and pleaded to be told the facts. 'If I'm going to be paralysed and in a wheelchair for the rest of my life, I'd much rather be given something and be put to sleep. I want euthanasia.'

Everyone, including Brock, turned bright red, which for some reason made me angry. Then the doctors repeated that I had to understand: health could not be hurried. I was getting a bit fed up with this. No one seemed to want to be honest with me.

In a very bad mood, I was wheeled back to my room by Fiona. She said nothing, but Brock did when he arrived a few minutes later. He was boiling with anger at my childishness. 'Look,' he said. 'This is your situation. You will be in a wheelchair for the rest of your life. You probably won't be able to move your left hand. You are, in fact, paralysed on your left side after a colossal stroke. A fine way of thanking them for all their kindness and help in trying to

get you better, to ask for euthanasia when you're not even in pain!'
I looked at him in shock. 'What do I do?' I asked. He said: 'Go
and have physio, and work really hard. See what *they* can do for
you and what *you* can do for them.'

At least I had the truth, flatly and unsparingly told. I now knew
that I would not walk again, or do anything with my left arm,
unless I tried to help myself, which meant going to the gym every
day and doing all the exercises which I loathed. However, I realized
I had to give it serious thought. I asked Fiona if she could alert the
physiotherapy team and say that I was coming down for a full
assessment. That evening, staring at the television, I came to terms
with my predicament. There was no alternative.

Down I went to the gym, to be met by two hearty young ladies.
They were welcoming and warm, but, by their expressions, doubtful
about what they could do for me. However, we persevered. The first
thing I was taught was how to transfer myself from my wheelchair to
the bed in the gym – not as easy as it looked, but after a couple of
days I began to crack it. On about the fourth morning, while
being wheeled to the gym, I had another attack. Again the floor
disappeared and I was in my 'corridor', choking and screaming.
The black door at the end was open. I fought like mad. At one
point I decided to give up. There wasn't much future for me, as
far as I could see. I might as well simply go through that door. But
I didn't. I battled on. And I found myself back in intensive care.
Apparently I had had an embolism, due no doubt to the exertion
I had been putting into the physiotherapy.

Despite the setback, things steadily improved. After a week, I
was returned to my room and stared at the Post Office Tower. I
was taken off the sloppy diet and allowed to eat a bit of toast, which
I did nervously but successfully. Once back on proper food, I began
to perk up. I had seen my face while trying to shave and thought
I looked like an El Greco saint. I was told to put on weight before
I could do any real exercises. So I ate porridge, toast, butter and
egg-and-bacon sandwiches, which I made with one hand, very
proudly.

The week before Christmas, I was allowed to come back to the flat, having been passed fit to cope – which was, to say the least, optimistic. Anyway, I was pleased to be rid of the Post Office Tower and the plum tree.

I was frightened of the prospect of the flat, after so long. All was in order, however. A very obliging nurse, who hated Christmas as much as I did, came back with me to see me over the first hurdle. The wheelchair in my sitting-room was not at all comfortable or easy to manoeuvre with one arm, but Brock and Kim had fitted the flat with all kinds of devices: rails for my bed, so I didn't fall out; hand-grabs all over the place; a commode; and just about every other reminder of indignity you can imagine – plus a mobile phone, which, although detestable, has proved useful.

A year or so later, here I still am, unable to do anything for myself. I am nursed day and night, and have to be turned. But there is the television and unlimited reading matter. As of this moment, however, a vague sense of feeling might be returning to my lower limb. We persevere with exercises. Writing is impossible: I can work only through dictation. Therefore, at John Coldstream's suggestion, we have put together this collection of work which has appeared in newspapers during the past two decades.

The first part of the book is a miscellany of articles, essays, obituaries and even a letter or two to the Editor. The second consists almost entirely of reviews commissioned for the Books Pages of the *Daily Telegraph* and the *Sunday Telegraph*, printed here in chronological order. This period of my writing life, as a critic, came about in an unexpected way.

In my sixth volume of autobiography, *A Short Walk from Harrods* (1993), I describe how, in the dark days of early 1988, I was back, miserably, in London after some twenty years in France. Forwood, my manager, was dying of cancer and the nurses had arrived to care for him. One evening a pleasant young man came round to the house for a drink. He was Nicholas Shakespeare, then the literary editor of the *Daily Telegraph*, and he asked if I would consider reviewing some books for him. The suggestion was so surprising, the meeting in the unhappy house so bizarre, that I agreed. Why not? I had to pretend that life would continue; all was really quite normal; there was no one in the room above fighting for life. I felt a mild glow of hope. I'd manage somehow.

One morning shortly afterwards, a package of books was delivered, with a note: 'About 750 words? By the 27th?' The result was a review of *Mr Harty's Grand Tour*, which appeared on 2 April 1988 – the first of about fifty notices to be published in the next six years. Nicholas didn't know it at the time, but it was he who chucked a plank across the ravine for me. He moved on, and his successor, John Coldstream, became the handrail.

The articles and reviews collected here constitute a 'body of work' which has surprised me, if only because of its bulk. In any case, it will have to do – at least for the time being . . .

DIRK BOGARDE London, 1998

PART ONE
MISCELLANEOUS ARTICLES

EARLIEST MEMORIES

Blue Remembered Frills

Memory: I scratch about like a hen in chaff. The first thing that I can recall is light: pale, opaque green, white spots drifting. Near my right eye long black shapes curling down and tickling gently.

Years later when I reported this memory to my parents they confirmed it. There had, apparently, been an extraordinary pea-soup fog: it had snowed at the same time. My mother had lifted me up to observe the phenomenon; the black feathers which wreathed her hat irritated my eye and I tried to pull them away. I was about two years old.

I remember lying on my back on the lawn behind the house in St George's Road. It was a brilliant day of high wind and scudding cloud. The tall house reeled away from me as the clouds whipped across the blue sky and I was afraid that it would fall down and crush me.

And later I saw our giant ginger cat – well, giant to me then – nailed alive to the tall wooden fence which separated us from an unfriendly neighbour. I remember my mother weeping: which frightened me far more than the sight of the dying cat, for I had not yet learned to recognize cruelty or death, but I was recognizing pain and distress on a human face for the first time.

It would not be the last.

The house in St George's Road was tall, ugly, built of grey-yellow bricks with a slate roof. It had the great advantage for my father, who was a painter, of a number of high-ceilinged rooms with perfect north light. It also had a long narrow garden with ancient trees.

An Irish woman lived in the basement with two children and cleaned the house from time to time. She had once been a maid to the Chesterfields, who lived in a very grand house not far away called The Lodge.

Sometimes I would see her crouching on a landing with a mop or a brush. There was an almost constant smell of cooking from the basement, and my father said it was Irish stew because that was what the Irish ate.

I suppose that made sense to me: at least I have remembered it.

My father was a prudent man, with little fortune, and he let off most of the rooms in the house to artist friends so that, apart from the prevailing smell of Irish stew, the place reeked of turpentine and linseed oil. The mixed scent of those two is the one which I remember best, and if I smell them anywhere I go, I am instantly at ease, familiar and secure.

One of his lodgers was, in fact, an artists' model who had been left behind, in a rather careless manner, by an artist who had wandered off to Italy to paint. I knew her as Aunt Kitty.

Tiny, vivid, a shock of bright red hair brushed high up from her forehead, brilliant green eyes heavily lined with kohl, she was loving, warm and exceptionally noisy. For some reason, which I can no longer recall, I always seemed to see her carrying a tall glass of Russian tea in a silver holder. I never knew why, or even what it was, then; and I never asked.

She had a small powder puff in a red leather bag which I found interesting, for it looked exactly like a fat little bun with an ivory ring in its middle. If you pulled the ring, out came the powder puff, of softest swan's-down, and the powder never spilled. It smelled warm, sweet and sickly. I liked it. Her room was dark nearly all the time, for she hated daylight, which she said gave her terrible headaches. So the room was lighted here and there with small lamps draped with coloured handkerchiefs; each had a stick of incense burning beside it – the handkerchiefs cast strange and beautiful patterns on the ceiling.

There was a gold-and-black striped divan. Cushions in profusion tumbled all about the floor for one to sit on or lie upon. She had no chairs. I found that exceptionally curious, as I did the polar-bear rug with roaring head, fearful teeth, glassy eyes and a pink plaster tongue, and the tall jars which were stuffed with the feathers from peacocks' tails.

It was the most exciting room in the house. She also had a portable gramophone which stood on a table with a broken leg, which she had supported with a pile of books. She would wind it up after each record, a cigarette hanging from her lips, hoop earrings swinging from her ears, dressed as I only ever remember her dressed: in long, rustling dressing gowns covered with flowers and bluebirds, bound around her waist with a wide tasselled sash. The tassels swung and danced as she moved.

On occasion she was distressed and wept hopelessly. Then my mother had to go down to the scented room and comfort her. Sometimes, too, she was rather strange. Leaning across to caress my cheek, for example, she would quite often miss me and crash to the floor in a heap. I found this worrying at first. However, she usually laughed and dragged herself upright by holding on to the nearest piece of furniture.

She once told me, leaning close to my face, that she had had 'one over the eight': I didn't know what she meant, and when I asked, my father bit his lower lip, a sign I knew to indicate anger, and said he did not know.

But I was pretty certain that he did.

Her dazzling eyes, the henna'd hair frizzed out about the pale, oval face, the coarse laughter, the tassels and the peacocks' feathers are still, after so many years, before me.

She offered me, in that crammed room, a sense of colour and beauty, and, even, although I was almost unaware at the time, excitement. I was uncomprehending of nearly all that she said, but I did realize that she was offering riches beyond price.

First had come light; after light, scent – originally of turpentine and linseed oil (hardly romantic, one might think); and now I was shown colour and, above all, made aware of texture.

'Touch it!' she would say. 'Touch the silk, it's so beautiful. Do you know that a million little worms worked to make this single piece?'

I didn't, of course: but the idea fascinated me. That something so fine, so sheer, so glorious should come from 'a million little worms' filled me with amazement, and I liked worms from then on.

Sometimes she would go away, and when I asked Mrs O'Connell where she had gone to she would only reply: 'A-voyagin'.' Which was no help. My parents, when questioned, said that she had gone on her holidays. I had an instant vision of buckets and spades, shrimping nets and long stretches of sand with the tide far out. And, in consequence, knowing that Aunt Kitty would be having a lovely time, I put her from my mind.

When she returned she came bearing amazing gifts. Silver rings for my mother, a basket of brilliant shells of all kinds and shapes for me, French cigarettes for my father who, I knew instinctively, liked them better than he liked Aunt Kitty.

She brought for herself rolls of coloured cloth: silks, voiles, cottons of every hue and design. These she would throw about her room in armfuls, so that they fell and covered the ugly furniture; then, with the cigarette hanging from her lip, she would wind up the gramophone, drape a length of cloth about her body and dance. Barefoot: her nails painted gold.

Mesmerized I would sit and watch the small feet with gold-tipped toes twist and spin among tumbles of brilliant silks and the spilled shells from my palm-leaf basket.

'Why Do I Love You?
Why Do You Love Mee . . . ?'

She told me, winding up the gramophone for the second side of the record, that the silks had come across the sands of Araby on the backs of camels, that she had seen monkeys swing among the branches of jacaranda trees, and flights of scarlet birds swoop across opal skies. I had not the least idea what she meant. But somewhere in my struggling mind the awareness was growing, from her words, that far beyond the confines of St George's Road, West End Lane, Hampstead, lay a world of magic and beauty.

Once I heard my father say that one day Aunt Kitty would not return from one of her 'voyages'.

And one day that is exactly what happened. She never came back again; the Ground Floor Front was locked. I asked where she had gone. My father said possibly into the belly of a crocodile: which distressed me for a whole morning.

Years later I was to discover that no crocodile had taken Aunt Kitty: she had gone off, willingly, with a rich Sultan from the East Indies.

When her room was opened it was exactly as she had left it. She had taken nothing with her, not even the silks. There was the gramophone, the draped lamps, the gold-striped divan, the bearskin and the little red leather powder puff wrapped in letter paper, on which she had printed a message to my mother, begging her to keep it always as a remembrance of her.

Which she did. For many years it lay at the bottom of her jewel case and sometimes I would take it out, with permission, pull the little ivory ring, release the swan's-down puff and the strange, musky scent. Naturally, over the years, the scent grew fainter and fainter until, eventually, there was only a ghostly odour, and the swan's-down puff grew thin, grey and finally moulted. But Aunt Kitty remains in my mind as clear as when she wound up her gramophone for me.

'We'll have a little dancy, ducky, shall we? Would that be lovely?'

Some time after she left us my sister Elizabeth was born. I was taken off to Scotland by my maternal grandmother Nelson, a friendly, firm, warm, straight-backed woman in black, to keep me 'out of the way'. I can only remember a new tweed coat with a velvet collar, of which I was inordinately proud, a railway compartment, and sitting with a round, black-lacquered wicker basket, painted with pink roses, which contained my sandwiches.

When I returned to the ugly house in St George's Road an enormous pram with wheels like dustbin lids stood in the front drive, and Mrs O'Connell said that I had a baby sister and that if they were not careful (they apparently being my parents) a cat would sit on the baby's face and smother it. Faithfully I reported this piece of information, and my howling sister was draped in netting.

With another member in the family, discipline was relaxed, and I was left free to wander from studio to studio, squashing tubes of paint, watching the 'Uncles' (they were all called 'Uncle', the resident artists who rented my father's rooms) painting their canvases, and being as tiresome as any child of four could be in a cluttered room full of sights and smells and bottles.

Bottles had a great attraction for me. I wonder why? I can remember, very clearly, taking down a full bottle of Owbridge's Lung Tonic and swallowing its contents. I liked, enormously, the taste of, I suppose, laudanum, or whatever the soothing drug was which it contained.

Though I well remember performing this wicked act, the time following it is obliterated.

I went into a coma for four days, and nothing, not even salt and water, mustard and water, or being given my father's pipe to smoke, apparently made any impression on me. No one was able to accomplish the essential task of forcing me to vomit up my stolen delight. I lay as for dead, heavily drugged. I recovered; and later drank a bottle of rose-water and glycerine to the dregs. I was thrashed for this by my father, who always did it rather apologetically with one of his paint brushes.

But it did not stop me. I stole from every bottle set high on shelves, or left, carelessly, standing about. The studios were forbidden territory. Not only did I squash the artists' paint tubes empty, I was obviously quite capable of scoffing their linseed oil and turpentine.

A 'handful' is what I was considered, and handfuls such as I had to be dealt with firmly.

But no one had much time to deal with me, so, apart from being locked out of all the Uncles' rooms, I was pretty well left on my own to play about in the garden and feed my sister with pebbles or anything else which came to hand. And, of course, got another walloping. People simply did not understand that I was being kind.

Some of these fragments I remember with intense clarity. Others less well. Memory, as far back as this, is rather like archaeology. Little scraps and shards are collected and put together to form a whole by dedicated people – in this case my parents – who filled in the sprawling design of my life at that early age, and made real the pattern.

Aunt Kitty's room, for example, I can see as a vague, shadowy place filled with sweet scents and the trembling shapes of feathers and handkerchiefs flickering high on the ceiling. And I remember the gold-and-black striped divan, for it was to become my own many years later, when we moved to the cottage. Equally I remember the polar-bear rug. It was the first time that I had dared to place a timid hand within the roaring mouth: for the simple reason that Aunt Kitty had assured me it would not bite. It did not. I trusted her from then on, implicitly.

I trusted everyone in sight. Unwisely.

I can remember the great spills of cloth, but not the stories of camels and Araby or the scarlet birds swooping across opal skies. These items were added much later by my parents – who had, doubtless, heard her recount them. But I do remember the worms; and the million it took to make a tiny scrap of glowing material. However, most of those very early years are simply the shards and scraps. Vivid none the less.

But from five years old onwards I have almost total recall: although I rather think that Elizabeth, with a feminine mind, has a far greater memory for detail than I.

Telegraph Sunday Magazine, 18 March 1984

Years of Innocence

My father grew restless in the grey-yellow brick house and decided that he wanted to move out to a quieter area. He suffered from catarrh; and also from hideous nightmares, which his experiences only a few years before on the Somme and at Passchendaele had engendered.

These of course I knew nothing about. Sudden shouts in the night, I can remember those – and my mother's anxious, caring face the following morning as he set off to his work at *The Times*, where he had become the first Art Editor at an absurdly young age.

So we moved away from the grey street in West End Lane, Hampstead, into a small but pleasant house among fields just outside Twickenham. It was the talk of the family, and of its friends, that the sale was a 'snip'. He had bought it extremely cheaply for some reason, and everyone was amazed. The reason was soon to become apparent.

One morning the dirt road in front of the house began shuddering with trucks and lorries of all descriptions; they droned and rumbled all day long, and when they left in the late evening we discovered the fields before us, and around us, stuck with scarlet wooden stakes and draped about with sagging ropes. My anguished father discovered too late that he had purchased a house in the exact centre of an enormous building development – which was the reason why it had been, as everyone said, 'so ridiculously' cheap. A 'snip'.

We were buried among bricks, lime, cement and piles of glossy scarlet tiles. The road was churned into a mud-slide and the windows rattled all day with thudding trucks.

Within the year the fields in front had yielded up a row of semi-detached villas, with bay windows and Tudor gables, their roofs, as yet untiled, looking like the pale yellow bones of a smoked haddock.

My father was in despair.

I was fascinated by all the work and upheaval and spent as much of my time as I possibly could clambering about in the unfinished foundations of suburbia. Although the workmen were friendly, and seemed not to mind me being among them, there came a time when they shouted at me to 'bugger orf', and once someone threw a half-brick.

Another time I got a hod-full of lime full in the face, rather like a custard pie. It was, of course, quite accidental and all I can remember is that it burned appallingly and I fled, blinded, from the half-built house, screaming at the top of my lungs, across the battered field and the rutted road. My distracted mother could not understand what had happened, naturally, and I was unable to tell her because I was yelling. She washed my face and hair and tried to get me to explain, to no avail.

At that moment an enormous man burst into the kitchen, pulled me on to his lap and licked, with his naked tongue, the lime from my eyes. Had he not done so, I have been assured, I should in all probability have been blinded for good. Counselling my distraught mother to bathe my eyes with milk and not let me out of her sight ever again, he left. I have often wondered who he was, and thought of him with gratitude.

I only stopped going to the half-built houses because I was warned that I'd be given a thrashing I'd never forget if I did. So I wandered off up the little path towards the deep rubbish-tip in the quarry. It was quieter there, no one came near, and I could explore the tumbled rubbish of Twickenham with complete freedom. Boxes and crates, broken chimney pots, old tin cans, a battered pram; pieces of wood, quantities of smashed tiles and earthen drainpipes; nothing smelly.

I remained always just at the edge, for it was very deep and I had a fear of falling in; which, one day, I did. I heard a kitten crying down at the bottom. Leaning too far over the slippery edge of broken tile and chimney pots I slid rapidly to the bottom and found the kitten, a skinny creature which had managed to get out of a sack, leaving the dead bodies of its companions. I sat down cradling my find, confident that someone would collect me.

I tried to clamber up, but found that impossible. Each step I took up the jagged slope of rubbish sent me slithering backwards; and there was no possibility of climbing, to me, the sheer sides with a frantic kitten.

Calling had no effect, either, I was soon to discover. For my thin voice never reached the lip of the pit, and my wretched mother, who had quickly discovered my absence, passed and repassed my prison without having the very least idea that her first-born was sitting below among the debris.

Eventually a search-party was formed from the builders and masons on the swiftly growing estate. I was discovered and dragged to the surface with the kitten. I think that my mother had been so frightened that she forgot to punish, or even scold, and I was permitted to keep the kitten, who grew into a fine creature which we called 'Minnehaha', unknowingly getting his sex wrong.

The little path through the grasses was not exactly out of bounds, although now the quarry was. But along the path a jungle of most attractive plants and grasses grew, and tiny green crickets scissored in the sun. I picked handfuls of bright black fruits from a small bush, ate them and stuffed my unprotesting sister full – with Deadly Nightshade.

Both of us, this time, went into a coma. There was a nurse and a doctor and enemas and thermometers; and the moment I was well enough to do so I upended the nursery fire-guard, shoved my sister into it as a patient, and we played 'Hospitals'. It was very exciting, but pretty dull without 'pills'.

So I consumed, because it was my turn to be a patient, a full bottle of aspirin. Another coma.

My mother was told that nothing could be done, I had taken such a massive overdose that I should either die or recover. All that she could do was lie with me, her hand on my heart, and if she felt the least change of rhythm she was to call the doctor instantly.

I slept like a lamb, my heart beating contentedly.

I do not think that I had suicidal tendencies. Certainly I had no murderous ones – then. However, my parents decided that the time was ready for me to have some kind of supervision and discipline in life: I had been altogether far too spoiled.

Miss Harris and her sister ran a genteel school for young children in a square Victorian house overlooking The Green. In their back garden, down among the laurels, and where the teachers parked their bikes, there was a long tin shed, painted dark red. This was the kindergarten.

I landed up there.

A blackboard, a big iron stove, tables. I remember nothing else. I imagine that one was instructed in the very basics: but I never bothered to learn them. Which has had serious consequences for me throughout my life.

Jealousy seething, anger mounting, I sat and thought only about 'Minnehaha', or how best to build an aquarium, or when we should next go down to Teddington Lock with net and jam jar to fish for sticklebacks.

I simply did not bother with Miss Harris and her silly kindergarten; my brain absolutely refused to see the connection between 'cat' and 'mat', and I frankly didn't give a damn which sat on which. As far as I was concerned it was a wasted morning.

My parents found it to be the same thing after one caustic report from Miss Harris herself: 'He doesn't try. Won't put himself out at all.'

He was not about to.

Stronger medicine was needed, and it was found in the form of a tall red building along the river, almost next door to Radnor Park. A convent school a-flutter with smiling nuns.

I was captivated by their swirling grey habits, by the glitter and splendour of the modest, but theatrically ravishing, chapel, the flickering lamps beneath the statues of the Virgin Mary and Joseph. It went to my head in a trice and I fell passionately in love with convent life.

I liked, above all, our classroom, a high-ceilinged, white-painted room with great mirrored doors which reflected the river, the trees

14

beyond and the boats. I worshipped Sister Veronica, with her gentle hands and the modest mole from which sprouted, fascinatingly, a single hair; and Sister Marie Joseph, who was fat and bustled, and stood no nonsense, but taught me my catechism and let me come into the chapel whenever I felt the need, which was often (not to pray, you understand, but to drown in the splendour of the lamps, candles, colours, a glowing Christ, and the smell of something in the stuffy air which reminded me of Aunt Kitty).

The colours, the singing of the choir, the altar-cloths shimmering with gold thread, filled my heart and my head with delight. I was lost: and decided, there and then, to be a priest.

Religion – certainly the Catholic religion – was not taught in our house. My father was born into a strongly Catholic family, with a staunch Catholic convert mother, and it was as a Catholic, firm in his belief, that he went to war in 1914. His belief, like that of so many other young men of that time, was shattered on the Somme, in Passchendaele and, finally, for all time when he pulled open the doors of a chapel after the battle of Capoaretto in Italy and was smothered in the rotting corpses of soldiers and civilians who had been massacred and stuffed high to the roof.

'Jesus,' he once told me, many years after, 'does not have his eye on the sparrows. But you follow whatever faith you wish. It is your life, not mine.'

And so Elizabeth and I grew up and flourished in a vaguely ambiguous atmosphere. We were sent to the convent on the riverside; I was allowed to have my own altar, which I built with intense care in a corner of the nursery; and we mumbled our 'Gentle Jesus' and the Lord's Prayer without interference. We were left to make up our own minds about God and Jesus, Joseph and the Virgin Mary.

It was not a difficult process for me, because I had fallen quite in love with everything that Catholic teaching had to offer: without, of course, realizing that what I had *actually* fallen in love with was the theatre. Not religion at all. The ritual, the singing, the light, the mystery, the glowing candles: all these were theatre, and theatre emerged from these things and engulfed me for the rest of my life.

Learning my catechism was, after all, merely the prelude to learning my 'lines'.

Like my father before me I laid aside my belief – not that it had ever been very strong, to be sure – for ever in my war.

Whenever I make a declaration of this kind I am inevitably swamped with letters from well-meaning people, usually women, who want to convert me to 'believing' again. I am bombarded with religious books, usually American paperbacks, of all possible permutations and persuasions.

One which turns up regularly is called *Wrestling with Christ*; which appears to be an enormous bestseller but fails to answer any of the questions which have concerned me over the years. I have absolutely no wish to wrestle with anyone: especially with Christ.

It is particularly hard to retain a shred of 'belief' standing in the middle of a battlefield, at the age of twenty-three, watching piles of dead, frequently mutilated soldiers, their bellies bloated with the gasses of decomposition, being bulldozed into a mass grave. I watched them tumble, spill, slither like old shirts in a spin-drier, and as I walked away retching in the stench of death I knew that, at last, I had come of age, and that I could never recover the happy platitudes of immortality.

Whatever happened, I wondered on another occasion, to that loving, comforting phrase, 'Suffer Little Children to Come unto Me'? And my first, appalled, uncomprehending sight of a concentration camp, two of the women guards smiling brightly and wearing scarlet nail-varnish among the decaying mounds of bodies, shredded to tatters whatever belief I had and dispersed it in the winds of fact, and hideous truth.

I always, however, said my prayers. I still do to this day. But it is a prayer to a greater force than the simpering plaster figures to which I once prayed so ardently.

However, to return to Twickenham and innocence: a priest I decided to be, and that was that. The fact that no one took my decision seriously, even beloved Sister Veronica herself, did not trouble me. I had time before me, and I was exceptionally happy.

There were other moments of happiness which I recall during

the Twickenham years. Days on the river in a punt. My father in white flannels and shirt, poling us along; my mother lying among cushions, a Japanese parasol shielding her face from the sun; Layton and Johnstone on the portable gramophone; a picnic hamper among the bathing towels; the smell of boat varnish and the excitement of getting to one of the locks and watching the rise and fall of the water.

Opposite our house were the Howards. A family of four: three boys and one girl, called Jessie. Jessie was one year older than I was and I liked her because she had a small tent in their back garden, a wilderness still of rutted mud and cement dust, and invited me to come and play with her.

It made a change from my sister, because Jessie was really pretty daring. She showed me a secret box in which she kept cigarette butts, and we sucked away at these for a time, without, of course, lighting them. They made me feel sick. So she rustled about and produced another tin box, battered but secure, in which she had a hoard of rotten apples, bits of cake and a whole tin of baked beans which, with an opener in the shape of a bull's-head (which I coveted instantly), we opened and ate cold.

I felt a little more sick, but better after a bit of mouldy cake. Then she pulled down her knickers and said that she would show me her 'thingy' on condition that I showed her mine. This surprised me slightly – we had only known each other for an afternoon – but I was still feeling a certain unease in my stomach and anyway I had seen Elizabeth naked in the bath every night, just as she, indeed, had seen me; so I was not fearfully interested, for I could hardly believe that I was about to witness something extraordinary.

I complied.

We regarded each other in silence.

'My brothers have got one like yours,' she said.

'My sister has one the same as yours, so there. I think I'll go home now,' I said.

Later I was extremely sick, and would not look at supper, which alerted my nanny to the fact that perhaps all was not well. She told my father that I had spent the afternoon with 'those dreadful people in the new houses. It's not fitting. They'll spoil his ways, and there is nothing that I can do on account of the fact that I have only one pair of hands and no eyes in the back of my head. He wanders.' My father was a just and kind man; he followed my anxious mother down to my room and asked me what had happened that day. 'We only want to know what has made you so ill, and then we can get it set to rights,' he said.

So I told him in detail, from sucking cigarette butts to eating mouldy cake and cold tinned beans and examining each other's 'thingys'.

He looked grim, but said nothing. My mother took my temperature, found that it was normal, and they said goodnight and went away.

A few weeks later we moved back to Hampstead.

And that is that. The first seven years of my life recalled as faithfully as I can remember, aided by others who have filled in the gaps.

The years of innocence. These, I am told, are the impressionable years, the formative ones during which all the things which one discovers, or is shown, stay with one for the rest of life and, as it were, one is moulded. One sets like a jelly. Perhaps not quite the right word. Cement? That sounds too heavy. Moulded, or fixed, must suffice.

I discovered light, scent, and, through Aunt Kitty, was made aware of colour and texture. Enduring senses for me all these years later.

I have, it would seem, left out a fifth most important one. Music.

Music was a constant part of my life in those years: my father's passion was music. Not always the kind that I particularly cared for, it must be said. His studio at the top of the house was filled with what I grew to learn, and detest, as chamber music. It was the music to which he painted. We called it, naturally enough, 'Po Music'.

But there was opera, too. Great ballooning sounds soared through the house; voices swept us from corner to corner, subliminally reached us in sleep. We were aware of music from our earliest moments, and in time, as is right and proper, the sounds which were incomprehensible between four and seven years, for example, began to take their own forms.

At the convent, of course, there were songs of praise and sonorous organs and those, too, became a part of the pattern of one's existence.

Music was everywhere: but I agreed with nanny fervently when she said that she 'did like a nice tune, something you can hum. And you can't hum much of your father's music, I can tell you.'

But, anyway, music.

Light, scent, colour, texture, music. I entered the next phase of life with a rich haul.

Telegraph Sunday Magazine, 25 March 1984

WAR

A Night to Remember

Perhaps, after so many years, this episode of my life may seem to be faintly trivial. Greater 'nights' have been set before me since, but none has moved me so intensely.

It was the darkest, coldest, winter just after the disaster of Arnhem. My Division never got to Arnhem, but stayed where it was, just across the river, watching the hideous death of a dream, a city and much of its population in helpless frustration. Uselessly one wept, or dragged muddied, soaking bodies up the slithering river banks, and watched as our youth (I was twenty-three) drained away into the swirling waters of the Rhine.

We settled into the battered buildings of a small village called Elst, just across the river from the terrible bridge which we had failed to hold. I stuck my camp-bed up under the roof of a shattered farmhouse in a dusty, tile-spattered attic which I shared with two aged men and a sad-faced, very plain girl of about twenty. Together we crawled up a ladder from the wreck of what had been the main room of the farm, having eaten part of my rations and some potatoes and turnips which the whey-faced girl had forced into some sort of a soup.

We were mostly silent, for no one spoke English and I spoke no Dutch. Apart from the slurping of soup from the old men and the whining of starving dogs (they were barely alive, and survived, I guessed, to serve as a basis for future soup), there was no sound. We were down to rock bottom. My army ration, spread among the four of us, was just enough to keep us alive.

Holland, up on the polders, is cold, colder than anywhere I had ever been. The ice in the mornings was finger-thick, the skinny blankets under which we huddled in the attic were beaded in the mornings with white pearls from our breath.

I was here from September until, I think, the end of November. Doing nothing apart from trying to keep warm, help any stray escapee who managed to get across the river, and file useless intelligence reports. Occasionally members of the Dutch Resistance slipped silently into our midst, faces blackened, intent on looting from a stalled goods-train stranded, packed with booty, on the Bemmel Polder not far away. One night the mortars got its range, hit it from end to end, left it blazing, and I was summonsed by field-telephone back to HQ in Eindhoven.

Eindhoven, war or no war, was alive. Lights were on, people walked about in the streets, there was some food (we drove into Belgium and brought out jeep-loads), and one night I saw to my amazement a poster stuck on a splintered tree which announced that ENSA, the highly abused 'entertainment for the troops', had finally reached us. That night, for seven nights, we were to see *The Merry Widow* at the Phillips Theatre, commandeered in town, and the stars were Madge Elliot and Cyril Ritchard, two ageing, but still gallant, Stars from the *real* West End.

I was almost first in line. After Elst, the darkness and the sadness across the river, the dead swinging silently in the current of the Rhine, *The Merry Widow* could not be missed. I sat enraptured in my plush seat, no heating, but snug-ish in a greatcoat; the orchestra crashed into the overture and sheer glory, magic, beauty, life and fun were there before us.

Madge and Cyril Ritchard burst into our delighted, amazed, deprived lives, sang and danced, were wondrous to behold, made us laugh, adore and cheer. OK, there were holes, if you looked, in the fishnet tights of the chorus, some of the costumes had got a bit frayed round the edges, perhaps the stars were not quite as lissom as once they had been.

But they were there; they gave us back the youth which we were in severe danger of losing for ever. Their laughter, their songs, their aliveness brought us all back to a daring belief that, perhaps, just perhaps, we could make it through to the end, that we might survive.

I went to every performance. I know the score by heart to this day and I learnt, that night in the Phillips Theatre, Eindhoven, just exactly what the theatre *really* meant. It was not some obtuse essay into 'Why or How', not Shakespeare, not Shaw. It was glorious, glowing, colour, laughter, light and life with the added splendour of music. Because of Cyril and Madge, and *The Merry Widow* which they and their company brought to us in that bitter cruel winter, I swear that hundreds of us survived.

The instant that I hear the first notes of 'Vilja' or 'We are going to Maxim's', I am instantly, for a second or so, back in Elst, with the crumping mortars, the blazing train on the polder, and the brilliance, the bravery, of Madge and Cyril Ritchard, whose laughter, delight and energy revived a battered, almost defeated group of wretched soldiers for ever; in my case, anyway.

Sunday Telegraph, 12 January 1992

FRANCE

The Pond

On a terrace some way from the house I noticed a patch of grass which was always lush and brilliant even during the greatest heat of July. Mint flourished there, tall reeds, even bull-rushes: the area was thick with spongy moss which squelched when you walked upon it. All around the land was sere and dry beneath the great olives, but parting the dense rushes I found a crystal spring bubbling furiously; a veritable oasis in the parched limestone earth.

I should have a pond here, I decided. A real English pond 500 metres up in the terraced hills of Provence. A pond where there had never been a pond before, brimming with clear water, speared with yellow flags, with water lilies and carp perhaps, or golden orfe: a place where I could sit on hot summer evenings and just feel the cool and watch the water lapping gently round the great boulders with which I should surround my little *pièce d'eau*. It would not be formal: quite the reverse, a natural, simple, country pond.

Armed with spades and barrows, with forks and wellingtons and high hearts we – the local builder and his son, and Ahmet from Tunis, who came twice a week to help on the land, plus any stray guests who happened to have wandered down from London or Paris or up from Nice and Cannes – set to work. We dug and carted, water spilled crystal about our feet which we sipped with relish, cool on burning days; pure water gushing from the land, ice cold, refreshing, natural. One day, digging on my own as the others were occupied elsewhere, I vaguely noticed a tiny fragment of paper swirl across my aged wellingtons. I ignored it until there was a second: this was rather harder to ignore, since it clearly bore a fragment of floral decoration very much the same as that which decorated the lavatory paper in the house.

On closer inspection it *was* the lavatory paper. No spring this.

26

No natural phenomenon. A savage leak in the pipe leading from the septic tank was just what it was.

Alerted, gentlemen arrived from Grasse and Antibes with bottles of brilliant dyes which they poured into the drains, pipes, sinks and lavatory pans. The spring took on the hues of Bonnard's palette. We all had injections because we had spent a considerable amount of time during our digging seeking refreshment from its apparently unending supply. Spades and barrows were put away, pipes laid and a new drainage system installed. The spring ceased abruptly. I surveyed sadly a wide, muddy pit.

But why not have a pond after all? The pit was there, much of the work had been done, the rushes flourished. I set to work again. The pond grew. Cemented carefully, lined with boulders and shards of local rock and stone, fed by a hidden waterpipe in a clump of nettles, and filled to the brim from the local mains, it shimmered in the summer evening. My sister brought me water lilies from her Sussex garden pond, my father packed roots of 'real English mint' in his sponge bag, someone else brought gnarled roots of water iris. I bought a plastic bag of little goldfish at one franc each from the Monoprix and a bunch of green Canadian pondweed. In two summers it was established; it was a real pond. The Monoprix fish went mad and became hundreds, the weeds flourished, the iris nodded in the speckled shade, the lilies were white cups with flat green saucers, the mint smothered the banks.

And then the strangers arrived, borne upon the wind one must suppose? The dreaded mare's tail, wall pennywort, the Canadian pondweed, so small in the bunch, became a vast viridian carpet. Then came the 'people' . . . voles and shrews plopped along the sedge, dragonflies of every size and colour darted across my pond, water wagtails came, the yellow and the grey, swallows and swifts and once, to my astonishment, a bewildered heron lost on his way to the Camargue. Waterboatmen, water beetles, dragonfly lava, water spiders and mosquito lava multiplied. I bought half a kilo of eels and three carp from the fishmonger. Small green frogs with gold eyes and yellow bellies sang in the mint and sprang from rush to rush with the dexterity of trapeze artists.

I sat entranced before my creation. Five hundred metres up in the limestone hills of Provence, among massive olives and jagged rock where no water had ever been before, I now had a lush English country pond.

And then came the toads.

They arrived in the second year as one pair. Locked together in ugly rapture, struggling valiantly up the steep hill. After some days of violent and uncontrolled waltzing together, the hen toad industriously laid her eggs, ropes of glossy black pearls strung and looped among the pondweed. In May I had two million tadpoles bustling through the water. I was enraptured. Each year more and more pairs arrived, locked together in a ghastly embrace of lust and determination, humping slowly over the land from God only knew where, through the thyme and broom over the rocks and straight into my pond. The water became ebony with billions of tadpoles:

all summer we slid and skidded on the squashed bodies of tiny toads who seethed like boiling black rice beneath our feet.

Rapture turned to wrath. Plants were uprooted everywhere by large toads desperate for cool and damp in the blazing sun. They crawled and hopped into the tiled sitting room, clambered ponderously up the stairs, hid behind doors, crouched in the woodshed. And every season others arrived from every nook and cranny in Provence, lumbering determinedly towards their breeding ground. In desperation, I erected a high wire fence around my once so natural English pond and caught them up in their dozens before they could clamber over, or dig under, and reach the water. Now it is my job, morning and evening in the spring, to bundle them, writhing, into a large plastic dustbin and cart them down to a stream some miles away in the valley below.

The 'catch' varies. Sometimes it can be as little as three pairs, sometimes twenty. Often more. What happens to them when they reach the stream I do not know: I am told that they will all make their way back to me, since I started the whole damned business in the first place.

But I am gradually winning the ecological war. So far this season only two pairs have managed to get over the wire. I managed to scoop them up just before the waltzing commenced. There will not be a single tadpole in the pond this May if I can help it. But I am still carting and dumping these toads in their hundreds.

I knew there would be a great many strange changes in my life when I came here to live ten years ago, but lugging dustbins filled with furious mating toads was not one of my expectations. Entirely my own fault, I know that. As far as I remember there was not a single toad in sight here then. In my opinion it is very foolhardy indeed to try to alter the ecology – even for a small, pleasant, English country pond. I may be winning my battle up here, but what of the unfortunate people who live in the valley near the Dustbin Stream? Already I have carted hundreds down there. They will be swamped. Will they sue?

Weekend Telegraph Magazine, 3 June 1979

Impressions in the Sand

They'll tell you that it is ruined: and they'll be right. They'll tell you that it is solid concrete from St Tropez to Monte Carlo; and that's nearly right. They'll tell you that it is a wild mixture of Blackpool and Atlantic City, and they aren't far off; and they'll also tell you that the people who throng the artificial beaches (the sand is brought down every winter from distant quarries and never gets near the cleansing of a tide: there *is* no tide in the Mediterranean) are pretty grim.

I find it hard to fault that as well, sadly. The glamorous people, under the onslaught of coach tours from everywhere in Europe and beyond, have long since relinquished their places in the sun and hurried off to start another life in the Caribbean.

There is a blue haze of petrol all along the coast. The pervading smells are of fried chips and hamburgers, melting tar and the paraffin which pours from the jets screaming down on Nice Airport (bringing yet more property developers and their women, Arabs, and haggard-looking American widows with plastic pixie-hoods and expert face-fixes).

All this is so. It cannot be denied. I have known the Riviera for more than forty years and lived on its fringes for nearly twenty. Certainly the place is a ruin now: there *is* a sea of concrete, there *are* ribbons of *autoroute*. Hideous little villas scab what was once sweet and gentle land with its ancient farms and noble pinewoods, and the people who go there, by and large, aren't much cop. You won't go a bundle on the cast even if you still quite like the scenery.

But. And this is a big BUT. The *magic* is still there as it always has been. Still there if you really want to see it and if you manage to keep away from the more obvious bits of desecration and greed. Still there for you to catch and to hold, to leave you breathless when you find the little corners which Progress has not yet managed to 'improve'. Try the view of the Esterel and the Baie des Anges, from the top step of the terrace of the Hôtel du Cap. If *that* doesn't leave you breathless you don't deserve to breathe anyway.

Whatever happens, the contours remain: the hills covered with tacky little villas still melt into the purple dusk, and the villas are drowned in deep colour so that all one can see is the hard outline of the hills against the sky. The hills don't change – though they did remove one, just above Nice, to use as an in-fill for a new airport runway. But that was just one pointed little mount among many: you'd hardly know it had gone. Hardly. Only if you remembered where it had been.

The Riviera was invented in 1925, so the legend has it, by a very rich, erudite, glamorous and civilized young American couple called Sara and Gerald Murphy. They arrived one day from Paris and fell in love with the little walled town of Antibes, which then sat in a quilt of rose and carnation farms, jasmine fields and cane breaks, its ramparts caressed by an as yet unpolluted sea. Enraptured, they rented a small house in a pinewood just above the empty beach known as La Garoupe. Patriotically, they renamed the house Villa America and invited their host of American friends from Paris, who would arrive on the night train in the golden dawn, fall under the spell and linger on and on. In time they all became a little too much. People had to be fed and wined; the picnics on La Garoupe had to be devised and catered for, and Sara's cast list was mostly very distinguished. And demanding, as holiday guests so often are.

The Fitzgeralds, Picasso and his monumental Mamma dressed, as always, in the deepest black plus high hat, Hemingway and whoever he brought with him, and a list of others all equally brilliant, glowing and glamorous: writers, painters, musicians and players. The Murphys asked the owners of the local hotel along the beach to stay open one summer to accommodate their guests. Normally the winter season finished at about the end of April, for no one wanted the heat and the blazing summer sunlight. The hotels would close until the cooler weather returned in September or October. The owners were somewhat astonished by the Murphys' suggestion, not believing that they would be filled, but they agreed to remain open for 'just one summer'. The trains brought, and continued to bring, the glittering crowds from Paris, the Hôtel du Cap remained open ever afterwards, and thus was 'the Riviera' born.

That is the story I have been told, that is the story I have read, and I'm staying with it. It suits me, and it's probably true.

By the time I first hit the Riviera, in 1948, it was a going concern of the greatest elegance and beauty – a mixture of extreme sophistication and the simplest peasant existence. Rolls-Royces inched politely past meandering hay-carts pulled by oxen; the air was sweet and calm, no one hurried and there was not a sodium lamp in miles. Cicadas sawed in every rough-barked tree in the heat of the afternoon, and down at Vallauris Picasso was working away at a rich seam of clay which he found suited his new bowls, plates and jugs, while Chagall mixed his colours up at Saint-Paul, where the village weaver made his rugs and shawls on an olivewood loom.

Aeroplanes did land at Nice, but on a grass strip. The departure lounge was a trellised terrace smothered with honeysuckle; the arrival lounge next door was drenched in a vicious Dorothy Perkins rose. The really glamorous people came down overnight on the Blue Train – or, better yet, by boat from New York to lie off in the bay of Cannes. Life was easier, simple, ordered: the rough-and-tumble of tourism had not yet fully struck, and the land lay serenely unaware of impending disaster; magical.

Magic has its components, and the most important of them here is the Light. Without the Light it is fair to say that the Riviera would not exist. In spite of the ruin and the greed along the coastal strip, the Light (and it deserves its capital letter) has not altered. The petrol haze on the seafront has merely dimmed it slightly. It still glows down, sparkling in sequinned disarray upon the deceptively clear sea; still scorches the pale bodies unwisely ignoring its power along the artificial beaches full of vermin. It exaggerates light and shade (shadows here are blacker than pitch) and enhances colour – fierce, harsh almost, brilliantly exploding colour that one never suspected could exist in nature, so that pink is suddenly carmine, the soft green of the maritime pines is viridian, tiled roofs burst with orange fire, and the dust under one's feet is a rich copper.

This of course is why Bonnard and Braque, Monet and Renoir and all the others came here, determined to 'capture the Light' and set it for all time on canvas. My own father was driven to desperation as a painter trying to catch the elusive colour of the olive trees. Was it green or was it silver? Was it blue or a mixture of the three? No two painters ever agreed, and my father, alas!, never caught it at all. For ever his olive trees were the sorry product of the sodden skies of his native England. They never lost the boiled green of broccoli and were a continuing disappointment to him.

The Paris painters were here long, long before Sara and Gerald Murphy 'discovered' the Riviera, pinning its magic on canvas. Van Gogh caught it earlier, and perhaps even better, than most of the others. At any rate he caught the violence of the mistral, that strange wind which hurls and screams down the Rhône valley, bending the cypresses and canes, then turns left above the Camargue to wrestle and rage its way along the coast. It blows itself finally into the sea, ragged and exhausted, somewhere in the direction of Cap Ferrat. And when it does that, *then* watch the light! Watch the clarity of the sky and the landscape scoured by the tearing wind: the brilliance is very nearly blinding. Every root, every tile; every rock and scrubby bush; every tree and church-tower; every clustered village high on its hill – all are startlingly cleansed of dust and haze. So sharp, so outlined, so pristine and clear does it appear that it's almost too much for the eye to take in.

Go into Cannes one morning early. Early like seven o'clock when the beaches are still deserted save for a lone swimmer or two, when the streets are silent except for a shopkeeper sleepily washing down his section of the pavement, and for the fishermen down by the old port hosing down the cobbles under the tables of the fish restaurants which line the quay. This is when you will discover the 'old Riviera' beneath the modern ruin.

Watch the big boxes of mussels, the tubs of oysters, pink prawns and jumping grey shrimps as they are swung off the lorries from the station, straight off the night train from Dieppe and the colder seas of the north. Follow rue Meynadier into the gigantic vaults of the Marché Forville, a tremendous concrete cathedral of aisled trestles piled high with every sort of fruit or vegetable you can imagine; and many you cannot. In season there are pyramids of peaches and nectarines, great green apples, oranges and lemons with the acid leaves still attached, potatoes and plums (the former as small as quail's eggs and golden in the morning light; the latter larger than hen's eggs and velvet blue). Early peas spill in glistening drifts and lettuce is piled in translucent tumbles of jade. Hens and rabbits, alive in small coops, cluck and rustle at one's feet among the cabbage stalks and fallen parsley.

It's not just fruit, vegetables and livestock that you'll find in the Marché. Cheese, too. Round and oblong, square and half-moon; some wrapped in vine leaves, others in the faded leaves of last autumn's Spanish chestnut; some tied in ribbons, others black with charcoal. It is said that the French produce more than 300 kinds of cheese. If that is so, you'll find them all here – plus a few others which have just been invented. And if you still don't fancy anything you see, go on back up rue d'Antibes to a tiny shop on the right hand side where Madame Agnèse has a few more for you to choose from.

Just aside from the flower-market is the fish – slithery spills gleaming fresh from the boats, the scent of brine mixing very pleasantly with the neighbouring roses and carnations. Not *just* with roses and carnations, but the humble marigold, lilies in armfuls, tuberoses, sweet william, mimosa and, in the early days of spring, huge sprays of almond or early cherry.

On the first of May there is lily of the valley – as pungent as cheap soap, as simple, clean and fresh as a mountain brook, yours only for a day or so before it crumples and fades.

Overlying all this is the pungency of roasting coffee, for the market has been open since 5 a.m. when the first trucks rumbled in and a thousand willing, gnarled and chapped hands began the setting up. By noon all this will have been swept away. Nothing

34

will remain to remind you that a vast market has taken place: perhaps just a small pile of rotting peaches, a scatter of spinach, a fallen potato. For the rest of the day the Marché Forville is a car-park for the ruined Riviera.

Back, then, to your hotel – ideally one of the modest ones off the Croisette. The Savoy, the Victoria or the Swiss will do you very well: no sea view, but pleasant little gardens and always a tree to cast speckled shade where it is most needed. You'll eat well here, not over-decorated designer meals but good simple produce such as you have seen at the Marché.

Naturally a visit to the Riviera must include a beach, and there are plenty along the curve of the Croisette and away down the coast past La Bocca. Unfortunately I cannot recommend any, for I have not set foot on a beach for thirty years; but most people find them fun and if you select one of the private concessions, paying a bit for the privilege of clean mattresses and bright umbrellas, you'll doubtless enjoy yourself even though your pockets may be quite a bit lighter by the end of the day.

The sea around Cannes is pretty well clear, the city fathers have seen to that, and each year more improvements are made, so as long as you don't swallow a bucketful you will come to no harm. There used to be a rather ominous little notice, in brass, tucked away on one of the great pillars in the main hall of one of the *grands palais* which flatly stated that no one would be responsible for you if you bathed from their beach. But I think that's been removed now: it would be comforting to know that it had.

After a time, beach life becomes wearing and expensive and you need to look about for other diversions. If you go up to the hills, within half an hour or forty minutes of the hubbub and racketing of the Riviera Strip, you will find unbelievable peace and content- ment in the small villages which top the many craggy mountains overlooking the sea. Greenness and coolth and, perhaps most im- portant of all, silence broken only by the clonking of a distant sheep bell or the cry of a kite or buzzard wheeling high above you in idle swooping circles. This land is still the Riviera, though it bears so little resemblance to the gaudy cities of the plain below.

Up here, in the clean air, the villages have hardly altered since the days when they were used for safety against the invading Saracens and Moors. The narrow streets twist and loop for shade in the summer heat, for warmth in the cold of winter and, above all, for security. The streets are dusty, you can walk barefoot in the powdery ruts or, better still, among the sheets of wild narcissi which cover the hillsides around Thorenc in the spring. Great white drifts which look like the last lingering vestiges of winter's snow until the overpowering scent reminds you that you are indeed treading through millions of flowers.

Further along the valley to the west, lying on a great plain dominated by a tremendous rock called Bauroux (a good 5480 feet high), is the tiny village of Caille – a single village street here, for this is on the plain. The village just huddles round its church under the towering rock, and the street trails out into fields surrounded by dense pinewoods. High among these woods there are secret fields which, like the ones at Thorenc, are sheeted with wild flowers, only here they are not white but gold with cowslips. Acres and acres of them so that you cannot walk without crushing the nodding bell-like heads alive with honey bees from the rows of skeps, or hives, along the edges of the wood.

It is impossible to believe one is so close to the raddled mass on the coast: nothing seems to have altered up here for centuries. Apart from the television aerials ubiquitously thrusting from every tiled roof, nothing very much has.

The people here are of the kindest and warmest. Curious about you, amused by you, but warm and ready to direct you or help you understand their patois, for these are the true people of the mountains and, incidentally, of the Riviera, who came with the Romans, the Italians, the Saracens and the Moors, and all the bloods have mixed together to produce a hardy, tough-living race of astonishingly varied peoples.

It is not everyone who gets any pleasure from walking barefoot in the red dust of the village lanes, or among the superfluity of wild flowers, or who can lie in the whispering mountain grasses listening for the sheep bell. But all this is within the belt called 'the Riviera',

36

and you can take your choice. Beyond Cannes there are ravishing villages like Fayance, Auribeau, Bargemon and Seillans, all with excellent restaurants or modest but extremely reasonable hotels. It's worth making the extra effort to heave yourself off the crowded beaches and go up into the hills: you'll find very few, if any, GB-registered cars. The French know the secrets of these lovely places and are wise to keep them to themselves.

If I write at length about Cannes and its hill-villages, it is only because I know this region better than anywhere else. For years I have had my hair cut here, been to the bank, gone to market, bought my plants and visited my dentist. Inevitably it is closer to my heart than Antibes or Cagnes or even the old whore down the coast, Nice.

Nice nevertheless is, I suppose, the heart of the Riviera proper. Cannes has the air of the faded gentry, with the ghosts of the Russian Court still lingering in an air of elegance and polite charm. Nice, on the other hand, is definitely raffish, vulgar and, for some, more attractive. A port city set on one of the most beautiful bays in the world, the bay of the Angels, with a background of snowy mountains hemming her in from the cruel northern winter, she flourishes among her lemon and orange trees like some lascivious slut, the skirts of her gown, so to speak, spread out around her in waves of ugly suburbia which flounce and trail over every hill and valley. Never closed, noisy and squalid with here and there great elements of beauty and relics of the past which still can catch you unawares and force you to hold your breath with delight. Stand in the very centre of the great Promenade des Anglais which curves around the enormous bay, and look to your left and right in wonder. The towering blocks of apartment buildings, the *frou-frou* and nonsense of the remaining *grands palais* all stuck about with wrought iron and lacy plaster-work, the immaculate gardens stiff with palms and flowering yuccas, the millions of coloured lights which flash and change as the great ball of a copper sun slides into the sea as surely as a penny slips into a slot machine. Darkness falls so quickly: there is almost no twilight here, and the whole promenade is suddenly lit by a tremendous necklace of diamonds. The old whore, defiant of her hidden squalor, radiant, beguiling, brash, beckoning. It is very hard to resist her tattered charms.

In the heat of the morning sun, wander into the old town. An Italian town this, since Nice was, and often still is, called Nizza and belonged to Italy until the late nineteenth century. Here they have very wisely rid the place of cars and trucks and petrol fumes. The old houses lean towards each other, sometimes six or seven storeys high (without lifts). Balconies looped with washing, surrounded with little cages of singing birds and stuffed with old pots and pans frothing with geraniums and petunias.

The streets are silent save for the cries of playing children, or feet hurrying, and the clatter and fluster of pigeons. You can wander into the bread shops (the hot smell of baking almost forces you to) to try a *real* pizza, not one of those dreadful mixtures they shove at you in London and New York, or eat *fougasses* made with anchovies and olives blended together in a thick paste with the sweet bready dough. It all looks, finally, like a piece of well-toasted fretwork. If you have never tried it, and think perhaps that you should, go for a slice of *tapenade*; here again the olive is an ingredient, together with capers and anchovies pounded by pestle and mortar and spread thickly over a slab of pizza-like pastry.

These, apart from the pasta and the fish, are the main delights of Nice from the point of view of gluttony. On the other hand you can just as well give them up and try your hand at the Casino. Both Nice and Cannes have their casinos and you can lose your shirt or win a wardrobe in a short evening.

If this is your kick, try it. You'll see the underbelly of both towns, the pale and anxious, the huddled rich, the Arab princes staking kingdoms, the resentful old women with raddled faces trying again and again to win.

Some do, some don't. That's the Riviera. There is no sympathy, a great deal of envy, some disdain. But no one really gives a tinker's gob: it's all up to you.

Be warned. The Riviera is not cheap. A bottle of fizzy lemonade on the beach at Cannes or at Nice can set you back three quid or more; the mattress on the sands, or on the shingle, and the parasol against the sun could, added together for two weeks, buy you a small car, if you know what I mean.

But, on the other hand, you can always pull yourself up from the wincingly painful pebbles and drive into the mountains behind the town. There, away from the stink of sun-oil, chip-oil and paraffin-oil, from the pleasure boats which are slowly destroying the glorious bay by killing off the fish, you can be high among the pine forests, the alpine flowers, the startled deer and the chubby marmots. It's altogether a different world but, as with Cannes, you can reach it in less than an hour, depending on your resistance to zig-zag roads and sheer drops. In springtime you could swim in the mornings and ski in the afternoons.

And that's really it: everything you need is there in that amazing stretch of land, from beauty and squalor to richness and poverty (of a kind – a gentle kind because poverty never seems quite so desperate in the warmth of the sun, or so I like to think).

For forty years I have said that each year would be the last: I'd never return. The place has become a ruin, the traffic impossible, the guests resistible, the beaches crowded and filthy, the prices beyond belief. Everything I knew years ago has become smothered in high-rise concrete and fast-lane tarmac; it's gone to hell. The entire place is a disaster area.

But. I've always gone back. And I always will. You see, it's the magic and the Light. And they still, in some unaccountable way, remain and pull one back, and whatever happens to the Riviera, as long as those two major attractions remain, it will always be, for all time, better than Rio, or Hong Kong, or Bermuda, or anywhere else in the world.

Sunday Times, 14 February 1988

RETURN TO LONDON

A Short Walk from Harrods

Sitting here, as presently I am, the nicotiana is higher than my head. Well, as high as. The scent is overwhelming, drifting out into the still evening air. I suppose that I should try to find a word other than 'drifting', but that is exactly what scents do on still summer evenings; so it remains. Drifting. It's all part of building up an illusion of peace and calm. I planted the things out in April, earlier than advised, but I did it anyway, and did it so that I should be able to sit one evening quite embowered by blossom and suffocated by heavy scent. And so I am.

A sort of peace descends. It would appear from all outward signs that stress has faded.

Only appear. I still jump like a loon if a book falls, a door bangs, the telephone rings. That's rare. The telephone hardly ever rings. Sometimes it doesn't make a sound for days. And never between Friday afternoon and Monday afternoon. People go away.

Sometimes on Sundays, if it gets really grim, I walk to the station to buy a newspaper I don't need, or want, and talk to the very friendly chap who runs the paper stall. His mate runs the flower stall. We speak of the weather, local football (about which I know nothing), and it breaks the silence.

Heigh-ho. A fat bee nudges rather hopelessly among the fluted white trumpets. If you could talk to a ruddy bee I'd tell it that it was out of luck. You won't get any pollen from that lot; the trumpet is far too narrow. But it's not after pollen. Nectar, that's the word. And it won't get that either.

Trying to engage a bee in conversation, or discuss the state of the day with a portrait, or the wallpaper, is an almost certain sign of incipient madness and/or senility. I don't honestly feel that I have reached either of those stations of the cross: but I have checked it out with others who live alone, and living alone, they assure me, gets you chatting up a storm. To no one.

Well, it fills the silences. Sometimes they are good, the silences, but at times they do get a bit heavy. Music helps, of course. I listen to more music now than ever before.

The evening sun is warm on my face, the terrace tiles still hot under my bare feet, hot from the glory of the day. It really is a kind of contentment. The bee, the nicotianas, the stillness and, high in the tree beyond, the kestrel.

He arrived like a silent dart a few moments ago. Below, on the close-mown grass two wood pigeons waddle about like a couple of blousy bag-ladies, aware, with the extraordinary vision which they possess, of the danger above, but, disinclined to fly until death swoops, they continue to waddle. Very British.

The tree frills in the slight breeze which arrives suddenly like a sigh. The kestrel sways gently, eyes still on me. The nicotiana, the white and yellow daisies, the scarlet bells of the fuchsia rustle and swing, and suddenly, as if the breeze had been a signal, the kestrel takes off in a long, low swoop, glides across the lawns, flustering the bag-ladies, planes upwards over the trees on the boundary and is lost to sight.

All is still. The breeze has dropped as suddenly as it arrived. The garden is still, fading gently into evening. The ice in my whisky chinks, almost convincing me with the serenity of its delicate sound that there is nothing for me to do, or nothing which has to *be* done. But I know very well that there is. The nightly watering chore has to commence. I do find it pretty boring, carting gallons of water about and trying not to bump into the furniture on the way. Dusk is falling slowly, my ice melting; through the fretwork of the tree the elegant shape of Peter Jones looms, sleek, proud, clearly bent on a collision course with the Royal Court Theatre across the square. Lights spring up somewhere on the top floor, an ambulance siren wails, a window is slammed shut, traffic mumbles distantly, a voice calls out, a woman laughs and feet clack-clack along the pavement.

I am back full circle. I'm where I started out on my journey at the meek and wondering age of seventeen.

Consider: at sixteen, the height of my ambition was to construct a cage from garden-bamboo for a pet linnet. Which I did; only to find that I had misjudged the widths of the bars, through which the bloody bird sped. Story of my life, you might say. But you'd be a bit wrong. At seventeen, refusing education of a higher kind, refusing all chances of becoming an office-boy or a runner at *The Times*, refusing, in fact, to follow my exceedingly clever father into his post as art editor, I agreed to an art school place at Chelsea Polytechnic. At seventeen I was a year too young, but apparently showed 'interesting talent', so they took me on, unaware of my lack of education and my cavalier method of measurements (check with bamboo bird cage above). However, I went. And sitting here I can almost see the spire of St Luke's, which was not so far from the school. Which is why I can say that I am back full circle. For this was my area, my manor if you like. I knew it, and loved it, well.

So, at seventeen an art student; at nineteen I was scrubbing out the vats and pots in the tin wash at Catterick camp; at twenty-seven, after a good bit of voyaging, I was back again, became a 'film star', and at fifty, deciding to take stock and readjust the seasoning of life, I left England for Provence and sat up on a mountain among my olives and sheep very contently until I was sixty-seven, when the heavens all of a sudden fell.

So I came back here. To the area in which I had begun to grow up. It was familiar territory: I walked among ghosts, pleasant ones, and felt not so strange, and people were initially very kind until I decided, quite by myself, that solitude was better by far than being 'in demand'. I cut adrift and went my way. A simple life again.

Victoria said: 'Darling. Now put it in your little book. Dinner on the 20th. We'll dine at eight. Too thrilling now that you've become a spare pair of trousers! Wonderfully in demand you'll be. Swamped.' I didn't, in all truth, feel elated. However.

Sheraton gleaming, silver, the usual orchid in that bloody twig

44

basket, clink and chink of cutlery on fine plate. Served by three sullen Filipinos, decent food. Always is at Victoria's.

At dinner I sat between Phillida and Margot. Margot had recently had a brutal nose job and in consequence wore a becoming black lace mask. When I say 'becoming' I wish to differentiate between Margot with a mask and without one. With was far more acceptable.

Opposite me sat Sir Timothy Deadend. Deaf and cross, but apparently brilliant at advising someone or other in the Cabinet. Beside him the Hon. Constance Pullinger, a little high on pot and smiling vaguely into space, crumbling a bread roll, nodding pleasantly at no one. There is no one to nod to here under sixty-five.

'Trodden on a marble,' says Deadend suddenly, blank blue eyes moving slowly in a head as bland, pink and shining as a porcelain doll. 'Who, darling Timmy? Who has trodden on a marble?' Deadend helps himself to salmon mousse, a generous scoop. 'Old Tin Knickers.'

Margot whispers through her black lace to me. 'Who does he mean?'

'Tin Knickers! Seen her run? Trodden on a marble this time. It'll bring her down this time. Splat!'

Phillida asks me if I went to someone's memorial service and I admit that I had avoided it. Apologize.

'Oh, don't apologize! Same old business. Same lot. Those awful songs! That one about building Jerusalem in England's green and pleasant . . . you know? I believe they sing it in the Women's Institutes, a sort of national hymn, and then that actor who always reads a bit of John Donne, and the fat one who looks like a farmer and blubs, and that silly idiot Meredith Dunwiddy sobbing out her heart as if she had *liked* the deceased. "Deceas-ed," they say. Too tiresome. Who was Timmy being vile about?'

'I rather think Mrs Thatcher again.'

Constance Pullinger suddenly came back from wherever she had been to and leant anxiously across the table.

'Who did a hatchet job? Oh, do tell!'

Victoria, behatted as was usual at her suppers, adjusted her little veil, clutched her pearls to prevent them swinging into the mayonnaise. 'Not a hatchet, darling. *Thatcher*. Mrs Thatcher. You know.'

Constance nodded obediently, like a child instructed on going on an errand. She waved the mousse away and then returned to wherever it was she had recently been.

Deadend wiped fleshy lips. 'Tripped on a marble. Mark what I say. Always something trivial that brings them down. Trivial. They all do it, that class. Can't carry corn. Easy to spot 'em. No fibre.'

Phillida was chasing morsels of mousse about her plate as if they were ruby chips; she nodded towards him, mouth full, crumbs of fish falling.

'Oh dear. The grandmother business. Too awful. And the breathless insincerity of it all. Can't someone tell her, Timmy? Shaking hands with all those poor foreigners in front of the fireplace . . . a headmistress at the end of term.'

Then Margot suddenly turned to me from her partner on her right. Cyril Dillford Pryce. 'Cyril tells me that you're living permanently in London. A flat? Sold up in France? Too sad . . . but divine for us poor hostesses! One can always find a *mass* of single women, the place is littered with them . . . but you'll be wildly in demand. Where are you?'

I told her and she nodded agreeably. Apparently I had passed whatever test she had set and I was certain there had been such a thing.

'Well. Not quite sw1, but not far off, and only a short walk from Harrods. Wonderful for you.' Satisfied, she turned back to Cyril.

Constance Pullinger suddenly wrenched open a small silver box, took a small pill, swigged it down with half her glass of white wine and shuddered as if she had taken cyanide. Perhaps she had.

She smiled wanly at me. 'Did someone say Harrods?'

'Yes. Margot asked me where I lived. She seemed pleased that I was so near Harrods.'

'Ah, I see. Yes. Frankly, I never go there now. Who wants to shop in a souk?'

Cyril Dillford Pryce (ex-colonial of some years, his accent all but obliterated except in moments of excitement or anger when errant vowels escaped his control) leant behind Margot's back and nudged me.

'Saw you on the box on Sunday. Simply frightful! Such tosh! I suppose you saw it, can't remember the name. Ages old, black and white.'

I assured him that I never watched myself perform on television. The Filipinos were starting to clear the mousse and re-lay for the next course. Victoria repinned her Cartier clips.

'Thrilling!' she said, one supposed to Cyril. 'I adore really *ancient* movies. We were all so naïve then. What fun it was.'

'Never watch yourself?' Cyril was persisting as his plate was removed.

'Never.'

'How odd! I never do, normally, but my man had it on in the kitchen, so I couldn't resist a peek.'

'A long time ago,' I said.

'Ah ha! I know. Only a dog returns to its own vomit. That it?'

He squealed with pleasure. Beaming around the table. I so hated him that I wished him violently dead.

Perhaps Margot recognized my hatred, for she placed a firm hand on my wrist. 'Look!' she cried happily and a little too loudly. 'Here come those delicious little quails' breasts which Antonia does so brilliantly.'

Suddenly the room was noisy with dishes and service.

I realized, with a thud, that I was actually sitting among the living dead, and I made a silent vow, there and then, never again to put on a dark suit to dine in a cemetery.

I gave up that kind of frivolity, preferring my own company and a large Scotch. No demands were made on me, I wasted no effort, nothing was taken from me, whatever energy yet remained to me was for my own use and pleasure. Far wiser. And so I went off and shopped for food; one has to.

It had not really hit me at first that shopping for one was a consuming business. One chop? One cod fillet? I had not the remotest idea how to cook such things; and I soon found out that in supermarkets things were packaged for two or more. At home, in France, it was far easier in the local market. You could buy one egg, if so you wished. One slice of pizza, a leek, a carrot; and one slice of ham was wrapped up with as much respect and reverence as if one had ordered breast of peacock. I was to learn in time. But just at the beginning it was a bit rum. For a while I existed on frozen packets of junk, on boiled things in bags. It was easy. I could understand the instructions. There was almost no washing-up. And I almost began to enjoy 'walking to the shops', as my sister Elizabeth used to say.

Along the pavement which ran beside the private gardens there was an ill-parked line of cars, looking for all the world like a scattered desert convoy. Mercedes, Jaguars, here and there a modest Volvo, two or three dashing Range Rovers, a Rolls or two. Beside the cars, scatters of women in little groups, chattering.

All the significant signs of moderate and immodest wealth were there. The Hermès scarf, the Chanel bag with chain, Armani pants (these women were waiting for their brats to emerge from the junior school) and sunglasses, heavy gold jangling on wrists, cockatoo-cries of recognition. 'Jessica! All well?' Hope, Trisha, Diana, Caroline, Tessa, Lucy, and on it went. The only ones silent were the raven-locked Lebanese ladies, hair flowing, magenta lips, haze of heavy scent, high heels, leather minis, arms a percussion of crashing gold and platinum.

Under the tree, where the crows nested, the paving stones were marbled with their evil black droppings. A boy of perhaps eight was dragging enormous feet through the muck, satchel slipping from hock-bottle shoulders, tie awry. A woman, possibly pretty although anger had soured her face, dug about in her Chanel bag by a meter. 'Jonathan! Don't do that! What did Miss Jessop say? Tell me?'

The child remained sullenly silent, sniggered only when his mother's car keys fell to the pavement. She cursed, I bent to retrieve them, she took them absently, concerned with Miss Jessop, I began to move off into the starling-chitter of the waiting mothers.

'What did she say?' and then calling to me: 'Oh. Thank you. Jonathan! For the last time . . .'

'Said I was a rotten little bugger.'

The strangled cry of 'Jonathan!' reached me at the same time almost as her follow-up cry of 'I say! Do you have change for the meter? I'm absolutely done for.'

She looked distraught, bag hanging open. Jonathan, scraping birdshit thoughtfully, said: 'I'm a disgrace to the school, she said.' There was a gleam of malice on his pinched face.

I set my plastic bags on the pavement and sorted out my small change.

'Don't I know you?'

I handed her a five pence piece.

'I don't think so. Will this do?'

She took the money, still looking at me intently, disturbed.

Jonathan kicked at the crow droppings.

He was being left out. 'That's what she said, Mum. To the whole class.'

She suddenly struck him swiftly; he ducked, sniggering. 'She *did*.'

The woman's face cleared. 'Brilliant! I know! You used to be Dirk Bogarde. Years ago. That Dickens thing at school. *How* we blubbed!' And as I turned away with my plastic bags, she said furiously: 'Don't call me *Mum*! Mother or Mummy if you must. Never Mum.' She called her thanks for the five pence as I became lost in the jabbering mass of small idiot children. I used to be someone. Who the hell was I now?

The next afternoon was a little different: I had promised to go and see Mae-Ellen. I was not passionate about the idea, but felt that the walk, almost to Sydney Street, would be good exercise, which I had promised my physiotherapist to attempt.

Mae-Ellen had freckles and red hair, cut in what she terms a 'bang'; she wore white stockings and neat little lace-up shoes. The stockings, which seem to be a favourite with certain kinds of American women (leaning to intellectualism) gave her legs the unhappy impression of upended milk bottles. She was very warm and welcoming. Offered me herbal tea which she was about to infuse, but I declined, and sat me down in a wickerwork chair while she moved about purposefully with teapot and kettle.

'It was so great to see you! Just bumping into you like that. When was the last time? At Ruthie's on Delfern Drive . . . that was just years ago. And you really haven't changed. I mean, we're *all* getting old but I still swim four lengths every day . . . I'm with the embassy right now. It's so worth while . . .' She poured water into the tin teapot. Caught up a mug. 'I counsel Army wives out on the bases. You know? I won't say *where*, but I guess you know . . . they really have a time, you know? It's lonely on the bases; they feel kinda trapped, you know? I suffer for them. I really do.'

I rather suffered for myself, as it happened. I hated where I was almost the instant that she had opened the narrow door. Seeing me look about the dingy room, she chattered off again.

'I just borrow this place from a girl I know. She's great. She's gone off to Uttar Pradesh or somewhere; there's a famine or a war, something, and Arlene can't resist offering her services. She's wild. Sure you won't take some mint tea?'

The room looked out over St Luke's churchyard. It was a dismal day, but it was equally dismal in the house. Bamboo and wicker furniture, dragged blue paint walls, a stark bunch of dried pink larkspur bound with twine, decaying in a basket. Mae-Ellen stirred her mug with a pencil.

'What I'm doing is really essential, I just talk to these women and they talk right back and we have a conversation and that releases them, you know? Stuck on that base, hostile women in the woods . . . well, they have the PX and movies and the medics and so on . . . but they don't feel at home in the United Kingdom. They never go out. It's spooky and sad. Those hostile people just outside the wire.'

I nod and agree. What else?

'I say to them when I visit, now look: there are so many wonderful compensations you got. You have your husbin, you have your children. I mean that is just so right, so traditional, so wonderful.

Now then. You have your husbin, you have kids, and they all love you, and that is one helluva deal. Do you know that? You want proof of that? Well, the very first proof of that love is the very first gift your kid gives you. Know what? That gift which the child will offer to the giver of life. You, its mother. And you know what that is? It is shit.'

She sat back and glittered at me in the dim room, triumphantly.

'Defecation is the very first "thank you" from your child. It is just automatic. I think it's kinda marvellous. Uplifting. Of course, in our terms we'd say it was an automatic reflex, but I say that it's the deep psychological desire, buried way deep down in the subconscious of the new-born, that insists on giving thanks for our life. Isn't that a marvellous thought? Sure you won't take mint tea? I'm making a fresh pot.'

I left Mae-Ellen's a little earlier than she had intended. But enough was enough. I pleaded the walk home and having to take it easy, and some shopping I'd remembered I had to do before the shop closed. I got out exhausted and grateful for the air outside.

The King's Road was still the King's Road. By that I mean that I first walked it in wonderment at seventeen and now, at seventy, it still has the same effect. In some strange way, it still *feels* the same. I still *feel* seventeen. I am surrounded by familiars, altered but recognizable. I said, earlier on, that I walked with ghosts. And so I do. Not all of whom I knew, or even met, but they must still be about. Oscar Wilde coming from Tite Street, Lillie Langtry going up to the Cadogans', Carlyle hurrying to his tobacconist, Augustus John in sagging dressing gown off to the Five Bells.

My parents were here too; when they were young and I just born. Walking down to the Good Intent, or to the Blue Cockatoo on the Embankment. Henry Moore bought his packets of vine-charcoal from the shop on the corner; and Graham and Kathleen Sutherland, elegance far beyond anything I had ever seen before. And Danuta must bounce along somewhere. I can see her now, heavy Polish breasts jiggling under her loose shirt, broad feet in flat sandals striding to the squalid little studio she had in a crumbling terrace of Regency houses where the fire station stands today. But

I very well remember her removing my virginity there, on the rug before her plopping gas-fire, and casting it, and finally me, aside as contemptuously as an old jacket. In 1939 she went home to Warsaw for the summer recess. And that was that.

So I am not unfamiliar with my area. It fits me, and even though the players have altered out of all recognition, the game, as it were, remains the same. There are black faces now among the white. Bedraggled girls in black tights and Doc Martens, shaven-headed youths crashing the kick-starts of their motor-bikes. There is a stink of greasy food, of cheap coffee, the beat of heavy metal thumping in the air. All, really, familiar. Different from the people we were at their age. But, remember, at their age I was making birdcages for a linnet.

The shop is still open. I take a wire basket and wander in, wondering what to eat for my supper. A fraught business. A tin of soup? Easy. No mess. One dish to wash. Perhaps some ham? Cold ham and boiled potatoes. Perhaps with a bit of chutney. I was, I realized, muttering aloud to myself. I tripped over one of those blasted shopping trolleys, usually tartan, which elderly ladies drag behind them in supermarkets. The woman, in a plum-cloth coat and pudding-basin hat, glared at me as if I had attempted to snatch her bag, shrugged off my apology and turned back to her companion, a thin woman in a knitted beret. 'You was sayin'?' she said to plum-cloth. 'Well. I said to 'im, well then I said. What's that lump doing there? Wasn't there lunchtime. Very nasty it looks. Very nasty. You watch your bleedin' mouth, 'e says to me. Don't meddle! Well, I says, you go to Boots cash chemist and get something to put on it. Get lorst! 'e says. Silly old cat. My own child! Own flesh and blood. Flabbergarsted, I was.' Considering ham or pie at the counter, listening with curiosity to the conversation behind me, I was all unaware of mounting irritation from the woman next to me. She started to push hard at my wire basket with her own.

'Do you frightfully mind?' Her voice icy with disdain. We had crossed the Great Divide, there would be no democratic encounter here between her mushroom hat, well-cut silk dress and tight grey hair, and my aged anorak, dirty jeans and trainers. I was ready for the sacrifice and, armed with this reassurance, she pressed forward. I did not budge. Not a millimetre. I willed her to have another bash at my basket and this she did, swinging at mine like a demolition ball and chain.

'I did ask you to move. I *am* trying to shop.'

'And I, madam.'

'Here before you. And I know exactly what I want. So.'

'And I do. Exactly.'

A youth hovered about behind the glass counter. She raised a jewelled fist to summon him.

'Young man! Smoked salmon. Scottish, not farmed. Eight ounces.'

She turned to me once again and demanded that I move. I said that I would.

When I had been served.

This trivial and unseemly squabble had reached the point where I thought she might see fit to swing her basket at my head, her eyes burned with such dislike and contempt, but at that instant Mr Collinson, crisp in white apron, eyes sparking with mischief, was quite suddenly in attendance.

'Ah! M'Lord! There you are. What can we do for you today? Pie?'

The mushroom hat and the silk dress moved swiftly away. She stared at me, white with hostility.

Mr Collinson, beaming at a minor victory, clasped his hands.

'The ham, m'Lord? Of course. Can I tempt you to three slices?'

Behind me in the queue a woman's voice said: 'Oh my dear . . . Gerald and I had to dine with them on Tuesday. They really won't do, you know. I mean, Christmas cards from Kensington Palace stuck all over the room. In June! Quite impossible.'

Takes all sorts in my manor. A goodly mix, as my father would say. At the check-out, plum-coat had beaten me to it.

'My own flesh and blood, Chrissie. Did you ever?'

Walk up to my square: sunlight freckling through the plane trees. But no dogs leaping in idiot welcome, no scent of freshly cut hay, no scuttering lizards on the stone walls. No voice from the terrace calling: 'Were the London papers in yet?'

Emptiness sings. Perfectly all right. No problem.

How the hell did I get here?

Independent on Sunday, 30 September 1990

Cricket Season

To the Editor of *The Times*

Sir: I was happy to see a 'singing cricket' hopping about among some weeds in a greenhouse last Tuesday ('Last stand for "singing cricket" depleted by the fickle summers', 4 September). He is a member of a small colony which gives endless delight to various nieces and nephews.

It, the colony, has been in the gardens for ages . . . and it is a good way from Petworth, but still in West Sussex. So that is another 'sighting'. All is not lost. Yet.

Sincerely

DIRK BOGARDE
London

The Times, 4 December 1992

55

My Favourite Bookshop

John Sandoe, London

I really can't remember when I first went into John Sandoe's shop in those squashed little cottages in Blacklands Terrace. I only know that it was years ago and that I was not, as I now am, a regular client.

I wandered in from time to time looking, usually, for something which was out of print or which no other bookseller had come around to stocking. I also went there when I had only the vaguest knowledge of what I wanted. 'It's got "Earth" in the title, it's not about hunting but there is a fox, and I can't remember the publisher.' That sort of idiocy. But I got my copy of *Gone to Earth* by Mary Webb (that's how long ago it was).

I believe that the shop in those days belonged to a Mr Chatto, who was youngish and obliging and who seemed permanently to be pushing through an avalanche of books. Just, indeed, as the present owners do today. I remember first seeing the shop when I was a student up the road at Chelsea Polytechnic. I was ambling down a calm King's Road to my bus stop outside Peter Jones, almost opposite the flat where Percy Grainger lived, and bought a packet of five Player's cigarettes from what was then a seedy little newsagent and tobacconist.

Later, much later, after the war, Mr Chatto was installed, and after him John Sandoe came along, in 1957, and that is when I first really took notice of what was soon to become a 'singular bookshop', as opposed to just a bookseller. There is, as we know today, a marked difference between them.

Living, as I did then, in the country and seldom coming into London, I made only rare visits to the crammed and cramped little shop, and sought, as always, something that was out of print, lost, or published the year before. Something, anyway, difficult to get.

Sandoe catered for those oddities wonderfully well, just as today his successors, Rubio, Johnny, Sean, Stewart and the engaging, encyclopedic Perina (whose name I never can remember and in consequence just call 'Lady'), do with undiminished fervour and flair.

The absolute love of books which this shop engenders is hugely joyous. One feels that two hours spent in one or other of the jammed little rooms – there are four as far as I remember at this instance: two down, one up, and one in the cellar – will be rewarding, refreshing and never questioned by the owners. Indeed, they will often join you in your quest, because, frankly, up in the paperback room the wealth of works, the sliding panels concealing book upon book, the spinning towers stacked with glossy pocket editions bewilder the most ardent browser.

But the staff seem to know, with uncanny skill, just exactly where Molly Keane, Belloc and Brontë hide, where the erudite tomes on whatever theme are to be found.

A bookshop should be a familiar place, somewhere one goes for the sheer love of books, for the smell and the feel of them, for the companionship of others who share the joy of touching, holding, reading and learning. In the supermarket booksellers with their dizzying displays, their pyramids of bestsellers, one is intimidated, constantly lost in the wealth of glittering titles, bemused by a request answered by a computer which indicates the number of copies held of the title one has asked for, the price, position on the shelf, shelf position in the shop. Tills ring, green lights flash, and buying a book becomes as simple and as uninvolving as buying a packet of envelopes.

John Sandoe's is not like this at all. I well remember starting out to learn how to cook, after sixty years of inertia, and asking 'Lady' for help. She instantly strode across the shop and took a book from among thousands and assured me that it contained all I would ever need to know about cooking for *ever*. She was right. I have used it until it has powdered. She knew instantly, among the bewildering wall of cookery books, the precise one for me.

Bookseller, 8 January 1993

Radio 4: Britain's Vital Lifeline

To the Editor of the *Daily Telegraph*

Sir: I am well aware that I endeavour to live as privately and quietly as possible in this now over-intrusive country of ours, but I am not dead, or unaware of the gangrenous erosion and decay to the standards and qualities of our life which are presently taking place with appalling rapidity.

However, I confess that I did miss out on the disastrous suggestion that Radio 4 should come off long wave, there to be replaced by an all-news network.

After spending over one-third of my life abroad, I am only too well aware of the urgent need we have for Radio 4. It was a lifeline for so many people who had no other immediate access to their own language.

It was vastly important to our local friends, neighbours and companions, who listened to it as avidly as we ourselves. I remember well the awfulness of the Heysel football disaster, when – for the first time ever – I saw that we were in all the headlines as *les hooligans anglais*. But even the impact of this dreadful action was mitigated to some degree by Radio 4. With the knowledge of this programme it was felt that something so shocking must surely be a terrible aberration.

After all, didn't we invent fair play? We were a cultured and civilized race. Our current affairs discussions, our idiosyncrasies, our humour, the elegance and perfection of our spoken word, our points of view most sensibly and calmly argued were always of immense value abroad.

I agree absolutely with Sir Roger de Grey that Radio 4 is perhaps the greatest public relations programme for Britain, the true Britain, that we have.

God knows, there is precious little else left now that is fit for export. To axe its existence would be to amputate yet another healthy and flourishing limb of our dying reputation and honour abroad.

DIRK BOGARDE
London

Daily Telegraph, 18 August 1993

A BIG ISSUE

The Right to Die with Dignity

Thirty-four years ago, at Roy Plomley's invitation, I chose my 'Desert Island Discs' for BBC Radio. At the end of 1989, I ill-advisedly agreed to appear on the programme again. Instead of a quiet, pleasant conversation, it had become a cross-examination. My manager had just died of cancer, and I was asked if I myself had fears of a slow and protracted death. I said no, I had taken care to sort that one out. Some days later, I was stopped in the street by a woman who asked if she had heard me right. I said, yes, she had. She then asked if I could assist her with her very ill husband. All I could do, alas, was to try to offer a few words of comfort.

The programme brought a great deal of mail, nearly all of it from people in distress requesting help. Among the letters was one from the Voluntary Euthanasia Society in London, asking if we could arrange a meeting. I agreed, and shortly afterwards found myself a vice-president of VES. It gradually got around that I was prepared to stand up and be counted.

About eighteen months later, the European Parliament debated a recommendation by a health and environmental sub-committee that 'assisted death' for intolerably incapacitated patients should be a legal 'last right'. In Britain a sixteen-strong all-party group of British MPs and peers met for the first time to discuss the issue. As they prepared for their inaugural session, I gave this interview to the Daily Telegraph.

Desperate people write to me, slip notes under my door or stop me in the street. Never is it to say: 'thank you for your book' or 'you were funny in so and so', but to ask: 'could you help?' They have a dying parent in shrieking pain, or daughter or relative who has been in a horrific traffic accident, and they are in despair.

It is extraordinary. Friends I have known for years now talk about how much they want to die peacefully and with dignity. They believe, as I do, that so long as we are *compos mentis*, we must be allowed the right to decide – but only as a last resort – to be assisted to die peacefully. Before I spoke out they did not like to bring up the subject because in this country, I believe, euthanasia is still as much a taboo as talking about anti-Semitism.

People may, as I have, sign an advance declaration or 'living will' to the effect that they do not want life-prolonging treatment if there is no chance of recovery from severe illness or they are incapable of rational existence. They also have a right to expect sufficient doses of pain-killers to relieve intolerable distress.

Even so, a doctor may only ease the path to the end. He cannot lawfully assist or deliberately speed up death with lethal doses of pain-killers. That is the grey area where death may be either eased or appallingly prolonged. And it is where there is a great deal of hypocrisy, particularly by doctors, many of whom are critical of me.

That is precisely what we must discuss more openly, and I hope that the new committee will set the ball rolling. One poll shows that nearly half of GPs would be prepared to assist death in appropriate circumstances if it were legal.

Of course there are 'good' doctors; kind and thoughtful people. One such helped the aunt of a friend. This gentle, religious woman was dying hideously with cancer and in such pain she pleaded with us over and over to be let go. We sat in her kitchen with the gramophone on trying to cover the noise of her deep anguish. Eventually the Roman Catholic nurse was instructed to give her a larger dose of pain-killer, followed by another larger dose.

It is not self-aggrandisement that has led me to take a public stance. If I was not also able to say: 'I have seen screaming pain', if I had not nursed it, seen the utter ruination it can cause both to the patients and those who care for them, or if I had not been asked to terminate a life, I would not be so vehement about the need to help people who are begging for death.

I experienced the despair when my manager and companion of fifty years lay dying in London, totally paralysed with Parkinson's disease and terminal cancer and virtually speechless. He was not shrieking, but was in deep, dire distress. When we lived in France I had promised that I would help him, but he had not put his request in writing, and we did not know about signing a 'living will'.

I would have done something – though I could not have stood in a court and proved that was what he wanted – but eventually he slipped into a coma. Almost his last words as his night nurse and I turned him were: 'If you did this to a dog they'd arrest you.'

My views were formulated as a 24-year-old officer in Normandy. The jeep in front of us went up and we flung ourselves down a bank. There was this chap in the long grass beside me and all I could make out were the words, 'Help, kill me.' He had no arms, face or legs. I took out my revolver, but as I did so he was taken away and somebody else dealt with him – I heard the noise.

As the war went on, I saw more people taking the law into their own hands and I was convinced by this and later natural selections that there is no sanctity of life in existing in great pain if you are never going to get better, or will be on a life support machine for ever, if your choice is to go. People in that state who say 'let me go' are not afraid. One friend was so paralysed by a stroke that the only evidence of any movement was a tear. Perhaps without modern medicine she could not have been kept alive.

We are told that no one need put up with or die in intolerable pain. That is absolute bunk. People do die in pain and you can't imagine the hideousness of it. Hospices are admirable in helping terminally ill people to a peaceful death, but they are not available for all, and pain relief at home can be appallingly ineffective.

I know that some people find the idea of active voluntary euthanasia morally reprehensible. Nor do I deny that there are different approaches to dying. For instance, Lee Remick, my friend of nearly thirty-five years, who died bitterly of cancer recently, would never have asked anyone to hasten her end. She was that kind of woman and fought to hang on.

But there are changing views about the current way of death and it is time to talk about them. If we continue bringing people before the courts and exonerate – or convict – when they have carried out a 'mercy killing', we will simply bumble on as before and brush the whole issue under the carpet.

I hope the new committee will trigger some fresh thinking among politicians. Many are terrified in case showing support for voluntary euthanasia makes them unpopular with their voters. Yet polls show that most people are in favour. Of course abuse is possible. Thus any change in the law must be accompanied by proper protection, as in Holland. It is also important to state that nowhere does the Voluntary Euthanasia Society advocate getting rid of handicapped babies or the elderly and infirm.

When it comes to it, I believe we are all quite capable of being trusted with making decisions about our own lives. We did not choose to be born, but it is our privilege, I believe, to decide how we enjoy, endure and finally end our lives.

Daily Telegraph, 16 July 1991

The Old are Funnier and Wiser

To the Editor of the *Daily Telegraph*

Sir: Do we really need a Centre For Policy on Ageing? What on earth is it doing? Who invented it and for what reason? Dr Eric Midwinter (an appropriate name one would think) feels that a whole new problem has arisen in society (report, 8 Nov.).

A twelve-million strong 'forgotten army' are, he suggests, creeping around in the shadows, being made abject fun of by the media.

Well, the media have always favoured stereotypes, and so indeed do most of the people who watch television. They feel uneasy if they are asked to watch anyone behaving in an unfamiliar manner. They don't care for elderly people who keep abreast of youth. Those people are considered with great scorn – 'mutton dressed as lamb'.

But if someone of my age, for instance, recommends a brand of beer or type of bread, it is generally felt, because of our vast experience and age, that we tortoise-people know what we're talking about. The viewer will nod in happy agreement and buy a bottle and the bread.

Dr Midwinter would have us believe that this 'forgotten army' is 'the most dramatic realignment. . . since the Industrial Revolution', which is, begging his pardon, a bit silly. The most dramatic realignment since the Industrial Revolution is that today hundreds of people can fly off to Tenerife, rent a timeshare in Alicante or just retire, out of the shadows, to the sun of Marbella – or nearly everyone who can afford to, and there is a vast group of tortoise-age who can. So he had better consider *that* happy band before he lumps us all together as the tired, lonely and forgotten.

Why on earth should 'the man with the chocolates who goes through hell and high water' deliver them to his mother-in-law rather than his girlfriend? What sort of terrible aberration can this be? Who would believe it? Who would buy the violet creams?

Older people are much funnier and wiser than the young; we have learned not to take ourselves so seriously, got over most of the uncertainty, the intensity and the desperation of youth, and have settled back.

Dr Midwinter confuses 'laughing at' with 'laughing with' – an important difference. 'Older people', he says, 'are deployed as the counterparts, the hollow husks of existence.'

Not in this house they aren't. We have a lot of mileage still left.

DIRK BOGARDE
London

Daily Telegraph, 9 November 1991

BACK TO WORK

The End of a Long Breather

A portrait of Bertrand Tavernier, who directed my final film,
Daddy Nostalgie (*These Foolish Things*)

We did the last shot on *Death in Venice* at noon one hot August day in a plum orchard high in the mountains above Bolzano. And that, after six months of exhausting work, was that. As far as I was concerned it was the temporary end to my acting career. After more than twenty years' effort I wanted a very long rest, and drove, that morning, down to France and the peasants' house which I had bought and to which I was determined to retreat. Not, as most British journalists insist, to 'retire'. Merely retreat for a breather, and perhaps, one day, to kick-start my acting life again. Meanwhile, I would concentrate on rest and, with any luck, writing.

There was no work for me in the UK. That was certain, and I no longer enjoyed the kind of work that was done there in the cinema. In Europe the whole thing was very different, very alive, very innovative, very exciting. But for the time being I was unworried.

I had started out in 1947 when our directors always wore blue suits and red carnations, and hurried us all off to the studio bar as soon as the lunch-break came up to have a pink gin or two. It was very much a social affair: hardly work at all. And deeply unsatisfying. After a raft of mainly tedious films, broken only by the magical arrival on my scene of Joseph Losey, with whom I worked with a passionate but ill-founded belief that we could together buck the system, I decided to pack up in England and try my luck abroad. Losey and I failed at the box-office but gained critically. Not at all the same thing, alas.

In Europe they took greater risks, and my first offer from that direction came from Jean Renoir in Paris. This failed, sadly, but other directors beckoned, and I heeded their calls happily. Visconti, Resnais, Cavani and Verneuil among others.

A whole new life emerged for me as far as the cinema was concerned, a new breath was taken, culminating, I suppose, with Rainer Werner Fassbinder, a maverick genius, who made a wonderful film from a novel by Nabokov and then, deliberately, for reasons best known to himself, cut it to shreds and destroyed perhaps the best film work I had ever done. In despair – which happened also to be the unhappy title of the film – I decided to lick my wounds and pull out again. It was a long haul this time: twelve years. But, quite suddenly, fate took a hand and altered my tracks.

One dull day a good friend telephoned me to ask for the private telephone number of an actor she was trying to contact in order to send him a script. She had an address, but felt that it was essential to speak to him as well. Naturally, even to a good friend, I could not divulge the actor's private number. Private, after all is said and done, is simply that. Private.

This caused a good deal of impatience. 'Oh, come on! I won't flog it to the *Sun*! It's terribly important. Bertrand Tavernier is just about to start work on a script and he wants to talk to Xyz. Just his number? Be sweet.'

At the mention of Tavernier's name I was instantly alert. Bells rang, the day was suddenly no longer dull. The actor whose name she wished to secure was more or less my age. That is to say, anything he could reasonably be expected to play I probably could. From the point of view of age anyway. Curiosity pushed me to the edge of discretion. I paused on the brink. Fell. 'What is the script? Do you know?'

'It's one you turned down five years ago, actually. They want to go ahead now, with Xyz.'

'And Tavernier?'

'And Tavernier. He has already cast the other two roles, now he wants to talk to . . .'

Memory drifted back. Five years ago or so I had indeed read a rather whimsy-cutesy script about a dying man, his sullen wife and his mournful daughter. There was rather a lot of 'Daddykins' and

'Pussykins' in it, and it didn't in all truth seem a role for me. So I set it aside.

More to the point, five years ago there was no sign of Tavernier being in any way connected with the project. I had seen almost every film he had ever made and knew, perfectly well, that I would walk barefoot across Antarctica for the chance to work with him.

Was my friend absolutely certain about Tavernier? She was. And Jane Birkin, a huge star in France, was to play the daughter.

Heedless of shame, I put the situation into turn-around on the spot. Could my friend tell Tavernier that I would like, very much, the chance to reconsider my ill-judged decision of five years ago and would play the role under his direction whatever the script was like? If, however, it was too late, and he was absolutely set on Xyz, I would give them the agent's number.

'Look, I'm just a friend of Jane Birkin's, I'm not a ruddy agent! She has asked me to get the number.'

'Be sweet. Could you find out for me?'

She did; I was accepted. And spent the next three days in a state of terror and joy. Terror that I would have to go back to the cinema again after a happy twelve-year holiday; joy that Tavernier had agreed to me and not my rival.

Why, I wonder, did I expect him to be neat, simian, dark, intense? A kind of Truffaut or Malle? I suppose the extreme elegance and intellectualism of his work had given me this completely false image of him. The man who arrived for lunch was quite the opposite. A bear-like man, tall, a shock of white hair, laughing eyes behind thickish glasses, a bursting laugh, perfect English, quite immaculate in tweeds and lace-up brogues (these I would not see again once work started).

This was a Professor, albeit a young one, not a Movie Director. It seemed that we talked together endlessly about my role: he was sympathetic to my doubts about the script, but offered a new version which was, indeed, a great deal better.

The 'Daddy' was far less aged and frail; I suggested that we try to make him rather more of a bourgeois fellow, a man who was not altogether lovable; ageing, lonely, afraid, and reaping the rewards of his solitude, of his selfishness and years of neglect of both his wife and his daughter. Brought face to face with a bleak, not to say improbable, future, he was trying to adjust. Not very well.

I wanted him to be a bit of a fibber rather than a downright liar, a man not lacking in charm, not unaware of the good things of life, desperately trying to hold on to the drifting wreckage of his life.

To all this Tavernier agreed. I knew that it was up to me to demonstrate this creature we had decided on, when we got to France and down to work. This was a director who would improvise as one improvised; as the character of 'Daddy' developed, so he would assist by adding or, perhaps, by subtracting. It was evident from the very beginning that it would be a joint venture. We would create together; I would not be left to wobble about alone. A merciful delight.

'Bring a suitcase full of all your old clothes. Ties, shoes, things you are comfortable in . . . that are worn, shabby. You have such things?'

I had. I carted an Oxfam shop's-worth of old clothing to Paris for his selection, which he picked through with extreme care, from ties to cardigans with holes in the sleeves and missing buttons. All we bought extra was one blue shirt, and that itself was secondhand.

Nothing, nothing at all, was film costume. The shoes were scuffed, the ties I had used in movies from 1953. Assembled, and with me inside, slightly heavy, hair unkempt, bald patch glowing like a dinner plate, 'Daddy' began to emerge.

Tavernier grunted his pleasure and turned his attention to the rest of the cast – Odette Laure, who played my wife, and Jane Birkin, my daughter. Here again the clothes were essential. Jane had a pair of men's khaki pants, darned in the seat, and an old V-neck pullover too large for her. Odette, because she was rather more social in the stultifying life of the little coastal town in which we lived, was slightly better dressed. She was a 'correct' little provincial wife.

If I emphasize the costumes here, it is for a reason. No detail was too small to engage Tavernier. The sugar on the table, the

73

oysters on the tray, the handkerchief in one's pocket, the wrinkled socks. This was the complete *auteur* at work: he supervised everything, from the plants in their pots to the lenses in the camera and the kind of sound he wanted (not always virginal: wind could intrude, traffic, birds). But, above all, what he wanted was the truth. Nothing else would satisfy him, and nothing else was offered. I remember, the first day we all met together in Paris, his last, vastly important warning: 'You will have to be very patient with me. You are three people in one very small villa in Bandol, and I am shooting a movie in Cinemascope!' Anywhere else this slender little story would have been shoved on to a 22-inch screen with a commercial break halfway through. But not Tavernier's film.

It has been written of him, countless times before, that he is an intellectual film-maker . . . which is probably true, but it doesn't intrude to the point of bewildering one with theory and science. He knows more about the cinema than practically any director I have ever worked with, Visconti coming a close second. He has seen, it would appear, every film ever made, knows every player, the directors, the lighting cameramen, even the great make-up artists . . . he revels in the cinema. In London I have seen him come into dinner clutching two enormous plastic bags bursting with rare videos which he has tracked down with all the intensity and excitement of Howard Carter at the tomb of Tutankhamun.

Tavernier has also been described as a Russian novelist, a Dutch painter, a blues singer and an Irish playwright. Well, perhaps he is: it's a little bit above my head to grant him all these attributes. I mean, I know what is meant, because I too have seen the qualities there in him myself, but it's a little arty-farty for someone who is intrinsically first and foremost a film-maker. Passionate about the cinema, he is also well aware of how to explore, with his camera, the very soul of the characters he places in his Cinemascope film.

You don't just act for him. You literally become: and if that sounds daft, that is precisely what happens. Or what is expected of you to make happen. You do not offer him, as it were, a packet of corn flakes, glossy and bright exterior, unknown contents. You do not play the cover: he insists that you play the contents. Far too many players in the cinema choose only to offer the cover of the package and never explore the contents. It's all show and no effect.

As with an onion, one is required to remove skin after skin after skin until, finally, away-down-there-at-the-bottom, the tender green shoot of life is exposed. It is not a painful experience under his probing eye. It is exhilarating. One ends ragged-out but satiated. A new person has been created.

No 'take' is ever the same. Variations take place. Something one may have done instinctively in one take he pounces on with excitement and adds to another, one molecule of work combining with another to form a new dimension in the character. It is a tremendously exciting experience, hard (we would stagger from bed at 6 a.m., no coffee, no comfort, rehearse until 8 a.m., and only then be allowed refreshment; and we worked, with one hour off for lunch, until 8 at night on occasions), but no one could possibly complain.

It is the truth which hits audiences in the gut when they watch a Tavernier film, the twisting of a tiny screw of remembrance, the feeling he imparts through his characters to the spectator that they have shared exactly the emotion, the joy, the despair, the wry fun, or the heartbreak he is offering. Because he knows all these things himself, and is aware of them in others. His concentration on set is intense, there is none of the idiotic reverence so often imposed upon a set by some directors, just a determined, silent desire to get on film exactly what is demanded of him. The best: recognition, awareness, above all, truth.

When the film was finally being edited, he discovered that there was the need for one extra, final scene. He called me to tell me, and to ask me to try to write for him a piece about pain and death. I had recently been witness to both, as indeed so had he. I said, almost despairingly: 'Bertrand . . . pain is not intellectual, you cannot rationalize it . . . It is like a bad neighbour, with you all the time.'

Bertrand interrupted me urgently on the line from Paris. 'That is it! Write it! Write that!' And we finished the film.

I have said, when asked, that Visconti is the Emperor of Film,

Losey is the King, Tavernier is the Genius. And, for me, so he is, a genius in the minutiae of life which he gets on to a cinema screen as no one else has ever done quite so brilliantly before. Nothing very much happens in a Tavernier film. Just all of life.

Sunday Telegraph, 5 May 1991

An Orderly Man Returns to the Pin-Spot

From my earliest days, say about three years old, I was constantly told by my parents and our Nanny that Little Boys Should Be Seen And Not Heard or, more to the point perhaps, that one must NEVER DRAW ATTENTION TO ONESELF.

It seems to me that I have been steadily doing my best for the last sixty-something years to ignore that sensible and good advice. I have spent ages forcing people to regard me, to be aware of me; standing centre-stage and in a pin-spot (when available), and, as I would have been told, drawing attention to myself and behaving in a most ungentlemanly manner.

If I say that I fled into the arms of the theatre because there was nothing else that I was any good for, you might well raise an eyebrow. Oscar Wilde said 'the stage is the refuge of the too charming,' and I have a hideous feeling that in this, as in so many other of his epigrams, he was absolutely correct. As a foul little boy I remember overhearing again and again the dreadful remark, 'He *is* very charming; don't worry about him,' as my distraught parents sought to get me educated.

Hopeless despair on my account was supreme in our family for years. Until one brilliant spring day when I marched up the hallowed steps at Sandhurst as a spick-and-span officer. Charm had once again come to my rescue, for there was precious little of anything else. I was very good at square-bashing, splendid at yelling orders and preventing an entire squad of men from marching determinedly into Aldershot town centre by a nifty, and brilliantly timed, 'Abooooout turn!'

My beaming smile, signifying disgusting conceit and a wholly smug 'I can do that', reaped rewards. I was disobeying the rules, drawing attention to myself and being seen and heard all at the one time. I would never have survived otherwise. Disgracefully, I am still 'at it'.

For some time, when I reached my mid-century, I abandoned this slightly reprehensible business, quit the Cinema and the Theatre and faded happily away into the bucolic life of a modest agriculturist in France. And when this came to an abrupt and unhappy end, as it had to, I found myself back in an almost alien land and a vastly altered city, London.

I was aghast. All the clichés were true. A fish out of water, high and dry, a stranger among his (very few by this time) friends. What to do? There was no possibility of the Cinema now, too old, and hated it anyway; no hope ever of returning to the Theatre (once you have lost your nerve it has gone for ever).

For something to do while I lived abroad, I had started to write. The long winter evenings dragged. There was no one around to 'charm' and nothing at all to do once the chores on the land had finished with the sunset. So, I wrote. And I had not the least idea that writing would entail the utter horror of public appearance; that I would have to go out and sell the product.

All that, I thought, had been done and forgotten when I quit the Cinema. There, I expected to promote the work; to suffer the Critic and the dwindling audiences who had to be whipped into the cinema with hysterical hype.

The worst prospect of my new career was the signing session. I had grown out of the publicity habit. I did my best to scuttle away. Impossible. You had to flog the book; your book; all your own work, not like a film which you shared with a great many others – strong backs to shoulder the blame with you.

Alone, sitting beside the dreadful till, faced with (if you were lucky) your readers as the money rang up loudly, was as near to absolute disgrace as anything I can remember. I did hear a woman in Harrods exclaim with disdain: 'My dear! *Look* what he's doing now! Selling himself in public!' Which was exactly, and precisely, what I was doing. It was an altogether shameful business.

Then, as these things do, it occurred to me that people with the good manners and interest to queue for miles through Software, Records and Lampshades should be offered a little more.

I had, in desperation, accepted an offer to commemorate the anniversary of the death of the writer Saki by reading one or two of his stories one evening at a platform performance at the National Theatre. Ill with fear, I managed. It went very well.

I was asked if I would do another, but this time 'answer questions and read a bit from your own books?' That worked, too. I had an enchanting lady to monitor the 'game', but quickly discovered that we did not need her. The audience began to take me over, and I began to take them into my confidence. It was an amazing experience. Quite new to me.

Why then couldn't we combine the two things? The awful Signing Sessions *plus* the Platform Show? At a Signing I never spoke to any reader beyond a fleeting smile and a muttered 'What name do you want me to use?' while the till clanged another sale. It was insulting to us all. So we decided to go to a proper theatre, do a couple of hours on stage with a few books for me to read from, and then be braced to answer *any* questions.

A brave thing to do? I tried it with a packed house, and it worked. It was hard, but exhilarating and fun. After the Show came the Signing. And because people had been laughing with me, thinking with me, listening to me, we were closer. It was far, far better than sitting in a heap at a table signing away next to the till. I shall never do that again.

I love my audience. They are no longer a mass of separate people in a large theatre looking at a single figure on an empty stage for a couple of hours. We are united, are together, join in the laughter and, sometimes (there are serious questions about cancer, strokes, death and old age; it is not all 'hilarity and mirth'), in the silences which follow a desperate, sad question which someone has had the immense courage to ask in public.

To share the worry, despair or anxiety with everyone is a wonderful, moving feeling. Something I would never have experienced had I not, all those years ago, decided to draw attention to myself. Sometimes one can be helpful, as well as amusing. I have discovered that for myself. I cannot imagine how I ever did without it in the past.

Daily Telegraph Cheltenham Festival of
Literature Supplement,
28 September 1993

Wrecked By Two Arduous Days' Reading

Before I had my second stroke and my speech was impaired, I used to read aloud most of my own books for audiocassette. This is how it worked.

The other day a girl with a black velvet hat crammed down to her eyebrows suddenly screamed at me in Lower Sloane Street: 'Hey! I'm listening to you! Amazing! Brilliant! There you are and I'm listening to you! Wow!' She could have been Lord Carnarvon, so wide with disbelief were her eyes.

I smiled inanely and she ran alongside me, jogging and squealing, wires flying, looking like a demented spaniel. In desperation, I fled into an antique shop and priced a marble table I could neither afford nor wished to purchase, and she ran on. One hoped, into the river.

Audiobooks, or talking books, are here – and to stay, it seems; particularly now that not only the abridged texts on two tapes, running for about three hours, but also unabridged versions lasting twelve hours or so – what I call the 'Full Whack' – are commercially available at a reasonable price and on standard-sized cassettes.

Every night my ex-nanny, Lally, listens to one of my books (abridged) about my childhood, in which she played a not unimportant part. She drops off to sleep, she says, 'in a twinkling, remembering those lovely, happy, days'. I can think of no better reason for reading to her than that. Especially as I do not have to be physically present. She can just potter about and get herself into bed without fuss and, as she says, with my voice to send her off to sleep. That is hugely rewarding to me. The actual process of bringing her this delight is different. Hellish, in fact.

To read an eight-cassette job (unabridged) takes me two full days. At the end I am usually wrecked. One sits in a tiny cell, soundproofed, airless, a table, a desk, a chair, the book-rest, the book, a sealed window on to the aquarium of the Control Room.

One starts with an eager joy. Then a pleasant voice on the intercom interrupts, very gently: 'Dirk? Tummy rumble. Sorry'; or 'page turning' or 'heard you cross your legs/arms/ankles'; or again, 'sleeve touched the desk', or 'raised your arm'. Until you are so frightened that to sit stark naked in cement seems the only way to carry on. It means that with each tiny hiccup you have to go all the way back to the paragraph, line, whatever, and start again. This can take hours. I now insist, if I make a verbal mistake, or cross my arms, or if any other unacceptable sound issues from my person, that I cry: 'Repeat!' and proceed. Appalling work for the poor editor, but at least I get my 'run' clear.

It is claustrophobic, tense and exhausting. Some people bash through a reading without a flutter. Others have to be given bottles of water, biscuits, barley sugar, glucose tablets, Kleenex to cope with the extra saliva they generate, or a mattress to lie on. At worst, a calming pill which reduces the hysteria, but equally the performance.

The abridged (or mutilated) version of a two-cassette job is far easier. I can do one in five hours. But the abridging, done in my case by the copy-editor of my books, Mark Handsley, is brutal, essential and apparently perfectly acceptable to the listener. The plot, the characters, the very essence of the subject somehow remain intact. You junk detail, characters who do not matter and descriptive stuff. Reducing 95,000 words to 25,000 is a marathon task.

There is an enormous difference between 'reading' and 'telling' a story. 'Telling' must be much more personal, 'for your ear only'. It must be a quiet complicity between the teller and the listener. 'Reading' is often distanced by great elegance of speech, perfect pronunciation, the beauty of the words and the theatrical self-awareness of the reader. This does not get to the gut and mind of the listener. The intimacy, buttonholing, the imperfections of speech (a slight laugh, a sigh, a caught word, a repeated word) bring him or her much closer.

Anyone can listen to a reader; only one person, or one small group-at-the-knee, can listen to a teller. That is what counts. One has to 'play' the story, bring it to life, totally involve the listener. One alters the voice, a token change rather than a grandiose burst of actorly prowess, an indication only – which is why, very often, actors are better than professional, or habitual, readers. Get the listener in the first three or four lines; hold his interest; do not let it wander from your voice; keep him alert, so he can settle back and think: 'This is specially for me! I am now being involved, and I can't prevent it.'

If you can establish that height of interest, familiarity, comfort even, the audiobook will flourish prodigiously. It is already starting to do so. But do people who listen to the abridged tape being read to them bother to buy the printed book? I wonder. Knowing people, probably they do not. I keep my fingers crossed.

Daily Telegraph, 17 December 1994

SOME SPECIAL RELATIONSHIPS

The Lifebelt of Gentle Praise

Obituary of Ian Dalrymple

I knew him as Dal. Those of us who were permitted to get fairly close to Ian Dalrymple in this unlovely profession of the cinema all knew him as that. He was modest, cautious, calm and in every way a gentle man. A gentleman is how he would best be described, but sadly that word is now out of date, perhaps one which he might have thought pretentious. Nevertheless that is what he was.

In 1947, after six years of an active war, I had an overnight success (the sort of idiot thing so commonplace today) in a small theatre in Notting Hill Gate. The critics lavished their praise, the world and his wife came to see us. I was paid £5 a week, and Ian Dalrymple one night was in the audience. I don't know exactly when he came, I only remember that he wrote, and said that he had liked my work and had I read, perchance, *Esther Waters* by George Moore. Of course I hadn't; I'd only just managed to survive my war years with *The Oxford Book of English Verse* and a paperback of *Forever Amber*.

Well, almost. He overlooked this crass error and signed me up for two films: *Esther Waters* and one to follow called *Once a Jolly Swagman*, about speedway riders. Not exactly my scene, or indeed his. He wrote, I quote from his letter of 25 June 1947:

> I didn't want to disturb you while your play was still running. When it comes off, shall we spend an evening together about our future plans for *Esther Waters* and *Once a Jolly Swagman*? Then, when you have read and thought about *Esther* and I've explained the storyline, we can have a good discussion about the character of 'William'. You are a bit young for it − or more probably I'm getting so antiquated that my juniors seem all children.

Note the delicacy in his use of the word 'our' and not 'my'. That was Dal's style. They were always *our* projects from the start and remained so. My head reeled with delight and the overwhelming desire to please him. We worked hard on *Esther*. The film was lavish in cast, sets, costumes and a minutely detailed re-creation of the 1885 Derby, and it was all a colossal failure.

We had done some 'tests' on film before starting work. He wrote on 18 July 1947:

> One or two things emerge from Wednesday's tests but far, far the most important was that, if we all keep calm, you will rocket into the firmament. So. When you're a Big Shot, remember that your celluloid birthplace lay in Wessex [his own company]. But I wonder, will you! Or are you as hard as all the rest?

I remembered, I remember. I went to his house in Bourton-on-the-Water for the good discussion about the character of 'William'. A tumbling family house, wellingtons and riding crops in the hall. I seem to remember tile floors, polished wood, green lawns, a great tree, chintz and worn leather, the walls stuck about with a great collection of paintings, none of which I had ever seen before. 'Lowry,' he said, pushing his glasses high on the bridge of his nose, drawing on the cigarette in its long paper holder. 'A great potential. I like him.'

We had the discussion on 'William' but it really didn't do much good. I was too raw, too inexperienced. He pretended not to notice, or, if he did, he never let it show, and I went on to the set that first terrible morning frightened out of my wits – but at least going to join my friend, not merely my director. 'What do I do?' I said, looking in horror at the gigantic camera. He removed his cigarette stub, crushed the paper holder in his fist. 'Good Lord! I don't know. You're supposed to be the actor.' He said this mildly, so I jumped in and swam, as it were, without water-wings.

That I did not instantly drown was entirely due to Dal. He praised quietly, counselled wisely, showered me with confidence, cosseted and laughed, and when necessary threw me the lifebelt of gentle praise. We were certain that 'our' film was to be a winner. It was a howling flop and came near to breaking his heart. But he never at any time blamed me.

On 3 October 1948 he wrote:

I'm sorry. But for you time will swiftly flow. Hold your head up until *Swagman* in December. I've copped it good and proper, not quite all of it justified. But my regrets are more for the artists and technicians who worked so nobly, and my loyal family and friends . . . It's my one big reverse in twenty-one years; so it was time for it, from now on I let all the clever boys do the work.

Swagman did better, it was rougher, tougher, more of its time, but Dal had suffered a desperate wound which bled and, although we worked once again together on a film of Arnold Bennett's *Mr Prohack*, he finally gave in and left the scene. We didn't lose touch, though our roads diverged.

He had launched me, he had seen some spark, and with his gentleness, his wry amusement, his shrewd eye, he watched me as I went along my often bumpy road. He set me on that path. His fault entirely. Thank goodness. We wrote, he read my books, he saw me on various dire TV chat shows, we sent Christmas cards. But not, alas, this year, and I shall mind that very much indeed.

Independent, 1 May 1989

The Look That Says Rampling

I remember being surprised, and showing it rather obviously when Luchino Visconti, reading through the cast of a film which I had just agreed to make with him, said: 'And finally I will use the English girl, Charlotte Rampling, for the young wife who is sent to the concentration camp . . .'

All that I knew of Rampling at that time, and this was twenty years ago, was that she had had a great personal success in a comedy film called *Georgy Girl*. She seemed rather odd casting for a heavily tragic role in *The Damned*, a sombre film about Germany in the turmoil of the thirties.

'Rampling! But why?' I remember saying tactlessly.

Visconti placed the forefinger and thumb of each hand around his eyes, framing them.

'For this,' he said. 'For The Look.'

As always, he was correct. I saw The Look myself one day on the enormous set which had been built to represent the Krupps' villa in Essen. We sat, Rampling and I, with the rest of the film 'family' watching a concert by members of the household which was taking place at exactly the same hour as the Reichstag building was burning in Berlin.

When the news was broken, in a breathless voice in the middle of the concert, Rampling suddenly turned to me, her eyes wide with horror at the terrible implication of what lay ahead, and I instantly saw the power of those wonderful eyes. Green, wide, appalled.

All terror was there: all the fear of a woman who instinctively knew that her family was doomed was instantly summed up. No words were used, only that Look. It was enough. I have never forgotten it.

The very first time I met her she was wearing the shortest mini-skirt possible, and a pair of boy's scarlet under-briefs, clearly visible beneath the skirt, a crumpled T-shirt and rather grubby bare feet. She seemed to laugh a lot.

Two hours later, however, a strange metamorphosis had taken place. Hairdressers, make-up and wardrobe had gone to work on this capering, joyful child and, astonishingly, a perfectly groomed, radiantly beautiful and sophisticated woman in a long slim-fitting lace evening gown, corsage on her shoulder, pearls at her throat, was there before me.

The transformation was complete. No longer the leggy foal, hair tumbling in a golden fall about her: this was a cool, composed adult woman moving with extreme poise and the grace of a panther towards me down the long studio corridor.

A few years later, when I was about to start *The Night Porter*, I remembered that first Look and insisted that Rampling played opposite me. She had just had her first child and was still nursing him; there was virtually no money to make the film, and it was going to be what we call a 'toughie'. Added to that, the producers wanted a bigger name than hers for the American market. However, I stuck to my decision, she accepted a derisory salary and got the role, becoming, in time, a part of cinema lore.

She was the perfect partner in a difficult film and in an almost impossible role. It was a compelling performance in every way: when she is on the screen it is almost impossible to look at anyone else.

I have seen The Look under many different circumstances. I have seen the glowing emerald eyes change to steel within a second; fade gently to the softest, tenderest, most doe-eyed bracken-brown when in the company of her husband, her children and her very close friends.

If, in her 'commercial life', she appears to be the temptress, in her private life none of this is apparent at all. Her clothes are simple: trimly cut, elegant and understated. She knows very well that she has a pair of the best legs in the business and is delighted that these should be made the most of. She is aware that she is a sex-symbol, but wears no jewellery, no feathers, frills or frou-frou.

Rampling keeps her sensuality well banked down. But one is constantly aware of the measured tread, the slender length of leg, the curve of neck and throat, but, perhaps most of all, The Look.

Daily Telegraph, 28 June 1987

A Genius in Love with Vulgarity

The secret Joseph Losey

My father always said that the first tremor I would feel as I slid towards 'old age' would be when I turned first to the obituary page in the newspapers. I've had the tremor now for ages.

Another ugly sign is when the biographers arrive to ask you questions about someone whom you thought you knew, or whom they, at any rate, thought you did. The time of the 'authorized biography' is upon us: one begins to feel rather lost, a lone survivor on the raft of life.

It has now happened to Joseph Losey. There is a fat tome about, in depth, detailed, superbly researched, a public flaying of a character as maddening and complicated as any I ever knew; or *thought* I knew, because the joke is I didn't know him. I never have 'known' anyone I worked with. Don't ask questions, obey directions (when they suit), keep yourself to yourself and don't get involved. It has been my rule for all of my playing life.

David Caute's biography, *Joseph Losey: A Revenge on Life* (Faber and Faber), will satisfy (and shock) the cine-buffs, amaze his fans, and would have driven him to apoplexy. It has left me with jaw agape. This is the old friend that I did not know but always suspected might be lurking about. It is a scrupulous dissection of a man who was, at times, an enigma – even to himself. 'What the hell am I doing . . . ?' he would often ask me, but he seldom assuaged his anxiety by accepting the advice I offered, always went down the road he had chosen himself. So who was he?

I first met him standing in slush on a winter's day in a car-park at Pinewood. I was to have a private screening of a movie he had made a couple of years before. It was the early fifties, and I had never heard of him. I was exhausted after three movies in a row, and frozen. I had no interest in watching his old movie, but had agreed to do so because if, after seeing it, I said I would work with him, he would get the money on my name to start his first major film in England. He awaited my verdict like an expectant father in the snow.

I wearily sat and looked at his offering. For twenty minutes, huddled in an overcoat, all alone, I watched the screen, then got up and called him in. Together we watched the film run through. I had been presented with magic.

I knew that afternoon that I would work with him even if he decided to shoot the A-to-Z map of London, or try a remake of *Way Down East*. I was hooked. I knew where greatness lay, even if I didn't know much about the man. Greatness, for better or for worse, was sitting in the seat beside me. In his own words:

> . . . we made *Sleeping Tiger* not easily and not pleasantly: I working anonymously [black-listed by McCarthy] and without knowledge of British idiosyncrasies and with little confidence excepting what Dirk gave me. Dirk, insofar as he understood any of my political opinions, certainly didn't agree with them, so it took much courage and much acceptance to perform the unselfish act which he did. Out of it grew a profound friendship and love which has endured much testing and some provocation.

It endured all right; sometimes I wondered how. The umbilical cord which joined us got pretty stretched at times, but was never entirely severed. I stayed pretty close to him until his death. Ten years after *The Sleeping Tiger* we worked again on a modest movie which no one wanted or would pay for. 'The Money,' Joe said, 'isn't bright even about money!' And so it was, all his career.

I had reminded him about a small book, which he had considered during our first film together: *The Servant*, which he thought he might buy for me. Ten years on, I was too old for the 'boy' and the book had become a film-script written by a rising young writer, Harold Pinter. 'Over-written dreadfully,' Losey said; but he met Pinter, they paired, a new script was written. I had to play the servant because there was no money for a star like Ralph Richardson.

93

Thus *The Servant* was, in his word, 'fought' on to film. Fought, because we had no support.

He got pneumonia in the first week, The Money tried to close us down and claim the insurance, and he begged me to take over directing until he was able to return. Harold, and the cast and crew, remained loyal and brave. The movie was made and I, at least, thought that he had done the impossible: switched points on the deadly predictable railway-line that was the British cinema.

Losey seemed to have broken through. Hailed by the critics, avoided by the mass audience, we won and lost. For a time, however, he prospered, his name writ large. Every film he attempted was a desperate battle to get the cash. No box-office, no backing. It was heart-breaking, desperate, but he fought on and, with Pinter, he seemed to be winning, at least critically and, if not in Britain, abroad.

We made five films together, eventually. Always under stress and pressure and lack of funds and, although we were as close as brothers, I never really knew how he ticked or who he was away from the set. I have said that I never ask questions of my friends, or question their beliefs in religion or politics. That way you get to keep them. So it was with Joe (or 'Joseph', as he later insisted on being called). But somehow we stayed together, with some fairly hairy periods here and there. We were both pretty volatile people after all.

I suppose I *did* think that I knew him. But his biographer has delved deep, and asked the questions I never dared. I realize now that I was wrong to assume that I knew him. So close. So distant. He altered greatly with success when it came – it was not an abrupt alteration; he had always been simmering away, but, until he hit the real 'big time', he kept his lid fairly tight.

With Harold Pinter, a spare, meticulous, controlled writer, he reached his peak. Pinter never permitted him to go to excess, which would have been fatal to his work. Given his head, which eventually he was, he rioted and brought himself down unaided.

In time, he did start to mellow. Unhappy in England, which he never really came to terms with, he went to Paris, where he was lionized by the cinema intellectuals and gave huge, in-depth, and not always accurate, interviews. He shocked many by declaring that he was, indeed, a Marxist. This I never really took seriously. I found it too hard to accept, given his love of the rich life and the luxury he always insisted on whenever he could. Rich hotels, richer foods and wines, elegance, the best couturiers, top doctors, beautiful furniture. He treated all waiters and staff dreadfully, despising them for being 'servants'; he was appalling to women, especially those he bedded, and even the four he married; he dumped his sons, cheated here and there, was a liar sometimes, a coward (he could never sack a player: he got someone else to do that); he was generous when he was rich; above all, he bullied the weak.

But he was respected and loved by the team with whom he worked, for the excellence of his work. In time, his demands became difficult to accept and, regretfully, people fell away. His Achilles' heel was his love of richness and vulgarity; even though he *knew* it was vulgar, it pleased him. The Burtons, at their peak, mesmerized him with ostentation and luxury; he wallowed in wastefulness and prodigality. The Mid-West boy, the Commie-intellectual-fighter, was overwhelmed far too easily by glitz.

A lot of people suffered from these bouts – if that is what they were – of self-indulgence, but the main victim, finally, was himself. The Burtons naturally meant that The Money was eager to back him almost for the first time. With funds came the largesse, lavishness as never before; but, alas, it did not mean box-office success, and finally the financiers, too, politely and firmly eased away from him and he was quietly abandoned.

He battled on undaunted: his 'greatness' lay in his courage, his vision, his whole cinema-intellect. It lay in the incredible feeling he had for texture, shape, light, rhythm and film-pace, in the acute awareness that the camera photographed *thought* as well as the object. His understanding of the camera, the use of sound, of silence even, was total. Working for him was telepathic; we spoke no words together.

Under duress, often ailing, always struggling against The Money, he was determined, calm, brave and never questioned success.

Eventually he won. But, with too much money, more than he could handle, his innate streak of vulgarity broadened, the brilliance dimmed, and really came back to him only towards the end of his working time with *Don Giovanni*.

As he faded in health he started to lose heart. Reluctantly, he was forced back to Britain. He bought two absurdly expensive houses in Chelsea, in which he sat, lost, brooding, morose. 'They knew who I was in Paris,' he said one day. 'I was respected there. No one knows me here now. No one gives a shit.'

He was almost right. He had returned to a British cinema that was drawing its last breaths, where The Money demanded tits and bums, bombs and bangs, smoke and grunts instead of words. He was distressed, floundering, still trying to get 'things set up', even to the extent of easing, uncomfortably, towards television.

Life with Losey was never easy, but I loved him. At his best he was inspiring, audacious, stylish. He cared and he dared. This is the Losey I knew: he and his work are almost forgotten today, overwhelmed by an audience weaned on short-span television attention.

When he died, the cinema lost a man who made films because he actually loved them. He may have been all kinds of a scoundrel, but he was, without doubt, a great film-maker. He is our loss.

Daily Telegraph, 15 January 1994

With Thanks to 'Thumper'

On the death of Theo Cowan

My dear Thumper:

Bet you never thought that I'd be doing this for you? Should have been the other way around. However, you went first. In the perfect scenario, of course, it would have been me, one of your earliest 'chicks'. So a 'thank you' letter seems to be in order.

Thank you for unstinting love and support for over forty years. I joined the Rank team (not charm school) in 1947 – April, I recall. You were pretty cool. ('Well frankly, I was used to more rugged types. Granger, Farrar, Mason. You were a bit of a shock.')

We got through a great many years together, bad movies, not-very-good movies, and here and there a reasonably respectable one. Only now and again.

But you were *always* there. Remember the National Tours? Trains to Newcastle, Liverpool, Leeds, Glasgow? Red carpets and station-masters in top hats? Black ties and eternal dinners with Mayors. Day after day from one city to another. You and me. Everything planned like clockwork, ready on time, never once late, not even the train, and knowing everyone's name. Even the names of their children ('She's called Alice, 8½. Their third child. Might be useful?'). You had researched it.

And we all talked together. I never forgot a name. I hope it made them come to the movie. If I got lost, turned in despair, you were always there. Tall, smiling the smile of reassurance, glasses glinting in the lights. Courage regained.

Discipline you taught; patience, humility and tact. You did amazingly well by doing exactly what you were not engaged to do – keeping me away from the worst excesses of the Popular Press.

Keeping me 'out' rather than 'in' the public eye, for which I will ever be grateful.

Those subtle warnings about X and Y who might look kind but couldn't be trusted with a fly-swat or a feather duster. The 'killers' of their time. How frightened we all were of them! But it was you who said: 'What they write today you'll eat your chips from tomorrow. Remember that through your tears.'

And it was so. Tell them from me, if they are up there with you, that you were right. And Thumper, apart from your insatiable hunger for any kind of food, particularly sandwiches and bridge-rolls full of tinned salmon or any kind of nourishment (never a drink, only tea), your strength, tact, good humour and your discretion made you highly respected and for a publicist amazingly loved.

I don't think there was anyone in our profession who did *not* know you, from here to Paris, Venice or LA. We were all encouraged by you and often shielded by you from the Tyranny of the Bosses.

When I joined Joe Losey to make 'different' films you willingly came too – at a vastly reduced salary. Proud we were to have you; proud you were to be associated with what you called 'a brave new attempt' which lasted for longer than we any of us expected.

When I quit the United Kingdom for new lands you were still with me, as ever, and still for no money at all, because I had none. 'We'll settle that later,' you said, but we never did.

But you liked my house, the olives, above all the sandwiches and the tea. Your tapping your 'sugar substitute' into your cup with fastidious care is one of my enduring memories.

Cannes, with all its jazzy, jokey nonsense, will never be the same without you, in your hideous khaki shorts and two-way sunglasses, bowling along the Croisette. You only ever dressed for Venice. 'Venice,' you said, 'it's different. Not a question of money here; question of worth and honour.'

Back here in London we had tea and sandwiches in this little flat. You brought me one of your self-grown amaryllis, in a too-small pot, but it flourished. In all the years we knew each other very closely I never knew anything about you. I only knew you lived 'somewhere near Primrose Hill' and that was that.

I asked no questions and you told me no more. It's all a question as you told us – your 'chicks' – of duty, discipline, discretion and good manners. Apart from talent!

You were coming in for tea and a sandwich 'sometime next week'. Have to take a rain-check on that.

Love, Dirk

Daily Telegraph, 17 September 1994

Non! Non! Non!

A portrait of Brigitte Bardot

More than forty years ago I was despatched to Paris in order to do some shopping. It wasn't long after the war, and any excuse to get out of a still-drab and depressed England was to be greatly welcomed. Especially in this case when the 'shopping' was for a leading lady to play opposite me in yet another film in the *Doctor* series.

This time we were to be at sea. A sexy, singing siren had to be discovered, preferably in France because they seemed to make the best models and because we simply did not have any of that kind of exotica flying about in Britain, least of all in the Rank Organisation, where a few pretty creatures were bolted into terrible steel-boned corsets. To hold one in one's arms was like holding a pillar-box. Scarlet lips as well.

So off I was sent by those splendid producers Betty Box and Ralph Thomas, with a list of, I think, three for me to choose from. A matter of height, colouring, English language and general gaiety. This creature had to entrap me, enrapture the whole audience and add 'exotic lustre' to the whole enterprise.

The first girl I met was working at a studio outside Paris. Her anxious and charming agent was with her – to '''elp wiz zee translation, I spik bad,' said the ravishing creature, with a sparkle in her eye which indicated very clearly that no English, no language in fact, was really necessary: she would manage very well without.

From where I sat in the cramped little dressing-room, this amazingly glowing child – she was seventeen at the time – wrestling furiously with a vast lurcher-type of dog called Clown, was all I needed for my duties as a valiant young doctor at sea. It would save trailing across Paris to see the other two.

The elegantly, if sparingly, dressed child with her vast dog gave little pouts and giggles, which could have been irritating but merely went happily along my ignited fuse until I sort of exploded and declared that Mademoiselle was ideal! Just what I wanted as a partner. She clapped her hands and her agent, Olga Horstig (who became mine for forty years), wiped away a tear and we all embraced. I kissed the hand of my ravishing partner, who was hitting Clown on the head with a rolled-up newspaper, and we all said 'au revoir' and 'à bientôt'. Brigitte Bardot was launched into the British cinema.

Poor child: at the time, she did not realize quite what she was in for, but, after her fitting for the dress in which she would sing the 'Big Number' – which, she murmured, was 'like singing my catechism' – and discovering that she could move quite independently within the confines of the white-satin, steel-covered corset, she became, controllably, hysterical.

She proved, before my eyes, that she could turn her body all the way round within the scarlet-sequinned, crimson-beaded gown, so that it remained absolutely rigid and nailed to the floor. Nothing moved, the breasts were cupped and ribbed in metal, the waist cinched in with iron rods, and the whole edifice looked, as it was, a static reminder of what a 'chantoose' might possibly have worn in 1930. It had nothing whatever to do with a liner on a happy holiday cruise in 1954.

One of the less repellent tabloids did at least have a valid point when it screamed RANK DESEXES BARDOT. They were absolutely on the ball. She was, at all times, sanguine. When in Britain, Do As The British Do. Otherwise, go abroad. I do not honestly know why she ever accepted this silly film. A chance to break into international cinema? Unlikely. We had, even then, no influence. Maybe just for the fun of it? And it always looked good on one's CV to have starred, which indeed she did, in one's first British movie.

Her English was, to say the least, minimal; we learned the script together like parrots. It demanded nothing more, anyway, and she got her tongue around the banalities. The one word in which she was absolutely fluent was 'No'. Not 'No thank you, but . . .'; not

'I'd love to, but, really, no . . .'; not even 'No, I have to learn my script tonight . . .' None of that nonsense; just 'No'. No explanation, no elaboration, no politesse. Just the one killer word, administered always with a charming smile: 'No.' Not even 'Thank you.'

It had devastating effects on the people who surrounded her. I learned that one trick from Brigitte, and have remembered it with gratitude all my life. Just say 'No.' There ain't anything anyone can do about it.

The press people wilted; wrung hands. She never explained. People begging her to open charity balls, raffles for the dying in wherever; the idiot women who wanted her for their centrespreads covered in beads, honey, bananas or just bikinis, or sprawled on slithery satin sheets with baskets of fruit over salient areas – all got the same, polite response: 'No.' It worked for her, and when I lifted it from her (to her amusement), it worked for me. 'Never tell them why! Never be understanding! Always be gentle, always say "No" to anything you don't consider *comme il faut.*' She was dead right.

Of course, after two days of press exposure, laid on by Rank, she was dubbed the 'Sex Kitten' and that was that. She thought it very odd, but understood just what was expected of her. From then on, at press conferences she put a finger to her pouting lips, lifted her skirt just an inch higher, and, if anyone asked her anything she preferred not to answer, simply whispered '*Non*' and leaned back provocatively. After years of Rank ladies wrapped in concrete and steel, this '*Ooh! La! La!*' (and alas there was a lot of that) was manna from Heaven.

The use of the word 'No' did not spoil her private fun; a number of assiduous gentlemen in and around Pinewood never really heard it and, if they did, they were so overwhelmed by her charms that they really seemed not to mind. She thought most of them were rather boring, frankly, and longed for each Friday evening when she could fly back to Paris and to Clown. Or whoever.

To work with, she was huge fun: professional, aware, absolutely no problem with her make-up, hairdresser, the usual gang. She swiftly ditched her wardrobe and wore only her own, far simpler, *far* sexier, outfits which she had brought from Paris. She was wise, funny and far in advance of anything we had at that time in the UK and, of course, we didn't know how to handle her, and she slipped, thankfully, away.

We have met, over the years, in some restaurants, on a beach and, the last time, in the long studio corridor at Boulogne-Billancourt in the late seventies. She came running towards me; we were both much older, but we were old friends. Trusted and respected.

I said I had just seen the final dub of *Despair* and that would be the last film for me. She had been dubbing *her* last film. We both agreed that it was a silly profession, and that it was time we grew up and left it to *les autres idiots*, which we did. (Some years later, I bullied myself into one final appearance for Bertrand Tavernier.)

I haven't seen her since, but I shall remember her always as the fresh, amused, vaguely astonished little girl I chose that day, so long ago, in the studio with Clown. It has not always been fun for her; in time, she became revolted by the exploitation of herself and her life. I cannot pretend I am not sorry she left this capricious profession, but I am saddened by what the profession did to her. And thankful only that she finally had the sense to quit. It'll kill you if you hang on in there.

Two books on her are about to appear in this country. I don't want to read either of them. But I *did* know her, and adored her. When they write whatever they do, I bet you they won't get it right. If Brigitte now fights for animals, it is only because they are a great deal more pleasant than humans and are in desperate need of help. I promise you, she knows just what she's doing.

Daily Telegraph, 13 August 1994

A Glowing Friendship
On the death of Kathleen Tynan

Kathleen:

On Monday I was standing by your bed, holding your hand, small as the folded wing of a tiny bat, cold and damp, your eyes sight-less, blue, empty, moving gently to the sound of my voice. I can't be certain that you knew I was there; I didn't stay longer than a moment so as not to exhaust the little time you still had left.

I may not have been your oldest friend, your closest one, or even your most intimate, but I know that you trusted me, that you loved me and that you knew always that I loved you and trusted you in exactly the same way.

It was the most glowing and prized friendship, filled at times with joyous laughter or quiet contentment; sometimes, wretchedly, with despair and misery (there has to be a 'B' side in life).

The magical thing about you was your complete femininity, blinding, golden, tenacious and, at times, maddeningly perverse and even contrary. But you were always wholly bewitching.

I shall miss your daring, and the wondrous way that you (perfectly correctly) put us, your friends, with great finesse into our separate boxes so that you could enjoy us without our bruising each other. I shall long remember your fastidious courage, your elegance and calm and your determination to drag the wreckage of life around you, after Ken died, so that you could shelter and succour your children.

Above all I will remember your quiet resolve to have your own life, to choose and keep your own friends, to give them always your unstinting love and loyalty.

Now that you have left us, closing the door behind you, the

rooms about us will grow cold and drab without the honey glow of your presence.

The brutal wretchedness of it all is that it happened far too soon to you. Ciao, darling.

Dirk

Daily Telegraph, 11 January 1995

A Lifetime's Love for Cinema

On the death of Dilys Powell

I started off as a movie star, name above the title and all the dreadful tra-la-la, in 1947. There were a thousand fearful traps on the studio floor, and alarming outside elements, like distributors, cinema owners, fans, and perhaps the most fearful of all, The Critics. They were, then anyway, held in awe by studios. Two were held as the Most Important Of All: C. A. Lejeune, of the *Observer*, and Dilys Powell.

They were fearful because they wrote for the 'informative' papers and spoke their minds bluntly, and if they ignored your film it was not desperate, but not terribly good either. They came to every press screening, sat apart from everyone, even from themselves, and hurried away after the lights went up.

Certainly nobody ever spoke, or dared to speak, to either. They were the 'intellectual' critics. It was a pretty exciting event if they praised the product. They were fair, honest, intellectual and didn't actually appear to like actors. As far as Dilys was concerned, this was just about true.

She adored films, loved the whole atmosphere of them, sat enraptured (unless a horse was shot, or fell over a cliff; that she could not entertain at any price). Cruelty to animals was implacably a no-no area. But she worshipped her cinema.

I don't think I have ever met anyone, here or abroad, who was as idiotic and delighted by her job as Dilys was, and she tried never to miss a screening.

She never knew how a film was made. 'I don't want to know that,' she said to me years later. 'That is not my job. I don't care how it's moved, cut, what angles are used. I only want to know if it has involved me and who has done so and why? Perhaps that is why I am so uncluttered! I'm really the child with the magic lantern: don't tell me how they lit the lamp. Just let me be enthralled.'

I didn't enthral her, it appeared, for ten long years. Then, in 1957 the BBC, in its wisdom, decided to put together a special programme about me. Dilys agreed to 'end the programme'.

Well, she was honest, as usual, and said that I showed great promise but that I hadn't quite proved myself, as she felt certain I would, one day. Of course I was a little depressed. Ten years in, playing everything from Victorian heavies to members of the IRA and idiotic light juvenile roles, I still hadn't been taken aboard Miss Powell's raft of goodies.

She was no fool, Dilys. She'd wait a little, until the glorious day when she wrote '. . . gives the commanding performance one has long expected from him . . .' That was for a film called *Victim*, and I remember saying aloud: 'I've done it! She's accepted me!' It was an amazing day.

I don't know just how many actors hung on the lines of her piece each week in the *Sunday Times*. How many of us longed, yearned as I did, for her approbation. But I know that if she had praised your work, you felt pretty good. She knew her 'wine', and if you were in her cellar you were particularly lucky. Nobody else's opinion was as important to me as hers. I knew that she understood deeply, and once she had accepted me I worked every time with hand on heart for her.

'Mr Bogarde, given too little to do, does far too much . . .' was spot on; I nodded at that in agreement and did less after that. And still she was a stranger. She was as aloof and silent and, frankly, shy as anyone I have ever met. After she described *The Servant* as 'flawless', I threw caution over my shoulder and wrote a brief note to thank her. She, dangerously, replied. From then on we were friends.

After *Death in Venice*, she asked to meet me. We did so in my sitting-room at the Connaught, but neither of us was much good, constricted by shyness and awe. A week later I wrote and asked her to lunch. She got my letter the same morning that I got hers begging me not to invite her to lunch because she was 'quite hopeless socially, and desperately shy'. But she accepted my invitation, though it was an ungainly lunch, awkward, but funny, and really only made possible for her when she saw Claudette Colbert and Rex Harrison together at the next table.

We wrote now: there was no shyness in writing, no shyness in exchanging thoughts, ideas; we were true friends at last. When Leonard Russell, her second husband, died, she closed herself away in their pretty house, and drew the blinds. I took a huge bunch of white hyacinths to remind her, with their sweet smell, of her beloved Greece. We sat in the twilight gloom of her sitting-room. Empty of life apart from a yapping little dog. We didn't speak at all. It was enough for me that I was there with her, and she accepted my presence with calm and affection.

Afterwards I was often invited to lunch. She was getting deaf, and for some reason we had a good deal of fun out of that. She wore an ugly machine, which hissed and squealed, and the wretched little dog, to whom she was devoted, yapped and ran about. Nobody else was ever present, just her kind Portuguese maid who cooked and washed up.

Dilys, I would discover, kept all her friends in separate compartments. We never discussed anyone else and spoke only of the cinema and the people in it.

It was a strange but close friendship. She took her time to accept me, watched curiously from her seat in the dark, approved when I had 'worked', cautiously disapproved when I had defaulted. When I told her I was retiring, that I would concentrate on trying to write, she merely nodded. 'It's all a very different world, gun and blood and people being shot or hit,' she said. 'It's quite hard to watch the screen now. I really only enjoy the old stuff. Myrna Loy, Cary Grant, they still delight me. Such style, that's all gone, it seems.' And with her death she has taken the last vestiges of it with her.

Sunday Times, 4 June 1995

THE WRITER

A Book That Changed Me

The Swiss Family Robinson by Johann David Wyss

My father, who was the first art editor of *The Times*, spent his Saturday mornings going about the junk shops of Lewes in Sussex near where we lived. I always went with him because in one particular junk shop I could buy bound copies of *Chatterbox* for a penny. Since I was desperately trying to be a writer I thought I'd better read, and *Chatterbox* was filled with a year's supply of literature.

One Saturday morning when I was thirteen, in 1934, something caught my eye among a pile of *Chatterboxes*. In a faded green leather cover with gold embossing was a picture of a young man of about my age struggling with a giant boa constrictor. I bought the book for a penny. It was crammed full of exciting illustrations of a family, father, mother and four boys, escaping from a terrific storm at sea. Their ship was wrecked, and they were the only survivors. They made a shelter from a sail on the first night and after that collected pieces from the sand which conveniently got washed ashore. It was all absolutely improbable and tremendously exciting, which is why I was passionate about it. They built themselves a house in a giant 'banyan tree' to protect themselves from wild beasts.

I longed to be a writer but unlike Jane Austen I found it impossible to write at 'a desk in the hall' – a wooden house such as Mr Robinson's would be perfect. So I decided to build a house for myself at the top of the orchard, where no one could come near me. I rather predictably called the house Trees. I built it from an old cold-frame and pieces of furniture from the house and from the rag-and-bone man in the village. I could write here (dreadful poetry and one-act monologue plays for myself to perform). At this stage in my life I wasn't sure whether to be just a writer, an actor or a poet – simple choices! However, Mr Robinson and his house in the trees pushed me in the direction of writing, which is why that book changed me. The poetry was incomprehensible and the monologues were pretty dire too – but at least I'd started.

I couldn't possibly read the book now. For years it was my bedside book, but the years led to the war and that led to a general break-up of everything, including my childhood. I couldn't recommend it to anyone unless they were passionate about wild animals and DIY and shipwrecks: no modern child would give it credence. But it's a rollicking good adventure, far better than *Kidnapped* or *Treasure Island*, and if you can find a copy you may be influenced to build your own private world, as I was.

It still has an influence on me today, to some degree. I tried acting and now I'm trying to write. I built my own house and sat in it and wrote my monologues and read them aloud for hours to the uncomprehending apple trees, and it changed me from an apathetic youth into an ambitious one, at least – if over-ambitious.

Independent on Sunday, 9 November 1997

A Sentimental Education

A writer's beginnings

I suppose that my beginning, as a writer, was pretty early. I mean I was very occupied in writing plays for my sibling and me to act in when I was about six. When I could use a pencil, spell words, read.

At nine, or about then, I sat before my father's solid and (to me) enormous Underwood up in his office, learning how to use it. To slot in a bit of paper and discover #@%& and the other magical things. I grew fairly good at it, in a woodpecker way. Well, not ever as fast as a woodpecker, really, and a bit hit and miss, but by the time I was thirteen or fourteen I had managed to compose my very first Epic Piece. This was a very long monologue for myself to read aloud. 'Man in the Hole' was its title, and it was all about a wounded soldier lying in no man's land in a shell hole dying and thinking about home.

I was greatly affected by the First World War at the time. Obsessed, really. I knew all the places and dates and years. Ypres, Poelkapelle, Béthune, Vimy were names which were as familiar to me as those of my nearest Sussex villages. I wrote constantly. I began, at about seventeen, to be seriously worried that the First World War would very soon give way to a second. With signs of a coming confrontation with Germany, I was forced then to write passionate if vaguely over-emotional poems. A little Rupert Brooke, an essence of Wilfred Owen. Notebooks were crammed tight with abandoned 'works'; here and there a really imposing one, some three pages long, would emerge. It was tosh, of course, but it was a beginning.

Then I was caught up, willy nilly, in a war of my very own. The great majority of what was called the 'Intake' at Catterick Camp was, to my astonishment, illiterate. Many of them were farm boys or young men who had hardly ever been to school and got shoved into some kind of factory. Or, on occasions, just drifted about. These were netted up for war and spilled out into huts all over Great Britain. My barrack room was jammed with tough fellows who yearned to communicate with Mum, their sisters or, most important of all, 'The Girl'. And they couldn't do anything about it for themselves. I became a cigarette millionaire very shortly after arriving in my hut by the simple virtue of my ability to write.

In corners of the hut, out on the range, marching out to Church Parade, lying about for a ten-minute break on route marches, all manner of private longings and expressions of love and misery were given to me to set down in my notebooks. I then had to write the things on small sheets of NAAFI letter paper which sometimes they signed laboriously or with merely a row of crosses along the bottom.

I remember pointing out that a single O could indicate a hug. Thus XXXOO or OOOXXX could be taken to mean hugs and kisses and I wrote to the recipient of that fact so that she would understand herself. 'Do you want to send hugs and kisses? Or just hugs?' became a standard phrase for me. Very often just a row of Os was requested.

It was useful to my mates that I had begun, years before, to 'write'. It was vastly useful to me to learn so much at first hand about my fellow men. I never ceased to be amazed that people who were more or less absolutely illiterate could use such beautiful language in the cause of love. It delighted and moved me, and I grew extremely fond of my 'job' and of my clients. It was always completely private and very secret.

Of course there were more exciting, frightening things, like being bombed or driven across hideous assault courses, which set my shaking hand to clasp its pencil and attest to the terror, agony, cowardice or relief which I had recently had to endure. I wrote it all down. Always. Grenade practice, throwing live grenades at a distant target, provided my first sight of real, not imagined, gore. After vomiting, I wrote.

The severed hand in the heather, the ashen astonishment of its one-time owner, the pallid faces of his mates, the smell of cordite and excreta – for the shock very often loosened the bowels. Down it all went into my notebook, crammed in among the suggested outlines for various plays which never got written. I didn't need now to imagine soldiers dying in shell holes and dreaming of home. They were doing it for real as I watched. It went on right through to the Normandy landings, which were so much 'for real' that there wasn't a lot of time to record them. But I did write every week to my father. He'd had a bloody war in his time, and I was sharing things with him.

To my astonishment I had two poems, two real poems, published about that time. One in the *TLS*, the other in *Poetry Today*. I had written them for a girl with whom I had considered myself to be very much in love. She lived in Belsize Park; she sent the poems on their way.

And then a new existence, after the war. Not as exciting or fascinating, but enjoyable in a way. I became a cinema actor. There wasn't much time for writing then. For years and years all I was able to do was 'mend' terrible scripts which I had to play in. I mended assiduously, causing great hostility among the writers, naturally, and often directors.

To be sure there were occasional moments which did not require my anxious, sometimes desperate, meddling. Harold Pinter was one. But he wrote glories for the actor. There was never any need (nor was one remotely permitted) to alter so much as a semi-colon. There were others which had all the vileness of a cheap Valentine card, but, whatever I did to them, I at least managed to appear 'real' for most of my time on the screen.

And then, sitting trapped in her host's drawing room on a dismal day, forced to endure *Match of the Day* and, later, the replay, Norah Smallwood, at that time the boss at Chatto and Windus, switched channels in fury and caught a chat show on which I was a guest talking about Bergen-Belsen and my appalled arrival there one bright April morning.

She wrote to say: 'If you can write as well as you appear to speak, we would be happy to publish you.' Just like that. Zonk. Out of the blue. I had written, as it happened, a few modest pieces for a woman I wrote to in America. These became the first three chapters of *A Postillion Struck by Lightning*. My first, and I then honestly believed, only, book.

The cinema began to disenchant me. It started to die anyway, and I realized that I was growing too old to play more than grandfathers, agonized and ageing men lusting for pretty girls, druids or senior monks. I was forced abroad, but Mrs Smallwood, and my typewriter, came along with me. I chucked the cinema and stayed with the writing.

A whole new world was set before me, much the same as the cinema in many ways. The absolute discipline, the drudgery, the joy, the promotions, the talks with the reps, the grisly book signings, which gradually became three-hour marathons of absolute delight before packed audiences who now read me instead of just watching me remotely on screen.

It was very much the same job: observation, words, economy, truth, technique, passion. The same resentful critics, the same panic before a 'performance', the same apprehension that the audience won't come.

Writing was marvellously private, if you wanted it to be so. It could even be mysterious; there was a definite cult of loneliness, solitude and learning. I confess that none of these things has come my way. I just write. One does need peace, although Jane Austen, one is told, wrote at a table in the front hall amid the bustle of family life. Odd.

That I could not do, but I love, passionately, what I now do, and I am constantly aware that I have to be eternally grateful to Mrs Smallwood's unthinking host, without whom I might be doing nothing more exciting than voice-overs for cheap holidays in Majorca or someone's lager. If this was a beginning, it was a magical one.

Observer, 28 March 1993

Books Are Better

I have appeared in only two screen adaptations of novels which are undisputed classics: Dickens's A Tale of Two Cities *and Thomas Mann's* Death in Venice *— one a failure in the cinema, the other a success. Therefore I really didn't think I was qualified to write with authority on the subject of classic books used as the basis of films. However . . .*

My name, I fear, held me back from being cast in classical films. Too foreign, too 'pop', too associated with lightweight stuff — funny doctors, sad-eyed subalterns, stern wing commanders, romantic 'juves' — ever to be considered for the loftier realms of the classic-book department. Anyway, they weren't making many. And when they did, the film chaps tended to use theatre people. It was assumed that they were better at classic work, on account of all the strutting and camping and the essential fact that they could 'carry a costume'. Cinema actors, such as I was, were fine for technical, cinematic stuff. We didn't 'over-project', which kept everyone comfortable. Theatre actors, though essential for the classics, did rather have to be 'pulled down' a bit. Which made filming them tiresome — and costly. All those retakes and things. I am, of course, talking about a long time ago. Things have altered now and all kinds of extraordinary cinema people are shoved into wigs and farthingales at the bang of a clapperboard. It seems almost to be the rule rather than the exception.

I did, I remember now, make a couple of adaptations of classic books for the screen: Dickens's *A Tale of Two Cities* for Rank here in the UK, and Thomas Mann's *Death in Venice* in that city for Visconti. They were interesting exceptions to my diet of charm, or what English critics called 'waspish wit and mannered movement'. As poor Sydney Carton, I fared pretty well with most critics,

116

but deliberately avoided any histrionics. This seemed to sadden them. They rather longed for a bit of that.

In *A Tale of Two Cities*, T. E. B. Clarke did a brilliant job on the adaptation; we had a most impressive cast of (mainly) theatre actors; enormous care was lavished on the authenticity of sets and costumes; we went all the way to Bourges in France and shot the film there. But even though it was a faithful 'reproduction' of Dickens, even though we spoke his words and delivered his rather preposterous plot perfectly to the screen, the film failed. My contention is that (A), they wanted Ronald Colman, and (B), we cut costs and made it in black and white. Although it drove a generation of schoolgirls into hysterics (my breeches were pretty tight) and still sends hordes of Japanese ladies (and some gentlemen) frantic to this day (for the same reason), the effort was not successful. Apart from in Japan, where people have very short legs. Mine were long. As a 'classic' adaptation, it could not be faulted, but it did not transfer to the screen of the late fifties. It was not of the time. And, I fear, because of my position in popular cinema then, it just came over as 'another Dirk Bogarde piece'. OK for the fans, but not really suitable for the nobs. In the UK anyway, my name stuck to a classic was the kiss of death. Abroad it was not. After all, mine was a foreign name, and abroad I had long been accepted as a serious player. I suppose because they had been mercifully spared most of the junk films I had had to make in the early years.

So when it came to Thomas Mann and Von Aschenbach no one curled sardonic lips. At least as far as I know. And the adaptation was fascinating. There was *no* script for the players. We were merely given the Penguin edition of *Death in Venice* and told that that was what we would shoot. Of course there *was* a script for the money people, production, set designers and costume people – a faithful, or as faithful as it could possibly be, replica of the book, with a couple of important alterations. Von Aschenbach became a musician and not a writer. This was for two reasons. A writer is pretty dull in what he does. On his bum at a typewriter or a desk. A musician has far more romantic connotations and, very useful this, he is producing (usually) glorious sounds which can flood the soundtrack of the film. Mann had seen, on a journey from Venice to Munich, a crumpled, hysterical, badly made-up elderly man, slumped in a corner seat, weeping silently. His name was Gustav Mahler and, he told Mann, he had finally seen 'absolute perfection, purity and beauty, in one person', and life no longer had any reason for him. That is the story Visconti was told (I will refrain from saying by whom) and that is the story that I was given on which to base my portrayal. I was made to *look* like Mahler, but, alas, the plastic nose I had to wear filled up with perspiration all the time and fell off, forcing me, at the last moment, to reject it and just stick on a moustache hastily found in a box. That was one change. The other was the introduction of a fellow composer in order to use a chunk of hefty polemic based on, but not written by, Thomas Mann.

We also had to eliminate the opening sequence of the book, which simply did not translate to film. But that is about all we did alter, and although one or two bow-tied musical critics squealed that it was 'dire!', it seemed to satisfy a great many people worldwide and made Mann far more accessible than he had been before to the general public. It also reintroduced Mahler to a completely new, adoring, audience. It also inspired an opera and a ballet. It was a successful 'opening-up' of a novel – and a classic one at that – to fit the screen.

But it has to be remembered that books are for reading and films are for reviewing. Books are usually read alone and in silence. One makes up one's own mind about the characters, how they look, what they wear, how they move. If that book, classic or not, is translated to visual terms, the imagination we use when we read is dispensed with. We lack a dimension. I dislike, in the main, the conversion of books to the screen. It seldom works. The germ of the story is used; the adapter is at liberty to hack away at the verbiage in order to get to this germ and in doing so, as with polished rice, destroys the nourishment. Blandness is the result. What an audience must see, a reader can *imagine*. It's far better in my opinion. I have been in so many films-of-the-book that I can't recall them all, but not one, and I am careful what I say here, was ever as good as the original book.

In the decade when I was Golden Boy, a book would be bought solely for me as a perfect 'Bogarde subject', even though I bore no physical relation to the written character. That was all rejigged by the film adapter. Mostly these were middle-aged ladies, of both genders, who knew exactly how to get a script out of the most daunting material. Later in my working life, after I had gained my training in these popular films for the Odeons, I was granted the magical chance of working with writers like Harold Pinter who adapted other writers' books with amazing brilliance.

But that has nothing to do with the subject I have been set, which is the adaptation of classic books for the screen. Well, in my opinion, it is usually a disaster, although, as I have said above, I have had little personal experience. Adapted novels, yes. Classic ones, no. I never finished reading *Middlemarch* when I was young; it bored me witless, just as the television series did. And that was as reverent an adaptation as you could have. I was so stunned by the overt attention to detail, to costume, to the careful pronouncing of Eliot's deathly dialogue, that it confirmed in me the determination, now that I am aged, to sit down and read the bloody book to see just what all the fuss was about.

To have one's own book adapted for the screen is an agony no writer should be forced to endure. Never again. At almost my first meeting with the clever Dicks who had acquired the rights, I was informed that 'all the dialogue will have to be changed, *no one* speaks like that now'. The sadness was that perhaps they don't in Pinner or Palmers Green, but there are a few pockets, thank God, where they do. And that, anyway, was the whole point of the plot – youth from the suburbs against age with an aristocratic background on Cap Ferrat. The main character was finally played by a middle-aged Jewish lady with dark hair and a sardonic French accent. *My* lady had been based on Diana Cooper, whom I adored. It came as a bit of a shock, frankly. But there you go. My book was no classic, but what on earth did they want the thing for? They'd have been far wiser to have written their own. Dialogue included. I feel certain there have been wonderful exceptions to the general rule, but by and large I really do think it is not advisable to have 'adapted for the screen' stuck on after the title.

Literary Review, July 1994

PART TWO
REVIEWS

INTRODUCTION

by Nicholas Shakespeare,
Literary Editor, *Daily Telegraph*, 1988–91;
Sunday Telegraph, 1989–91

It was a hunch, really, no more than that. I had recently been appointed literary editor and was wanting someone to drop fire-crackers into the book world's cosy lap. I was looking for an acceptable outsider. So when, in the spring of 1988, I learned that after twenty-two years abroad Dirk Bogarde had returned to London, I telephoned him.

I had admired the lucid frankness of his autobiographies: here was someone who came late to writing as if he had been practising since an infant. Also an interview he once granted Russell Harty. 'No one's ever possessed you?' Harty had asked during that programme. 'No,' said Bogarde, but his expression was that of someone asking what on earth can have possessed him to agree to this interview in the first place.

Other nuggets included an admission he was not so dear and cuddly ('I ain't') and that he did not much like acting ('That's a revolutionary remark,' said Harty hopefully). I thought, watching Bogarde preserve his irascible self: here is someone who tells the truth.

One Monday evening I knocked at a Queen Anne cottage off High Street, Kensington. I knew it was a bloody time for Bogarde – his manager and companion of fifty years lay ill upstairs, and the house smelt of nurses – but I was not to know how bloody. Earlier in the day Bogarde had learned the cancer had reached Forwood's lymph glands. It was simply a question of time. 'I suppose I should have called and asked you to cancel your meeting with me,' he wrote later. 'But for some strange reason I did not do so.'

He let me in and we sat in the drawing-room and he talked, without rancour, of a half-century's companionship crawling to its hideous end. 'Someone who's looked after you since you were eighteen,' he said. He was drinking whisky and his shirt was hanging out. 'You've got to stick with them, haven't you?'

We must have found other things to talk about on that sorry evening. I can't remember, but I know he was sharp, charming, uncertain, confident, likeable, and he had a bigger nose than I imagined. When at last I mentioned the possibility of reviewing books, he was diffident. He wasn't an intellectual. Yet if I thought he was up to it, all right, he'd give it a try.

We spoke again a week later. I said a book had arrived which might have his name on it. He warned: 'If it's no good, I'm not going to be unkind.'

'Just write what you think.'

Bogarde's first review was of *Mr Harty's Grand Tour*. As soon as I read the copy, I knew how correct had been my instinct. His spelling was atrocious, but the writing utterly professional, and it had the loud smack of honesty: 'This, [Russell Harty's] first book, is easily read, light, frothy, as digestible as the wafer on a vanilla ice-cream, and about as insubstantial.'

Thereafter Bogarde became a part of the team. He was not prima donna-ish about being edited and remained keen to learn, although I don't know what I could have taught him. He hated writing about the film world, but if half-nelsoned could be cajoled into not being too nice or cuddly about it. His respect was hard-earned, always – of Josephine Hart's novel, *Sin*: 'This is utter tosh. Sorry' – but precious when won.

His best reviews were those in which the book mined something valuable out of himself. The readers responded. A review of three memoirs of the Holocaust – he had been among those to liberate Bergen-Belsen – elicited 200 letters. 'No one ever poses the question which raced through my mind all the time: "Why?"' I could rely on Bogarde to pose the question. Somewhere in the tree-dappled shadow outside Hanover, his tent peg had slipped into a mass grave.

It must have been the most difficult review to write. It was unforgettable to read.

Daily Telegraph, 2 October 1993

Trivia's Jackdaw

Mr Harty's Grand Tour by Russell Harty (Century)

I owe Russell Harty an enormous debt. One which I don't suppose I will ever be able to repay, however hard I might try.

Years ago, in the early seventies, he invited me on to one of his television shows and permitted me to talk, uninterrupted, about myself for some forty minutes. What could have been more irresistible? Ego flourished like bindweed and I all but managed to smother the programme.

Some days later a publisher of high standing wrote to me and stated that if I could write as well as I had talked they would be 'delighted to publish you'. This offer naturally went straight to my head and I wrote seven books over a period of ten years or so.

Mr Harty was, therefore, midwife to a new, if modest, career and we have remained good friends ever since.

He is a warm, sensitive, curious, funny, canny, straight-down-the-line creature, and exceptionally good company, but, and this is the rub, I don't think that he writes nearly as well as he talks: somehow he doesn't 'come off the page' as robustly as he does on the screen or in the drawing-room. That is a very great pity indeed and I don't know where the fault lies.

This, his first book, is easily read, light, frothy, as digestible as the wafer on a vanilla ice-cream, and about as insubstantial. It leaves no lingering flavour behind; one has nothing to savour. Perhaps the awful phrase on the front cover, 'Now a Major TV Series', puts one off; perhaps it is one of the faults? Maybe Mr Harty is relying on the vision to give body to his tour rather than the written word? We shall no doubt see for ourselves.

For example, he *tells* us that Siena is glorious, but I never for an instant felt that he had taken me there and shared the glory with me. There is no feeling of colour, of scents, of heat, of light, of the ochre and plaster, the marble and brick. We are taken to the Palio and this is described in detail rather like a football match in Burnley, and lacks the slightest touch of magic. The thing takes all of three minutes and reads with a curious lack of occasion. It all gets a bit boring and more is made of his attempts to back down a one-way street where he gets a 'ticket'.

The main trouble is, I think, that he has made this Grand Tour to meet people rather than to see places, which was what the Grand Tours were all about, and he is not terribly good at capturing people on paper.

We have a fairly useless little chatter with Peter Ustinov (anyone who can make Ustinov boring needs treatment), a rather longer and perhaps more informative meeting with Harold Acton, a deeply tiresome one with a very tedious German film star.

We even have a sort of meal with Barbara Castle in what appears to be a self-service canteen in Brussels which gets none of us, including the author, anywhere, and then in Rome he stares at the Pope for an hour and a half and only remembers the man's shoes. Which seems a pity.

There is a good deal of chitter chatter about people as diverse as Sting, or Christopher Scaife and Lord Lambton, but we never get to know them, only hear muted mutterings about, really, not very much. However, in Gstaad he falls in with a garrulous laundress who fills him in with details which she gleans from the soiled linen she handles of the film stars, mercifully unavailable to our writer.

Mr Harty is no eagle, no hawk, swooping down on his delectable prey, tearing out the gut and the heart and making us see the cities and the places which he drifts through on this tour; rather he is a jackdaw, concerned with the glittering trivia.

We visit Brussels, Waterloo, Naples, Florence, Lucca, but you would hardly know it. In Milan we are never told that there is a cathedral of astonishing glory, but we do hear an awful lot of chat about a fashion designer called Armani, and the great fresco of the Last Supper almost goes unrecorded because the church in which it is painted was closed.

Well, that happens, but the great traveller on the Grand Tour goes back the next day, surely? Perhaps there wasn't time with all the TV people fussing.

But I found it irritating; as irritating as the fact that although we are taken to Oberammergau all that we ever get to know about it, or its extraordinary performance of the life of Christ, is that if you sit on the wooden benches in the theatre there you get bum-ache. And that's not enough, at least for me.

The best part of the book is the first chapter; funny, touching, shrewd, accurate and alive, full of wistful detail, but I have a sad feeling that we won't see this part on television. It's too good and it happened before the Grand Tour really got under way, which is a mighty pity.

However, the book is certain to sell well; people love to read 'the book of the TV series' and it'll fill in some of the detail which the camera may miss. Mr Harty tells us that teaching is his passion; well, to coin a phrase, after this ice-cream wafer has been read and digested, he 'must try harder'. I am very certain that he will the next time.

Daily Telegraph, 2 April 1988

This, my first review, distressed Russell enormously. I was very shattered: I had not realized at that moment – or had forgotten – how cruel the printed word could be. And after all my experience with the media! He was at the time ill. I didn't know how ill. And he died shortly afterwards.

Venomous Pen

Dorothy Parker: What Fresh Hell is This?
by Marion Meade (Heinemann)

I can tell you one thing: I'd have loathed Mrs Parker and she wouldn't have gone a bundle on me either. Born Dorothy Rothschild in a New York suburb of a Jewish father and a 'goy' – in her words – mother, she seems, according to Marion Meade's dauntingly researched book, to have left the womb bitching, biting and belittling until the day she died.

This is a brick of a book, like so many American biographies, when it could have been chiselled down to tile-thickness: none the less it's readable, takes no sides, and simply attempts to present to us a witty, unattractive lady with a deep grudge. What I fail to gather is precisely what made Dorothy tick? Why was she so disagreeable? Why the angst, the rage, the cruelty?

She had an ordinary, lower-middle-class suburban life with brothers and sisters and holidays by the sea. It can't have been that bad a deal. Yet clearly she detested her background and was never known to speak of it. As soon as she could, she married one Edwin Pond Parker II of excellent English stock, made his life hell, divorced him but hung on to the name.

Her mother died suddenly when she was five or six. A fairly normal business, but she was consumed with guilt that she had something to do with it. She had nothing to do with it at all. Her mother went over to the 'other side' with a perfectly valid passport from the Coroner: 'Artery disease'.

Her father remarried two years later, which was very bad luck for his bride. Dorothy loathed her deeply. She was only ever known as 'Mrs Rothschild' and died two years later of a cerebral haemorrhage; this was hardly surprising since Dorothy spent hours staring at her in sullen silence.

From this supposedly 'guilty' background the sharp, poisonous wit of Mrs Parker developed. There is no doubt at all that she *was* a witty woman, if not particularly in her writing. But it was the sharp, cruel wit of the New York Jewish cut-and-thrust sort which scarred and wounded deeply and at which observers laughed and rubbed their hands, as long as they were not the targets.

In 1925 she was one of a group of young writers (she had started writing captions for *Vogue*) who gathered at a round table in the Algonquin Hotel every day to say amusing things to, and about, each other. With them she started the *New Yorker* magazine. She became its drama critic in 1927, writing stinging and slighting reviews and advising her readers to bring either a book or their knitting.

She also wrote woeful poems about sadness, loneliness, hopelessness and suicide, all of which added to her power but did little to increase her belief in herself. She said of her verse at one time that she was 'always chasing Rimbauds'.

Much of her wit, as I say, was verbal: much of it she never uttered at all, and some was quite wrongly accredited to others. She *did* say 'Where does she find them?' when someone said that a certain hostess was always kind to her inferiors, but I still can't discover from Marion Meade's probing inquiry *why* the woman was so unpleasing.

She remarried an actor-cum-writer, Alan Campbell, eleven years her junior, with suppressed homosexual tendencies. In Hollywood they became a writing team and turned out a number of scripts, mostly unremarkable, and consumed quantities of alcohol.

In 1947 they divorced. Mrs Parker had become heavily involved in radical politics. She had already been to Spain during the Civil War and had behaved there rather well, unlike her bosom friend, Lillian Hellman, who, so it is said, spent all her time in a Madrid hotel bar, dry-mouthed with terror.

And then, predictably, Mrs P became involved with the Communist Party in Hollywood and New York and got herself into trouble during the hideous decade of McCarthyism.

By now drink, pills and suicide were the norm. Having fun for Mrs P meant merely being drunk: having *lots* of fun meant being stinking to the point of incapacity and grossness. She missed deadlines, lived in hotels with a series of wretched dogs, smoked incessantly and tragically outlived her fame.

She died alone in a hotel room in New York in 1967, having very unwisely made Lillian Hellman her literary executor: unwise because Lillian, who actually disliked Dorothy very much, refused ever to release anything to writers working on the subject of Mrs Parker.

Lillian Hellman took charge and had her 'friend' cremated, neglecting to inform her family, who only read about it in the newspapers. Dorothy's ashes ended up, neatly boxed, in the offices of a legal firm on Wall Street. Pending instructions from Miss Hellman, they were placed in a filing cabinet.

After more than twenty years they are still there. The twopenny sparkler at the firework show had burned out.

Daily Telegraph, 30 April 1988

Bed for Art's Sake

The Salad Days by Douglas Fairbanks Jnr (Collins)
A Life by Elia Kazan (Deutsch)
The Magic Lantern: An Autobiography by Ingmar Bergman.
Translated by Joan Tate (Hamish Hamilton)

'Selectivity! Selectivity. Hone to the bone. That's the secret of good autobiography.' The advice of my first publisher and editor, Norah Smallwood, might have been useful to a couple of the fellows under cramped review here. Ingmar Bergman, of course, knew it, but the other two gambol away like spring lambs in a meadow. Douglas Fairbanks Jnr, or Fayrebanks as he likes us to know him, is slightly more reserved than the Anatolian billy-goat Elia Kazan, who knows no bounds of reticence or selectivity or even, it appears, *decency*.

Fairbanks is a glossy, smooth, Man-Tanned, red-carnationed, ever-decent chap, who never uses a sour adjective in his 400 pages. Everyone is delicious, lovely, adorable, divine, glorious and alluring or ravishing. He slides in and out of his ladies' beds as smoothly and as coolly as an onyx lizard.

Married at nineteen to Joan Crawford, always only 'the second man', never quite the Star, he clambers on and up beyond the dismay and the shadow of an impossible father, and two pretty tiresome stepmothers, to make his way in the world. Does it well, too. Unkindly known as 'the Hillary of Social Climbers', he is still at it by the time this book ends in 1941 with the promise of another breathless saga.

From the many assorted ladies of Hollywood, a sort of Dairy Milk Selection, he eventually reaches his peak of splendour by nibbling at the fringes of British royalty, even managing to beard Churchill at the Savoy Grill with a letter from or to Roosevelt, I fear I have forgotten exactly which.

Golly! Years ago on wet Sundays in Scotland my grandmother, wearying of her patience cards, would send me off to the kitchens to 'See what Cook and Mollie have today. Perhaps a *News of the World* or an *Express*. All trivial tosh, but it whiles away an afternoon.' Cook and Mollie would have enjoyed *The Salad Days*. If they could have afforded it.

They'd have detested *A Life*, Kazan's extravagant epic, 800 pages of manic ego. Somewhere in this welter of self-congratulation, sexual bragging and cruel anecdotes about practically everyone he knew – among them Lee Strasberg and his odious wife Paula, Clifford Odets, James Dean, even Brando – and almost every woman he bedded, he does have the grace to suggest that '. . . from time to time you've thought my book unfair, ugly and hateful. Here and there it is vulgar, too, but that is a word from which I do not shrink.' Nor does he.

This son of a crafty Turkish carpet-dealer barges and weaves his way through the market place as to the manner born, fawning, stabbing, and dealing. I know he was responsible for *On the Waterfront*, for amazing performances of *A Streetcar Named Desire* and others, but he was equally responsible for the destruction of a number of good and honourable people whom he named as 'a friendly witness' before the House Committee on Un-American Activities, guaranteeing that they would be totally unemployable as long as the McCarthy Hunt was on, and long after.

I knew a number of them and worked with them. I knew their despisal of the man. In Paris at the première of a film I had made with Joseph Losey, for example, the theatre was packed; seats were set up in the aisles. 'So full! Amazing! Even Elia Kazan has to sit on a wooden chair!' said some idiot press woman. Losey suddenly dragged me from my seat and bustled me through the crowd into the street and down to Fouquet's where we dined. 'I'll be damned,' he said, 'if I let you sit with an informer.'

But Mr Kazan is not in the least concerned in his book about betrayal or informing; he is as happy as a boxer dog rolling in a cow-pat; covered in muck, he comes lolloping towards one, a trifle sheepishly, but, after all, he had only done it all to save Democracy.

And bedding actresses, especially married ones, is all part of the big fun too.

So. If you like this sort of tittle-tattle, this kissing-and-telling absolutely all, and if you have eighteen quid to spare for the thrill, then go ahead. Otherwise leave it strictly where it belongs. On the shelf.

Mr Bergman, on the other hand, has written a *real* autobiography. We have selectivity here, we have construction, we have grace and prose and a genius film-maker at work. Born of two hideously ill-matched parents into a dire Lutheran existence, bullied and beaten, scorned and constantly ill (and no wonder!) he somehow managed to survive the rigours of a Swedish upbringing and chan-nelled all his pain and despair into the works which were to follow and which have so influenced lesser directors. Like the others, but in a more delicate manner, he too bedded his leading ladies and they all seemed to enjoy it very much: it was all done for the love of the 'art', you understand: and 'art' was supreme.

The Magic Lantern moves backwards and forwards in time, focus-ing here and there, pulling back, going in close, obeying all the movements of a camera, and he observes with an eye like a scalpel. There are sharp and perfect portraits of his mother, of his various affairs, of his children, of his intense horror at the 'filthy mess' of London and practically everything in that city, and he is unsparing, and funny for a Swede, about his relationship with the Oliviers during his rehearsals for *Hedda Gabler* at the 'being built' National.

In their flat he found shelter from a dirty hotel, and it proved to be a disaster: '. . . sofas grubby, the wallpaper torn, interesting damp formations on the ceilings . . . breakfast cups were not washed up, glasses had lip marks on them . . .' and so on. The Swedes, we know, are clean as hell. Tired old London did not suit and he left, hating it with 'every fibre of my body'. Which is a pity.

But he has written a splendid book, and even though the names we read are hardly familiar to us, one reads on eagerly. There is one excruciating, and accurate, portrait of Ingrid Bergman, dying of cancer but fighting on and fighting *him*. He wins. Her perform-ance in *Autumn Sonata* was one of the finest things she has ever done, and she knew this to be so in a letter to me. 'At *last!*' she wrote. 'I have done something I can be proud of after all these years. I have worked with Bergman. I never thought I'd get the chance.'

She did, finally, when it was almost too late. But she had worked with greatness, and that Ingmar Bergman certainly has. This is a passionate, caring book about a very particular man. I urge you to read it.

Daily Telegraph, 11 June 1988

Efric Spice

Middlepost by Antony Sher (Chatto)
A Twist in the Tale: Twelve Short Stories by Jeffrey Archer (Hodder)

I have a nagging feeling that I have, somewhere along the line, missed the point of this book by the multi-talented Antony Sher. And I don't for the life of me know why.

Middlepost is excellently written, deeply researched, as dense and patterned as an Axminster rug. It has one or two very evocative and economical drawings by the author, and it has a beginning, a middle – more or less – and an end. So where have I gone wrong? I wish that I could like it all a great deal more.

Let's start at the beginning. The cover, again by the author, is pretty daunting. A group of ostrich-necked grotesques weave about in a strange seaweed-like manner. And all in the most hideous shades of baby-lotion brown-beige. Someone should have advised Mr Sher that brown is a brute for a cover, and doesn't look so good on bookstalls: at least that is what Graham Sutherland, who used to try to teach me illustration many years ago, used to say. Red, blue, greens (white and black are not strictly colours) – but on no account use brown.

Perhaps what I dislike about it so much are the 'grotesques' themselves. They are, I presume, portraits of the characters we shall meet within these ugly covers, and pretty they ain't.

Storyline? Well, it is familiar to anyone who has read his Malamud. Little Jew, with straggly beard, 'matted hair' and an unpronounceable name, peels off from Middle Europe – and the 'rising tide' of anti-Semitism – with a suitcase and not one word of English. Which might not matter except that he makes for South Africa, a change from America or Australia, but as far as the people and topography are concerned, not that much different. And English he will need.

He manages to get through the whole book with a few words – 'Bye-bye', 'Bokswater', 'Gooood' and a couple of others – while all around him people chatter away in a Babel of Languages. But he manages all right, which is jolly clever, both of him and his writer, who almost convinces us it would be possible.

It is 1902, the British have savaged the Boers, the war is over and everyone has to begin again. Under these circumstances we also get, naturally, a 'cast of thousands': British thugs, Boer bigots, bushmen and bushwomen of lustreless hue. We even get a couple of comic Italians, fat and hysterical, and a black servant, male, called, oh dear yes, April, who spouts gobs of Shakespeare like bubble-gum. But it all hangs together and I bet I am the only one who doesn't quite see what it's all about.

I'm much too delicate, of course. I dislike reading about people who 'defecate', are 'constipated' or, even more, sit stuck 'in their own dung'; we get our fair share of this, plus the birth under a tree of a baby which is instantly buried in a small pit and walloped with a stick. Apparently that is the best way of disposal in Seth Efrica – anyway it was at that time – and if it was black . . .

We get a sort of homosexual advance which is made and, properly, resisted by our straggly bearded Jew, and we even have the obligatory 'pearl' of semen held, quiveringly, in the astonished hero's hand after a fairly close encounter with a black lady who, I gathered, resents his desire.

But basically the story is about a new start, a new world, a second chance. Hope is there, the sky is starred with millions of tiny lights, the great veld stretches out apparently for ever, empty, ready, waiting.

Our hero watches the stars in wonder: '. . . giant swarms shifting the heavens. He gasped, for now there was no doubt: the world was leaning into its tumbling, twisting fall . . . he kept his balance, treading, hopping, dancing, as oceans and continents swept beneath him . . .' – and that's about it.

The book ends on this note of high hope; the hero realizes that life can start again, that the universe is filled with treasures, scent and light and that he is at the centre of it all and it is all within his grasp. In fact, dear reader, you'll probably enjoy every word.

Now, Jeffrey Archer, as one might guess, has a very jolly cover for *his* book, *A Twist in the Tale*. Light, clear, easily spotted on the counter. We even have a full-frontal picture of the author on the back. No simple 'mug shot' this, but a glossy portrait rather like something from a BHS catalogue: from highly polished shoes right up to the Cheshire-cat grin.

But alas! This is no Maugham, no Dahl, no Saki . . . not even a Capote. A bundle of little stories with all the bite and crispness of tinned asparagus. I fear that I guessed the so-called 'twists' in the tale pretty quickly. Good aeroplane reading if you are doing the shuttle to Glasgow, but don't take it to Gatwick.

Daily Telegraph, 10 September 1988

Sweet Vapours

The High Road by Edna O'Brien (Weidenfeld)
Working for Love by Tessa Dahl (Michael Joseph)

My word, Edna O'Brien whips up a huge romantic whirlwind, and she *can* write – even if she is a lazy writer. It's taken her eleven years to get this one going. But she is a writer, despite forgetting some of the rules. 'Plonked' and 'thwack' seem a little sloppy, especially as 'thwack' is used during sexual intercourse. Ladies to Ladies, you understand? And then we have the following: 'It had begun to rain, drops that did not get heavy, but fell silently, were eked out of the sky.' Well, all right, if she must. But 'eked'?

Anyway, romance we have here in yards, with only a few 'begorras' and 'top o' the mornin's' to make one shudder. This is a very Irish-Romantic-Trip. None of your dainty bodice-heaving, eye-fluttering from the delicate paws of a Magenta-Persian, pussy-patting Mrs Cartland. You've got a real woman up there, with a lived-in face.

The story. A lady of a certain age quits London in despair and failure (sexual) to 'find herself'. She ends up on some unidentified Spanish island (Minorca was never so beguiling), alive with falling oranges, honey-coloured skies, sun zig-zagging over bare arms (female), the scent of flowers overwhelming all about. We even have the usual Irish Drifter for local colour, and, among the picturesque wreckage of foreigners washed up on this glowing land, the aged Sloane Ranger who has retired to plant beanshoots and weed her garden. We also have, ah ha!, the irresistible Local Girl who is a bit of a riot in bed with the ladies, has a quite remarkable range of language and finally causes all sorts of troubles.

This is strictly a woman's world and not for a feller at all. *The High Road* is well written, well constructed, and awash with verbs and close observation. When Miss O'Brien sees a loaf it isn't just a loaf. It's a loaf with raisins in it. And we have them described in translucent detail. Frankly, I just can't get on with this description of Middle-Aged Lady coupling with ravishing Local Girl: '. . . slipping through a wall of flesh, eclipsed, inside the womb of the world, and throughout it all her words, faint, sweet as vapour.'

Well, come on now. *What* vapour? Is it always sweet, Miss O'Brien? And what the hell is 'the womb of the world'? Nonsense, dear. Everything ends, naturally enough, in sultry Spain, in mince-meat, and the true plot is finally revealed. This *is* Romance, and there is absolutely nothing wrong with that. Only don't believe a word.

Now Tessa Dahl isn't really into the writing scene, yet. But there is no question that she is on her way. Although she strongly denies it, her first novel, *Working for Love*, is pure autobiography, and very compelling stuff it is. She's altered a few names, jigged it about, and, I hope, written out her desperate sense of loss and betrayal by Mummy and Daddy and various gentlemen along the way. But she writes cleanly and economically, as with a scalpel. There is no fluffy detail here. We get on with the savagery of sadness and cruelty.

It is a book flowing over with an astonishing candour of hopeless-ness, of loss and of recovery. Above all, it is a blistering account of a young woman who has sought quite desperately for love and affection all her life and just got the sums wrong. When she has sorted out this *roman à clef*, got it out of her gut, and *if* she can find another, wider, subject to stab away at, she will be very well worth watching.

Daily Telegraph, 29 October 1988

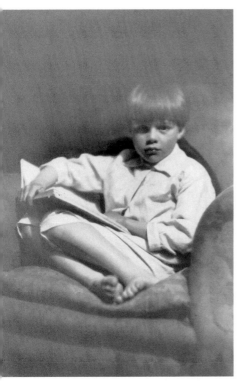

Hampstead, 1926, aged five

This reprehensible photograph was taken by my father on my last 48-hour leave, just before -Day. I am wearing his boots and breeches from the Royal Artillery in the First World War, d my own tunic from the Queen's Royal Regiment. The disgraceful mix of uniforms I cannot plain. Maybe I had been riding that morning on the Downs?

3. With Bertrand Tavernier on the set of *Daddy Nostalgie* (*These Foolish Things*) in Bandol, south west France, in 1991

4. At the Olivier Theatre, during one of half a dozen sold-out 'concerts' which I gave there in the course of book promotion in 1993

Charlotte Rampling photographing me for *Elle* magazine in the Long Room at Le Pigeonnier
June 1985

With Joseph Losey, who had just come out of hospital, filming *The Servant* on location in
Royal Avenue in 1962

7. Theo 'Thumper' Cowan in 1976

8. With Brigitte Bardot
Pinewood in 1954

With Kathleen Tynan on Venice Beach, California, during the filming of *The Patricia Neal* *ory* in January 1981

. At a Hatchards signing in the nineties. Editor's choice!

11. With Katharine Whitehorn aft[er] receiving our Honorary Doctorat[e] of Letters at St Andrews Universi[ty] on 4 July 1985

12. Russell Harty and 'The Drummer Bo[y]' on the terrace of Le Pigeonnier during t[he] shooting of the Yorkshire Television speci[al] in 1986

With Luchino Visconti at the Hôtel des Bains, Venice, in 1970

. With Norah Smallwood, my first editor, at Le Pigeonnier in 1980

15. With Glenda Jackson beside the pond at Le Pigeonnier, shortly after our wretched experien« in Hollywood in 1981

16. With my English mastiff, Candida, in the early sixties

Out of the Shadows of Hell

The Journey Back from Hell: Conversations with Concentration Camp Survivors by Anton Gill (Grafton)
I Shall Live: Surviving the Holocaust 1939–1945
by Henry Orenstein (OUP)
A Cup of Tears: A Diary of the Warsaw Ghetto by Abraham Lewin.
Edited by Antony Polonsky (Blackwell)

I can remember the day very well, even after all these years. It was a clear, cold, April morning. The 17th or 18th, not certain of the date, one seldom was in the war. But someone said that the Germans had pulled back a few kilometres, abandoning a large concentration camp, and we ought to 'swan off' and have a look. I was anxious, I recall, to acquire a pair of German boots . . . better than ours, and I had no more idea in my mind than that. We got the unexpired portions of the daily ration (bully beef sandwiches, thick and inedible unless starving) and set off in the jeep to Bergen-Belsen.

I don't know what I expected to see. I had known for some time that the camps existed – we saw them on our aerial photographs often enough – but it didn't really occur to me that through the greening larches and under a clear, hard, blue sky, the last traces of snow melting in the woods, I would be entering a hell which I should never forget and about which, for many years, I would be unable to speak. Sometimes, perhaps if I'd had a drop too much, I might try to explain and usually ended in unmanly tears. People anyway didn't want to hear about the camps, and if they did listen, it was always with a slight look of embarrassed disbelief. Which made me angrier and sillier. So I stopped trying to explain.

Now, reluctantly, I have agreed to read three books on the subject of the final extermination of the Jews. Bergen-Belsen was not an extermination camp. They just got it so overcrowded by moving people away from the Russian advance that typhoid and typhus flourished and people died in their thousands from that and from starvation, and not all of them were Jews; there were all kinds of people, Albanians, Dutch, Greeks, Italians, French, gypsies, socialists, homosexuals – all manner of men and women who had been rounded up. But, mainly, they *were* Jews.

I Shall Live by Henry Orenstein, *A Cup of Tears* by Abraham Lewin and, the best of these, *The Journey Back from Hell* by Anton Gill. These are the books. Mr Gill's is a hefty one. Nearly 500 pages of agonizing reporting. Wisely he has left the survivors to speak for themselves without any kind of interruption. The result is terrible in its very matter-of-factness. Unspeakable things are spoken of casually. Children, too small for burning, are flung alive into the gutters of running fat from the bodies of the adults. The fat was used for soap. A man standing shoeless in the freezing cold for hours on the Appellplatz is dragged away finally, leaving his feet behind him, glued by the ice to the bitter earth. Nothing to it. A tiny part of the day's infamy. Far worse things were happening all over Europe in the camps. Thousands and thousands were stripped, shaved, shoved into the gas chambers, the children thrust over their heads to fill up any space, and suffered an agonizing death, which usually lasted about forty minutes. Later they got it down to a convenient quarter of an hour.

Well: all right. Now we all know what happened to the Jews in detail. We know how many were destroyed, how few survived, and many of those who have survived are in Mr Gill's excellent book. They have come out of the shadows of the past to speak clearly, calmly, bravely. And with an amazing lack of hatred in general. But the absolute terror and fear of the Germans still persists, not so much for the younger Germans, who could not be held responsible, but for the big, noisy Germans, male and female, of that hideous generation.

They are still there; I have seen them and I too feel fear and revulsion. I remember very well Fassbinder, the director, warning me in Germany never to ask anyone of my age and generation what they did in the war. And even now, on the fiftieth anniversary of the dreadful Kristallnacht, in Bonn the following was stated: 'As far as the Jews were concerned, had they not aspired in the past to a role which should not have been theirs . . . had they not perhaps even deserved to be put in their place?'

'. . . put in their place'! *Why* is the Jew so loathed? Why is that tribe so feared and hated? I asked myself this again and again after that terrible April day in '45 . . . watching the cheerful women guards, trim and neat in uniform, blond hair in immaculate waves and curls, red nail varnish gleaming, chucking (two to a corpse) the dead into pits squashy with slime and decay. *'Juden kaput!'* one called up to our blanched faces.

One of the main things which went against them was their total lack of assimilation. They simply wouldn't join or become a part of their community and this was resented bitterly. But there was bile-rising jealousy of them too: they were successful in all they attempted: the newspapers, the theatre, the cinema, the music, medicine, business of all kinds, from the stall in the market to the fifty-storey building exuding prosperity and profit. And the other thing which was so detested was the nepotism. And the fact that, whatever country they lived in, it was always felt that they were 'foreign' and came, originally, from somewhere vaguely 'north of India'. And, alas, the fear and the dislike still exist today, especially in Austria, in Poland, in France, and even here in our own country, Great Britain.

I had two wonderful servants, in the early 1950s and 1960s. They were from Vienna. He had fought, and was severely wounded, at Stalingrad. Gentle, kind, warm and deeply loving, they were a part of my life for eleven years. Eventually they found a better job, for far more money than I could afford, in the United States. I took them, weeping, to the boat train and helped them with their luggage into the compartment. There were two rabbis sitting in a corner. Helmut spat viciously into both their faces and, with his sobbing wife, sat on his luggage in the corridor all the way to Southampton.

And could it happen here? In England's green and pleasant land, we asked each other this, in the jeep bumping back from the camp, and we agreed, in 1945, that, yes it could. 'Wembley Stadium to start with, then shove them all off to Catterick Camp or any other military hell-hole; you'd get all the guards you needed to beat the hell out of them and then ship them all back to wherever they came from.'

No one was absolutely certain where that might be. But 'abroad' – for in '45 'abroad' was indeed that, and 'foreigners' were 'foreigners' and 'if you give 'em an inch they'll take an ell . . . am I right?'

I remember this conversation vividly. I was swimming with tears, sick twice, and dreamt of it all for nights and months of nights.

But I had it easy: Belsen was a holiday camp in comparison to Treblinka. There, in one day from 6 a.m. until 5 p.m., they drove the naked Jews into pits which they had had to dig themselves to the blaring of dance music and jolly marching songs: 17,000 were finished off in this way.

I was twenty-four then; now I am sixty-seven. My actions are a little more controlled. I just leave the elevator if a German enters. It's the voice which disturbs me so dreadfully; rather a futile gesture, but I make it none the less. These three books might have the same effect on you.

Daily Telegraph, 26 November 1988

Book of the Year

There were actually two in my opinion . . . but I'm only allowed the one so it has to be without question, *Love in the Time of Cholera* (Cape) by Gabriel García Márquez. He has written the most gloriously heart-wrenching story of love that I have, perhaps, ever read. Gentle, subtle, persuasive and as elegant and fastidious as his heroine, Fermina Daza; as atmospheric and nostalgic as the opening of a long-closed chest redolent of the faded scents of camphor, cedar and lavender.

It haunts, lingers in the mind and in the mind's eye, long after the covers have been reluctantly closed. A marvel of a book which for me no one has come near to in the whole year – except Molly Keane, with *Loving and Giving* (Deutsch), which, as a sort of delicious 'chaser', is quite the best she has ever written in a long and victorious career. Can't really leave her out. Not really.

Daily Telegraph, 29 November 1988

A Sea Elephant in Mink

Lilly: Reminiscences of Lillian Hellman by Peter Feibleman (Chatto)

I saw Lillian Hellman only once: across a crowded New York restaurant. She reminded me, forcibly, of a sea elephant in mink. But not as kindly looking as a sea elephant: leathery, small cruel eyes, a gash of spite for a mouth. Not at all attractive. Arrogant, dictatorial, a chain smoker with a voice like iron wheels crushing gravel.

We were not introduced.

But some said that she was brilliant, some that they even liked her (not many on this count, actually). Others praised her wit, fun, generosity, courage. The usual guff that party-people use so glibly. They only told the 'truth' after her death.

Well, here is a spiffing book by a gentleman who really *does* know rather more about her than anyone else. He had known her since he was ten years old and she some thirty-five. Eventually, as a young man, in spite of the 25-year difference, he fell hopelessly (I use the word advisedly) in love with her and so remained until her death.

To say that she was spiteful, wayward, bombastic, opinionated, vulgar, lewd, oversexed and brutally ugly is not giving you a full picture. She was also a liar, a literary thief, a cheat, often funny, sometimes gentle (according to the author), always jealous and larger, by far, than life. And Peter Feibleman went along with all this, constantly on the verge of mental, physical and moral castration.

A lower-middle-class Jewess, born in New Orleans, Hellman quickly came to terms with her lack of beauty (in the conventional sense) and fought without shame for her place in the sun. She wrote. And she wrote exceedingly well.

In America there aren't, or weren't at that time anyway, many lady writers of note. Hellman set that to rights. She got three very fine plays out of her guts and on to the stage. *The Children's Hour*, *The Little Foxes* and *Autumn Gardens* are 'lasters' that will endure however badly they are played (and they frequently are, alas). But they are plays which she could be, and was, very proud of having written.

She had a respectable bash at some others, but they really haven't held up. She is left with these three as her main output, plus her prose, some of which she shamefully cobbled together from the experiences of others, claiming those experiences as her own. She was found out eventually, of course, and wasn't best pleased. But her arrogance saved her face, if not her reputation.

I used to read the prose avidly. However, something in the style of her writing gave me the vague impression that I was being conned. I can't imagine why: it was a shaky feeling of insecurity, rather like crossing a pond on thin ice, relieved to reach the bank. An odd feeling.

The plays – I saw four actually in my time, in various performances – have always seemed to me to be marvellous theatre, strongly plotted, tough and with superb parts for actors. But I don't think she was the towering force in the theatre which is claimed for her. And I don't think either, as the blurb will have us believe, that she was 'the wildest and wittiest' woman writer America ever produced.

The great achievement of Mr Feibleman's book is that he has, with intense and intimate knowledge, given us a 'living portrait' of an extraordinary woman. It is as funny as hell in places; warm, generous, often very moving, and sometimes astonishingly awful. Hellman's cruelty, her vulgarity, her meanness surge forward and almost engulf the reader in repugnance. Almost, because somehow Mr Feibleman never quite lets this happen.

He is a marvellous artist and 'paints', in bright, viscous, primary colours, the words, the warts and the wit (for there was wit in this wretched woman) and the wrongs. And there were plenty of those, too. If her wit was frequently laced with caustic soda, Mr Feibleman nevertheless loved her. That he loved her equally as a mother-figure is pretty clear also. That he loved her as 'a chum' comes through

blindingly. He knew the black and the white; he also knew the occasionally stunningly simple, and fearful, woman buried under the rubble of envy, greed, wobbly politics and, above all, unreasoning jealousy. All these things he knew, and puts before us to contemplate. If you don't limit your reading to *The Field*, Jane Austen or Jeffrey Archer, you might just find this a quite fascinating book.

I don't often laugh aloud when I read, but Mr Feibleman, with his dry American-Jewish humour, his wry wit, his self-awareness and, above all, his absolute understanding of the woman he loved (and at times almost hated), made me on occasion laugh aloud with glee.

When she died she left him her entire estate, plus the house on

Martha's Vineyard where they lived together. She and he were both raving food-nuts, concocting little suppers, picnics, parties, and dinners and lunches with epicurean delight. One day he asked the gardener with what Miss Hellman had nourished the horseradish plants that flourished in incredible lushness in her garden. The reply was that they didn't need anything, they just grew.

> 'They are famous plants,' I said. 'People from all over the world used to write letters asking Miss Hellman for some horseradish.'
>
> 'So I'm told,' Melvin said.
>
> 'One thing I just noticed,' I said. 'The plants are growing in a perfect circle.'
>
> 'They'd better be,' said Melvin. 'She planted them round the cesspool.'
>
> That was Lilly, all right.

The book is more a novel than a biography, and all the better for it . . . Thanks to the use of tape-recordings of conversations one 'hears' that gravelly voice, laughs or winces according to taste; but what the author does supremely well is to convince the reader, as he closes the covers finally, that somehow, in a strange way, he has 'seen' Hellman quite clearly and not found her as awful as all that. In fact, that had she ever accepted one (not at all likely), one might have fallen under the spell.

John Marquand Jr said: 'She was awful and she was worth it.' I think he was right.

Daily Telegraph, 25 February 1989

Recording Every Wrinkle

Willie: The Life of W. Somerset Maugham
by Robert Calder (Heinemann)

I don't know if you have ever done it, but should you stand about two feet away from even the most glorious tapestry in the world for more than a few minutes the whole thing simply becomes a beige blur – even the stitches. And thus it is with this exhaustingly researched, academic and generous book on the wretched W. Somerset Maugham. There is just too much detail to absorb; it's a beige blur.

I say 'wretched' only because this is yet another in-depth study of the writer, and heaven knows there have already been enough. We have examined the stutter, the lovers, the 'callous' treatment of the wife and daughter, the writing and the early years in medical school. On it goes.

The present author, Robert Calder, has even had an earlier bash at his subject with *W. Somerset Maugham and the Quest for Freedom* (1972). That title already causes one to tremble.

Clearly Calder's curiosity – perhaps even affection? – is insatiable. He goes at this latest autopsy like an insectologist pulling the eyelashes from a fly. We are spared absolutely nothing.

No book for a fireside chair, for your bedside reading, for a shady tree, this is for a long sea voyage (it is 400 pages long) or the silence of a reading-room in some university.

But we *know* it all: from the short stories to the suspect nonsense written by his nephew Robin Maugham in *Conversations with Willie* and his own volumes on his life, *The Summing Up* and *A Writer's Notebook*. Nothing in this fat book is better than those two.

So why bother to pick and probe and attempt to discover what made him tick? He who has given infinite pleasure and left us a splendour of writing which will remain for as long as the written English word is permitted to exist (even if at times it may go out of fashion with the grim intellectuals who shuffle through his work as disdainfully as schoolboys crunching through leaves).

Isn't it enough to be grateful for the elegance of the language, the spareness of the descriptions, as vivid and economical as an Impressionist canvas, for the variety of his stories, the elegance of his plays, the profundity of his 'notebooks'?

Someone said plaintively the other day: 'Why can't people write biographies about people they *know*?' Potty, of course, but I know the feeling. In a nutshell, so to speak, here is a sort of cigarette-card bio as far as I can sort it from the mass before me:

Born Paris, 25 January 1874. Mother, Edith, whom he adored. Papa, Robert, who seemed dullish but not unkind. Mum dies when Maugham is eight . . . And from that moment, according to Calder, and it is probably so, from time to time until almost the day he died 'he wept with the tears pouring down his face'.

That this death was a catastrophe for him is evident. It is suggested that his stammer stemmed from the shock, and that his homo-sexuality, or the 'temperament', began to incubate. Well, perhaps it did.

We all function in different ways, but homosexuality is used here like a sledgehammer to drive home the message of his works. One gets numbed. It is the reason for his entire life, his cruelty, his 'mordant wit', his cynicism and his selfishness.

The fact that he was not at ease with some women is clear, and from what one discovers of his wife, the tiresome Syrie, it is hardly surprising. But it is absurd to suggest that he only wrote 'masculine' women.

He wrote about women quite marvellously – they were not all 'monsters' or 'fellers', and Bette Davis and Joan Crawford didn't get to play them all, whatever the writers may care to say. Sadie Thompson and Rosie in *Cakes and Ale* are two of the most perfectly realized, and understood, women in modern fiction.

Although Calder's book is about as exhausting to read as sawdust is to chew, it does perk up a bit in the last third. We get, naturally,

the male companions, the good and the evil ones, the tales of wife and daughter, the selling of the paintings, the final, agonizing, if ill-judged, howl of fury and pain of his Lear-like rage against his personal Regan and Goneril in his infamous piece 'Looking Back'.

All is there, and so too is the amazing dedication of the great writer, the fastidious choice of words, the coolness of the prose, the discipline of his work: not for him a couple of hours at the table in a Notting Hill Gate kitchen and then a quick whirl round with the Hoover. Here is the master writer alive and well, until finally senility slammed him as shut as a door.

This is a thoroughly respectable book, but buy his words and

154

read them – they'll tell you all you want to know. Stand back from the tapestry and take a long cool look. You will be wonderfully rewarded.

Daily Telegraph, 1 April 1989

The Crushing Life of a Bloomsberry

Carrington: A Life of Dora Carrington 1893–1932
by Gretchen Gerzina (Murray)

Well, all right then. If you really do want to know any more about the tiresome Bloomsberries, Gretchen Gerzina's splendidly researched, dry-as-old-bones, fully detailed, unwitty, light-as-a-school-dumpling but scholarly, even loving in a way, book is for you.

Another American academic unearthing the British Eccentrics. But not in the same wretched manner as the writers of the recent Kipling and Maugham books. While not a scrap as good as Ellmann, Gerzina will do to be going on with. She has taken immense pains to set it all down, and even for those of us who know the sorry saga of this exceptionally irritating woman Dora Carrington (and for that matter everyone else in the cast of this peculiar little *pièce du théâtre*) it still has the power to hold the attention.

Carrington (she preferred this name to 'Dora'; less feminine, more aggressively masculine, which suited her) was born of a severely repressed mother and an ageing father (sixty-one – hardly in full fig, but obviously quite capable, since he sired five children). She loathed her mother, adored Papa, doted on one brother, Teddy – who became a kind of sexual symbol for her in later life – cut off her hair before anyone else of her time, and went off to art school to learn how to paint. Which she did very, very well indeed.

Strangely, Gerzina places her on the fringe of the Bloomsbury set, which is a bit dotty when you realize that the players were leaping all around her and that she was caught in the eye of the storm.

Consider for a moment: the Woolfs, poky-nosed, intellectual, barren sexually, patronizing, successful with their little Hogarth

Press and influential. Then poor, silly Ottoline Morrell, scorned, vilified, used as a cheap (but expensive for the Morrells) haven for safe discussion, wine, food and argument far from the horrors and odours of the war.

There were the rather dreary Garnetts; the Bells painting away like anything every lampshade and mantelshelf in primary colours and 'simplified forms'; the awful Gerald Brenan, selfish and whining; the hysterical Gertler who really needed a swift kick up the backside, and the rugger-bugger Partridge (plus pacifist chick) all trying to woo, secure, make safe or even merely bed this scatty, breathless, chunky milkmaid-cum-pantry-mouse, Carrington.

She loathed her femininity, hated the 'lumps of flesh which hang before me' and detested, at least to begin with, any form of sexuality. But goodness, she could paint. Painting provided almost the whole structure for her life, and Gerzina makes this clear without passing a great deal of comment beyond some predictable Freudian suggestions.

So this shy *faux*-cock-teaser, this shrew, this timid child, pranced and leapt around her Bloomsbury maypole clutching the ribbons, the Gertler, the Brenan, the two Woolfs, the Partridges and, to many people's consternation, an absurd sailor who instructed her, as she put it, in 'lust'. Beakus Penrose was thicker than three planks.

Well: there we are. She danced and capered with all her ribbons, mixing them up greatly, getting into a terrible tangle, while the centre of the maypole – one can say the pole itself which held the whole thing together – was in truth the complete love of her life, amazingly, until the day that she died: Lytton Strachey.

A tall, stooping, bearded figure, older by far than herself, with granny-glasses and the bending frailty of a folding ruler, he adored her for the rest of his life and they were joined at the hip. Strachey was homosexual, preferring pretty boys to tender doting ladies, but he settled down to live a completely contented life with Carrington, and she with him, cosseting, loving, caring for him deeply.

No one else really mattered to her. Although she flirted and was bedded, she rebuffed, and recalled, with tiresome regularity, a long series of lovers both male and female. She chucked her Augustus-

John-image gipsy skirts, off-the-shoulder blouses, for breeches and hacking jackets, and cantered over the downs when she wasn't painting, falling in love, or driving someone mad or writing her wonderfully misspelled letters, brilliantly revealing of the creature, but not prominent here. For that you must turn to David Garnett's *Carrington* of 1970, the collected letters, to get the full flavour of this extraordinary hoyden-given brilliance.

A fellow student at the Slade dismissed Carrington once to me rather sweepingly: 'Silly old Dotty Carry-on, we called her . . .' But there was a lot more to her than that, and those paintings which have survived prove she was unique in her time. Nearer to Nevinson and Nash than John or Laura Knight! Her work today still catches at the heart in its simplicity and its brilliant use of colour.

Eventually she and Strachey set up house with the unlikely Partridge, a returnee from the hell of Flanders, who wanted her desperately. Strachey, on the other hand, was rather keen to have Partridge. But he never made base.

This strange *ménage à trois* endured and eventually, under extreme pressure, Carrington became Mrs Partridge and survived a pretty tempestuous relationship, an on-and-off affair conducted at all times under the benign eye of Strachey, who seemed not to mind so long as he was fed and watered, loved and cosseted, allowed to get on with his writing and permitted to go abroad from time to time to indulge his sexual needs.

It all seemed set, safe and fairly serene. Carrington cooked, rode, painted and leapt in and out of beds when 'lust' got the better of her, although she was not absolutely mad about that part. However, they could have joyfully capered on into old age except that Partridge fell for another and married her. The strings of the maypole got badly tangled, Carrington was left only with her pole, Strachey, and settled happily for that, for he adored her. But that happiness was brutally snatched away when Strachey died of cancer, leaving her alone in a hideous vacuum.

Loneliness is a killer. It killed Carrington. She wrote, one day: 'He first deceased, she for a little tried/to live without him, liked it not and died.' Attempting to shoot a rabbit one evening from her bedroom window, she somehow slipped and shot herself.

Can a person love another so desperately? They can. The book ends with the line: 'Love is love and hard enough to find.' Carrington found it and could not bear to have it wrenched away. Life was unendurable without Strachey, so she left. Simple as that.

Sunday Telegraph, 18 June 1989

The Way We Were

The New Yorker Book of War Pieces: London 1939 to Hiroshima 1945 (Bloomsbury)

The only time I see the *New Yorker* now is in some dentist's or doctor's waiting-room. Thumbed nervously, tattered, out of date; a skimpy little booklet stuffed with leering advertising for Imported Everything: from Chanel to chandeliers, from gin to Aran sweaters, or 'live lobsters from Maine' and lumps of 'Aunt Tabitha's Original Fruit Cakes'. Or whatever.

Embedded in this unseemly riot of sales-tease you might just come across a decent piece of writing. Some prose, a poem perhaps, a cartoon or a film review from its acidic critic. But honestly, by the time you have waded through the sweaters and fruit cakes, sublime in their vulgarity, you will be called to have your blood-pressure taken. And you won't have missed a great deal, I assure you.

But there was a time – oh! indeed there was – when the *New Yorker* stood supreme. (Only the very best need apply. Only the very best did.) And here is a collection of some of the war pieces published between September 1939 and that appalling August day when innocence and charity were dispersed for ever in the dust of Hiroshima. I suppose the book will appeal most to those of us who are comfortably over forty. You won't know what the hell it is all about if you are in your thirties: still less if you have just hit twenty.

But for the sheer splendour of the writing and the reporting of a time lost for ever, it is almost essential reading. No matter that you were 'not there at the time' or 'can't identify', you will be amazed that we were so damned innocent: so simple, so pleasant, so *unbelievable* in comparison with today's grab-all, ugly, streetwise, utter-fall-from-grace-people who now surround us.

We were really pretty nice idiots who went to war and badly burned our fingers. Then, in 1939, Princess Paul Sapieha toured her estates in Poland in her chauffeur-driven car plus children and nanny never to return. That's how it *was*. Her account is written with calm good sense, the ease of 'position', the knowledge that there would be no looking back. Worse, no going back. Ever!

It is a good way to start the book. John Hersey finishes it with his cool, calm, dreadful account of the murder of Hiroshima. Not one word too much here; no excess. It haunts by its simplicity.

This is glorious, clean journalism which today almost no longer exists because it is not *permitted* to exist. Everything must now be written in colour-supplement language which knows that the reader has only a thirty-second attention span and must be clobbered over the head with all the subtlety of a crack with a cricket bat.

One of the most famous of the contributors to this magazine was Janet Flanner, with her 'Letter from Paris'. Her brisk, startling account of Mrs Jeffrey's escape from Paris over the border to Spain should be a compulsory piece in every anthology of the greatest short stories. It is riveting. So, too, is Mollie Panter Downs with her 'Letter from London'. Beautiful, simple reporting which reads quite unbelievably today like Mrs Miniver's work. Until you suddenly realize that it is about real Mrs Minivers, of all classes, who *did* exist.

One almost disbelieves, and then recalls that we *were* like that. There *were* Cockneys, there *were* stiff-upper-lips, people *did* celebrate death and birth and wounds and loss with 'a nice cup of tea', and V-2s did thud down at rose shows and Wapping was a real place – not a centre for office blocks, newspapers, rubber plants and Porsches, but a vibrant part of a living city where some people lived in rows of little cottages, with outdoor privies and sometimes a bit of raggedy garden with cabbage and dahlias – and a tin bath for Friday hanging on a nail in the brick wall.

All were awaiting obliteration, which arrived on a still September evening. Now everyone is in tower blocks; they don't know their neighbours; they aren't even Cockneys.

The Americans arrived, a little late as usual, but when they did they inspired awe with their simplicity, respect for their firepower, affection for their generosity, and gratitude. And they fought with us to the death.

You must not miss A. J. Liebling's account of the D-day landing and after; or John Lardner, to whose memory this book is dedicated (he was killed at Aachen), and his account, funny and desperately sad, of the landing at Anzio. And there are many others too: Iwo Jima; Phillip Hamburger's letters from Rome (8 May 1945) and Berchtesgaden (1 June); and the empty echoing of Berlin raped, are shattering.

You will not read of concentration camps here, of the Holocaust, of Dresden, of the evil things that happened to the victims of infamous Yalta, or of the officers at Katyn, because these terrible things were only just emerging with the discovery, one cool April morning, of the monstrosity that was Belsen. There had been rumours. We were aware that there were worms beneath the stones. There were whispered stories, murmured hints of dreadfulness ahead, but just at that time we had not entirely kicked the stones over.

The *New Yorker* did not cover Stalingrad. There are no reports from China, of Wingate and his Chindits. But this is not a history book. There is no serious academic lesson or lecture in its pages. All it might do is remind you what really brilliant and brave reporting, and glorious writing, was like, and just how much our generation, and indeed yours, lost along with it all. I doubt you'll see its like again. *You* lost splendid writing; *we* lost that and all our innocence.

A hell of a lot.

Daily Telegraph, 29 July 1989

One and Only

Capote: A Biography by Gerald Clarke (Cardinal)

Capote said of himself: 'There's the one and only TC. There was nobody like me before, and there ain't gonna be anybody like me after I'm gone.'

He was right on all points.

Start reading this splendidly constructed, very moving, often funny book of Gerald Clarke's and you won't want to set it aside. It is compulsive reading, with all the tenacity of a good novel and the incredibly researched detail of a thorough biography. It proves, if it had to be proved, that in this singular case 'it *is* a great help to know the person about whom you are writing.'

Clarke knew Capote in the last years of his life and had to watch the appalling decline of his subject into decay, ruin and ultimate death. Helpless to assist, he could only attend at the bier.

This is the unhappy story of a genius–gone–wrong, the destruction of a could-be glorious machine, of a brilliance tarnished and corroded far too early. A sad creature born of imbecilically hopeless parents in Alabama, who was as hopelessly lost and adrift in life as they were, he eventually managed to get away from them, adopted the name of his stepfather, Capote, and got himself to New York.

Undersized, high-voiced, effeminate, almost-pretty when young, homosexual and fairly repellent on drugs and drink when older, he wrote. And *how* he wrote! The output was modest, but it was marked with an astonishing originality, and his first major work, *Other Voices, Other Rooms*, secured his position. He coursed along on this *oeuvre* for quite a while, chucked in *Breakfast at Tiffany's* and odd bits and pieces, and became the cherished 'collectable' of the Smart-set and the Literary-louts.

He spent most of his time flitting like a dark, silent bat from love

163

to lover, potion to potions, county to country, pill to needles; he was, in fact, on a downward path from the second that he wriggled free of his mother's resentful womb. He knew about words, about sex and people, and how they ticked and *why* they did.

Capable of great affection and blistering cruelty, he was often described as Puck or Merlin, or merely as a 'bloody witch'. He began to believe his own myth, not a sensible thing to do at the best of times, and his times were mostly the worst.

His masterpiece is, however, *In Cold Blood*, the true story of the wanton, aimless slaughter of a small-town family in Kansas. The story became his obsession for almost half a decade; he lived among the witnesses, knew the killers, was marked by the experience for the rest of his life.

Gerald Clarke's massively researched account of this unhappy writer is like a police torch probing cruelly with a blinding light into the darkest recesses of a thieves' attic, revealing all the evidence needed as well as nuggets of sheer splendour, to prove the word 'genius'.

He makes it perfectly clear that Capote was correct when he stated: 'There ain't gonna be anybody like me after I'm gone.'

There ain't.

Sunday Telegraph, 13 August 1989

The Rum Mister Goldfish

Goldwyn: A Biography by A. Scott Berg (Hamish Hamilton)

Here is a triumphant biography. A. Scott Berg's last one was about Maxwell Perkins (the Genius Editor) but this is about a very different fellow, a rum fish indeed, but nevertheless a Titan. More or less illiterate, speaking only Yiddish and some Polish, at sixteen he walked from Warsaw, via Hamburg, London (dossing in Hyde Park) and Birmingham (where he had an aunt), and finally reached North America (£95 steerage).

There is no record of him having set foot in the United States. There is, on the other hand, a belief that he probably landed in Canada. We must assume he slipped across a wild frontier and reached his Utopia. Determination, guts and raw ruthlessness remained with him all his long, and raging, life.

I'm not going to tell you the story here, nor shall I attempt to analyse this extraordinary man. Scott Berg does that. His book is no less triumphant than his biography of Perkins: scrupulously researched, witty, moving even, amazing at all times, wry and utterly absorbing.

Schmuel Gelbfisz was the eldest of six children born to gentle Aaron and extremely ugly 'Big Hannah' (victims of an unhappy 'arranged' marriage). He spent his early life in two rooms on the edge of starvation and the Jewish Quarter of Warsaw. The family never *quite* starved, although they once had to survive for a week on a handful of potatoes; life was a constant battle against fear, pogroms, conscriptions for the Tsar's army, hunger and virulent anti-Semitism. Schmuel, reasonably, decided it was time to get out.

He was not alone: at the same time almost every harassed Jew in Eastern Europe had the same dream, and as Schmuel started on his marathon trip to Hamburg other families were on the move.

The migration to the West had begun. The Mayers left Vilna, the Zeleznicks (Selznicks later) quit Kiev, the Warners got out of Poland, the Zukors fled Hungary and Carl Laemmle slipped out of Germany – all within 500 miles of Warsaw, all to meet and found a very different ghetto in the desert sun of California; a remarkable event which would change popular entertainment for ever.

However, before the Golden Ghetto could come into being, these founding fathers were forced to earn a living in their promised land. Louis B. Mayer became a junk dealer in New Brunswick, Zukor a furrier in Chicago, Selznick a jeweller in Pittsburgh, Laemmle a clothier in Oshkosh. The Warner brothers' father opened a bicycle shop in Youngstown and Sam Goldfish (as he was now called) went off to Gloversville, where he learned all you need to know about making, buying and selling gloves: *and* wheeling and dealing.

He prospered. They all prospered. None of them would ever look back. Rather, they looked ahead with glittering eyes at a new vision which had appeared before them: the penny arcade, the nickelodeon which would make their fortunes. But just for a time Goldfish had to trail about as a commercial traveller for Elite Gloves. In his journeys he met a plump-faced little fellow who had a cornet act in Vaudeville. His name was Jesse Lasky, he had a sister called Blanche. Sam, at thirty, married Blanche, twenty-seven.

It was a miserable marriage. He was later to say: 'She couldn't stand the sight of me.' He was certainly no Donatello David: tall, balding, mean-eyed and mean-mouthed. However, they managed to have a daughter, Ruth, and struggled on. In time, with a more or less reluctant Lasky plus a new member of the group 'who knew a bit about making movies', one Cecil B. de Mille, they secured the rights to a stage play, *The Squaw Man*, and began making movies in a rented barn in an orange grove in California. The barn was in the middle of an almost defunct housing development (homes for the retired) on the outskirts of Los Angeles. It was called Hollywood.

The Squaw Man was not the first film to have been made in Hollywood, but it was the first time that a determined group of people decided to settle there and found an industry. The place was ideal – almost constant sunlight (this was before lights were used), desert, jungle, mountains and the sea. Here they would remain, joined by a horde who heard the drumbeat of success and flowed from the East. The cinema had begun. The peasants employed peasants to amuse peasants.

A simple, outrageous formula, but it worked. The Golden Ghetto spread across the dusty flats and up into the canyons, and Samuel Goldfish was its leader. In a short time he dumped Blanche, denied Ruth until she was almost middle-aged, changed his name by swiping half that of one of his partners, thus becoming Gold*wyn*, and began to carve the career which secured him until he died a multi-millionaire, an avid collector of art, decorated by his President (in this instance, Nixon) with the highest honour his country could bestow, the Medal of Freedom, when he was well into his nineties.

Not bad for a ruthless, petty-minded, cunning, cruel, whining, semi-literate and ugly man whose patched-together name stood, amazingly, for elegance, breeding, glamour and good taste – what the Americans call 'class'. He had little of these qualities himself, but he *knew* what they were, and he saw to it that they were put up on the screen. Goldwyn *was* style.

He imported the best writers from the East and Europe, wooed Chanel from Paris to design for him, almost invented the white-on-white of the thirties and, unlike many of his rivals, attempted always to employ 'ladies' and 'gentlemen' of the acting fraternity in his films. He made some stinkers, some astonishingly good films, and some ghastly malapropisms which became known as 'Goldwyn-isms'. 'Whatever happened,' he once asked Myrna Loy (one of his ladies), 'to that little guy from Ethiopia? Hail Salesia?' And walking on a beach with William Paley, who had stopped to look at a flight of birds with an amazed cry of 'Look at all those gulls!', he said: 'How do you know they ain't boys?'

Trying to purchase the rights of *The Little Foxes* from Lillian Hellman (who detested him) he was assured that it was a very caustic story, but he shrugged and said it didn't matter what it cost: just buy it. (He did, and made a killing.) And once, poor Loretta

Young, disliking her right profile, said she would only be 'shot' in future on her left, and good, one. Goldwyn agreed with dangerous cordiality: 'You give me half a face, I give you half a salary.' He won.

He married again, a pleasant, Gentile woman named Frances, who bore him a son. This gave him infinite pleasure, but the boy was virtually ignored, or bullied, or suddenly lavished with weepy, loving letters. There was little fatherly love around. That was considered weakness, and weakness was abhorrent to the man. Late in her life he admitted the banished Ruth back to the 'family', but he never forgave poor Blanche.

Eventually he won his coveted Oscar for perhaps his greatest film, *The Best Years of Our Lives*. This was based on a news item which Frances had read in *Time* magazine. He was discovered, late at night, sitting in his darkened study, weeping copiously, clutching his Oscar like a talisman. Which is exactly what it was as far as he was concerned.

It had been a very long walk from Warsaw to that moment. He was sentimental, harsh, a thief of other people's ideas, works, or even their employees if he needed them, snake-mean and childish. At croquet:

> . . . he just wanted to win – to hit his ball through the wickets and smash his opponents' balls to kingdom come. He cheated by moving his ball whenever he thought no-one was looking . . . made up house rules that were to his immediate advantage.

If he got caught, he would bluster and shout like a frilled lizard. If seriously challenged, he'd weep copiously. I never played croquet with Mr Goldwyn, never dined at Laurel Lane, but I spent time with some of his contemporaries, sitting on the white shaggy carpets in sitting-rooms all across the Golden Ghetto among the Monets, Manets, Sisleys, Picasso blues, Bonnards and Cézannes.

I even hung my coat on the bronze, outstretched arm of Degas's little dancer in the net tutu. She was in the hall. One of my hosts, a good and kindly man, sat with me revelling in his loot. His first job, he told me, on arriving in America at the age of ten, was to work on the pulp-barges removing hooks and eyes and buttons from rags before they were pulped.

'Can you *believe* that? Hooks and eyes and all this. It's *amazing*, wouldn't you say? Just *amazing*.'

And so was Mr Goldwyn.

Sunday Telegraph, 17 September 1989

The Blazing Radiator

Young Entry by M. J. Farrell (Virago)

Someone who spent a great deal of his adult life interviewing people for one of those television hideous chat shows encountered, to his delighted astonishment, Molly Keane. Later he said to me: 'Molly Keane is a blazing radiator; whereas most of the others I've had to deal with are drains.'

One sees instantly what he means merely from reading her work. Take any book by Molly Keane and I guarantee you will be delighted, charmed and sustained with pleasures. You will not be drained, bewildered or in constant need of a dictionary as you make your irritated way through pages of convoluted prose.

Young Entry was written in 1928 under her pen-name of M. J. Farrell when Molly Keane was twenty-four. It is, as you will readily note, a 'young book'; by that I mean it is full of things which the writer, wiser and wittier and harsher with herself, would probably have tidied up a bit, but it is a gentle delight nevertheless.

What I want to know, above all else, is how was she able to write so amazingly well? So confidently, so shrewdly? How did she manage her construction so brilliantly, set wit to her pages, life to her characters? How the hell did she *know* what to do?

Well: the point is that the woman is a born writer. It is something, I gather from Diana Petre's excellent new introduction, which causes Molly Keane a certain degree of discomfort if the fact is stated. Well, I suppose it might. The lady is modest and well brought up; she'd no more admit to being a born writer than she would to being a born lady. However, the marks tell equally.

This is a perfectly ordinary, good old-fashioned story, right down the line and, frankly, you must know the plot – they say that there are only seven anyway, so you'll be familiar with it. But that in no way spoils the joy.

Ravishing Prudence, horsey-go-jumping, flirting madly, is an orphan in Anglo-Irish society, brought up by unfeeling, aged guardians, about to inherit a fortune (plus crumbling great house) at twenty-one; she is headstrong, delicious, feather-brained, a splendid horsewoman, with a perfect eye for a hound and a pretty wide open one for eligible gentlemen.

They are all lithe-limbed, grey-eyed, impeccably dressed good riders, and the hero has what she calls 'blocky' eyelashes, so we know that he's ready for the picking. The story is strewn with the familiar Keane characters: the elegant dowagers, the shuffling crone casting spells in dark cabins on the bog, the lunatic girl with a secret child, the house servants all a little more than barking mad, and above all, the superb descriptions of the hunt itself. The hunt, hounds and horses are really the main characters in this tale anyway.

All in all, a delightful book, almost shocking in the way that it reminds you of a time lost to us for ever.

Sunday Telegraph, 24 September 1989

Book of the Year

A year crammed with splendours: Sybille Bedford, Kazuo Ishiguro, Julian Barnes, A. Scott Berg. What a spoiling! But I think I have to decide on Bruce Chatwin and *What am I Doing Here* (Cape). It gave me intense pleasure in the very spareness and beauty of its prose, its astonishing, and deceptive, simplicity and the detailed pictures which it set before my eyes.

Daily Telegraph, 25 November 1989

In Pursuit of Sticklebacks

At Home and Abroad by V. S. Pritchett (Chatto)

It would be absurdly presumptuous of me to try to criticize this collection of glorious articles by, perhaps, the greatest writer of pure English prose alive, thank goodness, today.★

All that I can do is to recommend it to you urgently and to consider the delights set before us – and persuade you to enjoy the words which, over the years, have become so hideously debased but which here are offered to us fresh-minted, as it were, so that once again one can read the beauty of the English language intact, glittering, clear and simple, as if nothing appalling had ever happened to our mother tongue.

These articles, which date from the late twenties through to the late sixties, range from South America to London, Greece to the Seine, and, most wonderfully, the Appalachian Mountains.

Here you will never read that someone has 'washed down his meal' with wine; no one 'opines', no one ever reaches 'the end of the day', no sun sinks 'into the wine dark sea like a giant orange/ ball of fire/flaming sphere'.

Food, when described, is never 'lashings of', nothing ever happens 'at this moment in time', and no one 'oozes' with charm – or anything else for that matter – nor does anyone or anything 'drool', and nothing is 'pricey'. Nothing is vulgar, nothing debased, every word refreshes and offers us the most vivid picture, unclouded by excess.

Oh! the relief. The joy of rediscovering what Mr Fowler has always said with such force: 'Shortness is a merit in words . . . they are more powerful in effect.' And they are in V. S. Pritchett's writings.

★ Sir V. S. Pritchett died on 20 March 1997

As you will discover from reading him in the Appalachians, he hunts and chases words in very much the same way that one used to chase tadpoles and sticklebacks to tip into jam jars and carry home in triumph.

But these essays are not only about places: rivers, mountains, jungles and savannahs. They are about the people who inhabit these places. Pritchett, the shrewd, friendly, aware observer, knows them well. Try him with the Americans, for example.

For more years than I care to remember, the Americans have constantly eluded me as a race. Although I am amazed and delighted by their wonderful country, they have often bewildered, irritated and bemused me, save for the closest and most beloved friends. I return to shabby Europe in relief, but, sadly, always aware that I have somehow failed in my journey towards comprehension.

Consider this extract: '. . . generalising about the American character or temper is a perennial international game . . . I have read more books by Americans on the American scene and character during this time than by writers of any other nation about themselves; and one thing has struck me immediately . . . what for generations we Europeans have called the boastfulness of Americans was really the self-dramatisation of a lonely people, an acute and often painful consciousness of themselves.' And there you have it. Now tolerance and awareness will take the place of irritation and sometimes, I confess with head hung low, stifled anger in my breast.

Pritchett has worked, and lived, among the people he writes about. He has not merely, as most of us have, stayed a little time and come to an often too hasty decision. In this book I can take his hand and run with him along the Seine, from the source of the Thames to the mouth, across Exmoor, about London, and in and out of the many towns and cities which he mentions in his essay on the Mediterranean. That is a shared joy. I have been there too.

But I don't know the people he knows, or why they behave, live and fight as they do. I have not seen them in such detailed dissection as he has. I read with dawning awareness: why have I been such a bigot? So unaware so often?

Pritchett approaches his people in much the same way as he

approaches his towns, cities and countries. In the same way that he hunts his 'words' like moths and strange beetles. With curiosity, with dignity, tolerance and, above all, with love and the deepest understanding of a completely unprejudiced mind.

He goes towards them all with arms wide open. Dangerous, you may well think. How many foolhardy, but passionate, people in the business, say, of Religion, have tried this guileless method and ended up simmering away without the Oxo? But Pritchett always seems to win.

He calls the Germans 'The Secret People', and with reason; he writes in 1964 of the German Experience beginning all over again. The hideous Wall was still intact, the land still divided. But the German, West or East, is implacably the same as ever he was, and he will never change. Innocent, plump and pink, as sugar mice. West and East cry in surprise: 'Guilt? What Guilt? Why should we feel any guilt for what our parents may have done? Why?'

That was in 1964. Today the dreadful Wall lies in designer-chunks all about the coffee tables of the West, the Brandenburg Gate is now open and it is not only my heart which sinks at the idea of a reunited Germany.

Pritchett's last line of that piece fills one with a sense of acute unease: 'The most hopeful thing is that this younger generation is at any rate not as sick as the Hitler generation was.'

He writes of sweeter things, particularly of the England he so very clearly loves and knows well and which is so horrifyingly being lost to us. Forget, if you can, the toxic waste, the dying North Sea, the concrete ribbons of traffic, the Ridley-rapes of the housing estates, the caravan parks and the dead villages, home now to stockbrokers, pop stars, designers and their ilk.

Remember it through his eyes: 'The oak and the ash close in on sudden ravines where fast black streams worry and curdle among the rocks under the old stone bridges. The rhododendron empurples the woods . . . and the leaves of the woods shine.'

Written in 1958. History almost now. A great deal of water has gone under the stone bridges of Exmoor, but that tiny piece of prose leaves us with the fragment of a memory of an England that was, once, which some of us have known, and which, if you seek carefully, still manages to exist here and there: somewhere in the woods where 'the leaves shine'.

This is a perfectly lovely collection: go for it, you'll regret it bitterly if you don't.

Sunday Telegraph, 18 February 1990

Dust and Déjà Vu

The Last Word and Other Stories by Graham Greene (Reinhardt)

Years ago, my very first literary editor gave me sterling advice: 'If you cannot find anything agreeable to say about a book I send you, do not review it. No point.' Simple advice. But was he really right? Anyway, I am in a dilemma. My new literary editor has already reprimanded me for declining to review two volumes, not, I hasten to add, because they were books which I disliked but merely because I did not think that I was capable. They were much too advanced for me.

Now I have been sent this collection of short stories, *The Last Word*, written by, without doubt, one of the greatest writers of prose alive today.* The book has been submitted to me, I would guess, because it is not very long – 149 pages – and is perfectly simple to read. Surely such a collection should not be beyond my capabilities?

But, alas, I sit and struggle to review Graham Greene's personal selection; I really cannot find anything positively agreeable enough to say about this wistful little cluster of tales. To start with, I cannot help thinking that the price (£11.95) is a bit steep.

Of course the book is stuffed with all the absolute, essential Greenery: I can't deny that. God, of course, religion naturally, South America, spies, wicked generals in unnamed Eastern European countries, and, of course, suburban homes in cosy areas of the Home Counties in which quite unspeakable agonies take place behind the Dulux and Dralon.

There are, as you must expect, the Americans; either sweet and silly, or just naïve and perhaps evil. It is all delicious, familiar ground,

* Graham Greene died on 3 April 1991

177

all ready to rediscover. For it is pretty certain that you have been there before. There are, to be sure, echoes of the wondrous works he has given us, like, for example, *The Power and the Glory*; of *The Third Man, Our Man in Havana*; and, from one book which I loved above the others, a purely personal reaction: *The Heart of the Matter*; there are even very distant echoes of *Brighton Rock* but, to be perfectly honest, I realize, writing this, that they are more like whispers than echoes.

Threads of memory tumbled into a mixed ball of silks, a scatter of seed pearls fallen from the garments of an emperor rather than jewels from his crown. And as such they are not to be scorned.

And I do not scorn them: I don't know how I have the temerity to pass judgement on this packet of tales from a mastercraftsman – it's just that when I had finished one I could hear myself say, aloud: 'Well, so what?' Or, worse still: 'So what was that all about?' A general feeling of déjà vu and dust.

One story held my attention firmly. Although written as long ago as 1940 and, perhaps, dated, it still has immense power to move and hold one. 'The News in English' is, in this lot, the very best; far and away more compelling than the title story, which just does not seem to work very well. Perhaps one is over-familiar with the pattern. I don't know, but 'The News in English' still chills the heart far more than the newer stuff.

'Murder for the Wrong Reason' is a pretty predictable tale, and I, unlike its author, who read it after some years, twigged the murderer far too early on – Mr Greene says he did not discover 'who' until the murderer was disclosed.

I find 'The Lieutenant Died Last' okayish. Rather implausible, not because it is a story of a German parachute landing of troops in modest numbers on an isolated part of the English countryside, but simply because it didn't hold water, it doesn't *feel* true, and it has a rather wobbly end, which makes it all the more irritating.

I am nitpicking: there is still much to admire, and envy even, in this slender book. The scraped-bone economy with words, the coolness, sometimes almost coldness, the instant, tidy descriptions, the very deceptively simple construction going on; but in some strange way the heart is never really touched, nerves are not shaken; one does not – or at least I did not – set the book aside and say: 'That is true. I know that feeling, person, place, dilemma.' One is not spellbound.

Perhaps one asks too much? The spellbinding has been going on for a very long time and one should be grateful for the splendours of the past after all. Greed is an ugly vice.

But this is not a book for a long flight to Tokyo, for a tedious train journey anywhere at all in the British Isles, even to take to bed with a 'go' of flu. It does not, in short, satisfy; one does not *long* to read the following story, and one is not contented.

As one switches off the light and settles down for the night, there is no feeling of being satiated and comfortably ready for sleep. It will do, until the next time, but it is curiously unsatisfying. One feels empty, sad; in need of sustenance or dreams even.

Oddly, I have been reading, strictly for pleasure, a cruelly over-looked book by P. Y. Betts called *People Who Say Goodbye: Memories of Childhood* (Souvenir), which has given the greatest pleasure and fulfilled all the demands I have made of Mr Greene's book and which I did not find there. The odd thing is that Mr Greene has written a most handsome quote, which is used on the cover, and it is comforting to think that we both were joined in our delight and amusement at least on a different kind of book. A mutual sharing.

The Last Word is not my best book, but it very well may be yours. After all, as I have said, one does not scorn the crumbs from the master's table. There is bound to be a next time. One rather looks forward to that.

Daily Telegraph, 7 July 1990

When Screen Fame Wears a Jealous Face

Garbo: Her Story by Antoni Gronowicz (Viking)
The Legend of Greta Garbo by Peter Haining (W. H. Allen)

Forensic scientists know very well what 'corpse maggots' are: they are an inevitable part of death, normal to decay, ugly to behold. I have seen them scattered like rice across a shattered face, or, depending on the weather and the temperature (they appear to proliferate in the heat), fat and bloated. But it is not only the pathologists who know this ugly metamorphosis from living flesh to maggot-death. It often flourishes in journalism.

Once death has claimed the subject, and therefore when no libel action can be perpetrated, journalistic imagination quickly soars. The greater the celebrity, the greater the feast or demolition job. Many kinds of secret jealousies, longings, yearnings and envies are freely let loose and the victim, chilling in its coffin, is very soon set upon by the unpleasant phenomena.

There is always a few quid to be made from setting before the public that which they – we are solemnly assured – have the 'right' to know about their once adored idols. If they *are* idols it is essential to show the worshippers that, in truth, their feet were of clay. And clay, usually, of the most perverse kind.

These creatures have writhed away in the bodies of Gable and Garland, Monroe, Davis, Crawford, Burton, Grant and Clift and many, many others. And they continue to thrive and grow fat, for there is always food for them. Here you will not find a biographer. No A. N. Wilson or G. Painter, no V. S. Pritchett, Frances Donaldson, Antonia Fraser; nor will you find a Sybille Bedford, a Scott Berg, or a Richard Ellmann or any writer of that ilk. But if you find the workings of the creatures to your liking, if that is your preference, then *Garbo* by one Antoni Gronowicz is just the book for you.

It is only fair to warn you that in very small print the publishers do admit that 'Neither Ms Garbo nor her estate authorized the publication of this book.' You can bet your life on that. The writer, now himself deceased, claims that he got to know the unfortunate victim of his imagination and cruel pen as early as 1938 and that they became intimate friends. He uses what is known as the 'first person literary device to emulate the voice of Greta Garbo' and many will consider this a worrying mistake.

From that decision on, he is in deep trouble: how on earth is it remotely possible to recall conversations in shattering detail from as long ago as 1917, or even 1937? Well, we get them all here, plus the most intimate thoughts of all the characters we are to meet.

I only met Greta Garbo once, in an elevator in New York in 1956. We nodded at each other shyly, and that was that. Mr Gronowicz gets much closer than I did in the elevator, and, by page 20, he opens wide his generous heart and shares his most intimate moments with us all. As well as hers. Thus: 'Since her blouse didn't yield to my fingers, she helped me. I began to kiss her breasts, but I did not feel her shiver.'

One must pause there to reflect that while she may not have done so, we do. But she seemed immune to the gross impertinence of this passionate Pole. For he continues: 'I pulled down her skirt, unwrapping perfectly proportioned legs. Pressing my lips to hers, I began feverishly to undress.'

With variations on gender and location, this kind of stuff goes on for most of the next 400 pages. Here and there shafts of light fall on the reader to lift the gloom, but I reckon that you may have got the gist of things from this indelicate, not to say, acrobatic, opening. 'Unwrapping perfectly proportioned legs' seems to have a distinct smack of a family butcher, or, perhaps, your local friendly pathologist.

As a matter of fact, her legs were not really very good and her feet very large. But who the hell cares? The magic she distilled up there on the screen overcame these minor deficiencies and, in any case, she was hardly ever seen out of a long skirt and,

with the glory of her eyes, who ever looked at her feet? No matter.

Born Greta Gustafsson of peasant parents in a working-class area of Stockholm. Papa a drunken dreamer, Mama, apparently sexually deprived (by said drunken Papa), hefty, hardworking, bullying, who would – according to this effort – prance about the flat naked, holding heavy breasts before her like lard-filled gourds in a desperate endeavour to ignite a spark from slumbering mate. Garbo grew up desperately anxious to leave this unpleasing atmosphere. There were two siblings, a boy and girl, but they apparently hardly counted for much.

At a reasonable age, Greta got a job in the local barber's shop, lathering the neighbours for their weekly shave, then moved on to model hats in the local department store, made a modest appearance in an advertising film, got herself into the Royal Dramatic Academy, was seen by the man who became her Svengali (for want of a better phrase), one Mauritz Stiller, who launched her into the world in a film he made called *Gosta Berling*.

She, and the film, were minor, but important successes; they were carted off to Hollywood by MGM (shopping for talent in Europe), where she was 'put under wraps' for a time and he was dumped.

And then the process started from cygnet to glorious swan. Greta Garbo began. I stop short, here, of using the word Legend, but of course that is exactly what she became in a very short period of time – under twenty years to be precise.

Garbo was not an actress, as she so inaccurately is called; she was an 'instinctive' and a 'behaviourist' – very different things altogether.

Acting, as such, is surface; 'behaving' is interior and only surfaces in thought. The camera photographs thought as readily as it photographs acting, but it sets both on the screen, and the result which most often touches the audience is the 'thought' rather than the histrionics. Garbo had thought in abundance.

It is not an intellectual thing, it is simply a 'gut' thing. She also, being a shrewd Swede, took the infinite trouble to learn the

183

technical details, essential – unless one remains *only* an actor – to absorb so that the mind is untrammelled, is clear, open, for the 'thinking'.

If one watches Garbo today after all the years, it is blazingly obvious, even to the basest viewer, that she is dateless. She has no mannerisms to hide behind, she simply *IS*. She thinks, ergo the 'thought' is photographed, conveyed to the screen, delivered to the audience. There has never been anyone quite like her since, and there very probably never will be. One thinks, perhaps, of Simone Signoret or, at some moments when she is controlled, Vanessa Redgrave, but there are very few people around who can channel that startling originality.

She never won an Oscar, was not paid as much as lesser stars, did not fit in remotely with the average Hollywood product – mainly recruited from drug stores, gas stations, the chorus line, or Broadway successes – and spent most of her time trying to avoid the crass vulgarity of her surroundings. When Stiller was dumped, she was quite alone in that comic-strip-glitter-city.

She stayed aloof, speaking poor English, with a minimal education, lonely (Swedes do not easily assimilate in hot climates . . . I recall, with affection, my friend Ingrid Bergman, who suffered almost as badly there), and, intensely physical, she decided pretty early on that she would remain apart.

And apart she stayed, sharing her life with the few people she trusted, and who would not take advantage of her privacy – a treasure greater than rubies in that hideous place.

It is possible that she had lovers of both sexes, not unusual even in Pinner and Morecambe Bay, and this *ugly* book gives you full value in that direction. And does it honestly matter a tinker's gob to us now? What she did, with whom, or how? After all the riches which she bestowed upon us with her work, unique in the world; the magic, the joy, the glamour, the ageless perfection of an art beautifully honed.

Should we now demand to see her disfigured, sullied, brought down to the gutter of popular press writing? Because she was selective, chose solitude rather than the common herd, because she chose the company of friends she trusted and who amused her, must we revile her and insist that she was a recluse?

Merely because she showed good taste, a yearning for privacy which every mortal has the right to secure; because she chose to read, to learn, to see beyond the confines of that restricted world of cinema; because she stayed away from parties and restaurants, remained loyal to a handful of directors and technicians who were trustworthy, honourable and knew how to present the amazing gifts she was able to offer, and because, above all, she decided to quit the cinema at the exact moment that Hollywood became aware that a war raged in Europe, decimating their profits, and that they had to make a different kind of movie for the hard-pressed and free European market.

Because of these simple, obvious facts, Garbo became a Legend.

For no other reason. She had always been unavailable, cautious, remote, whatever word you choose to use. Unafraid to say 'No', which did not make her popular in a 'Yes' city, and as she was a sensible, tough Swede, she could see the future and, after a final very poor film, which she disliked making, she simply stayed away, unwilling and uncertain how next to move into a new era.

So she left.

Few players are as sensible. They hang on playing smaller roles, 'mothers' and 'fathers', and finally just 'guesting'.

Rusted, finished.

Garbo left shining like diamonds.

And remained so. A Legend; avoiding people and press, the curious and the spurious. And finally had books written about her like this one. Who can resist what they call an 'enigma'?

There is another version of this so-called 'enigma' in *The Legend of Greta Garbo*. A perfectly respectable scissors-and-paste job, no hatchet here, consisting of pieces from journals and papers of the day.

George Cukor, who directed her in *Camille* and in her final film, and who was a close personal friend, gives you a far clearer account of the woman in a few pages than Antoni Gronowicz can manage in all his laboured 400.

There is a familiar saying among theatre and film people, which runs like this: 'You've either got it or you've had it.' Miss Garbo had it a-plenty, her biographer not at all, and if you believe his stuff, you'll believe anything.

Daily Telegraph, 18 August 1990

American Thirst

The New Yorker Book of Covers (Chatto/Cape)

The first copy of the *New Yorker* hit the bookstands on 21 February 1925, price 15 cents, and, in this vast volume which must weigh kilos and is best accommodated on a coffee table, every single cover is represented, in glorious colour, up until and including 20 February 1989 (price $1.75). Here they all are, marvellous weekly comments on the way of life in America, a social history of that great nation.

If the United States did not already have as many museums as they need, and probably more, there really should be another devoted entirely to these 3,277 splendid covers. They should be framed, enlarged, and set apart in rooms of the year, for we can see the amazing alteration in that society from the end of one war up to and including another as fearful, and on towards probable Armageddon. It could be called the National American Gallery; why not? Nothing has been overlooked here; everything is represented, from the Jazz Age to the Walk on the Moon, from garage sales in suburban Connecticut, to the American thirst for Culture, from pointed political comment to the epitome of suburban life; for America is, after all, one gigantic suburb, from Long Island to Orange County. You will not dodge the Wall Street Crash or the American discovery of Europe during the last war – the European ties still trail ribbons of memory.

You will discover, very gradually, how the black man takes his place in this enormous mixing bowl. In the early twenties he is merely set in the jazz bands or in the theatre and cabarets; it is only *much* later that he takes his place in a commuter train, in a restaurant, or fighting in Vietnam.

There is irony in these covers, political comment, nostalgia and wit. Perhaps, above all, it is the *wit* which so delights. There is shrewdness here as well as sobriety, nothing is overlooked, all is set down by artists who make the Europeans look impoverished.

We have no Peter Arno with his astonished playboys and *grandes-dames*; no Mary Petty with her frilly maids and dowagers in rococo palaces; no glorious Helen Hopkinson and her tribe of bewildered, bothered, bewitched suburban ladies; no wondrously frightening Charles Addams spying witches on broomsticks above the sky-scrapers; and no one can offer the beautiful architectural simplicity of Gretchen Dow Simpson's compositions in simple form, light, and shade. It is a rich land indeed, and these covers – sometimes deliriously funny, sometimes shockingly reproving – will tell you a great deal more about America than a heavy book by an historian.

But, after all, these covers are *drawn* by historians; that is why they tell the story so beautifully. It is really very well worth a look.

Daily Telegraph, 17 November 1990

The Mountain and the Magician

Luchino Visconti: The Flames of Passion by Laurence Schifano.
Translated by William S. Byron (Collins)

The cabin trunk was a splendid affair. Beautifully crafted in olive-green leather. Lined in watered silk of the same colour, embellished with the initials of Gustav von Aschenbach in gothic-gold. The drawers were fitted with every kind of bottle and pommade-pot, all in crystal, all engraved, all silver-stoppered. The mirrors and the hairbrushes were silver-backed, coat-hangers swung gently in quilted silk to match the lining. The locks and hinges were polished brass.

In all probability no one would see this splendour, for it was only to be used once in the gondola or while it was being carried up to the apartment of von Aschenbach in the Hôtel des Bains. That was all. I remember saying, in amazed bewilderment: 'But Luchino! So much glory! Who will ever see it?'

His eyes, those fine, hooded, black-agate eyes, regarded me with a flick of irritation at my crassness.

'You,' he said.

And he was right, as usual. I did see it. I *knew* it, and I was aware all through the work to come that the cabin trunk stood for the complete background of the man I was to play. Elegant, expensive, luxurious, spoiled and vain. Fastidious, correct. Everything in its place. Visconti was not incorrect in providing me with such a valuable item of 'instruction'. I learned.

I am always anxious, and often with good reason, when I am faced with the biography of someone I have known, even loved. Especially when the biographer has clearly only met the subject a couple of times (or even not at all) and has relied on the testimony of 'friends' and others for information, the rest gleaned from the

189

clippings-file. On such slender strings hangs the fabric of many biographies. Accuracy mixes wildly with inaccuracy and gossip.

Rumours are forced from seedling to forest giant; the portrait offered is too often the image of the victim the biographer *thinks* he has seen, the subject set down in vivid colour. Pastel becomes Picasso. There can be little fear of retribution as the victims are most often dead, and then only outraged families, wives or lovers can protest despairingly. And helplessly. One trembles in advance.

However, in this case, joy reigns. There is absolutely no need to have trembled before Laurence Schifano's triumphant biography of Luchino Visconti. As far as I can be sure of anything, I am sure that he himself would have approved. It was awarded the French Academy's award for Biography last year and fully merited that honour.

We are in good, caring hands here. Not one false step, no hint of envy or malice, no shadows of cruel inaccuracy. Professor Schifano is compassionate, understanding and fully aware of the *grandeur* of her subject. Never in awe of his complexities, sympathetic to his follies and foibles, alert to the towering rages (and they could indeed tower when necessary), equally aware of the quite touching gentleness, the arrogance, the astonishing humbleness of her prince. For prince he was.

To those of us fortunate enough to have known him – and to know him was to have worked with him – this book is very much like being once again in his company. Closing the covers one can say, and I did: 'Yes. That is how he was, that is who he was, that is how he did it.' No one, in my entire life, has affected me as he did.

Luchino Visconti was born on 2 November 1906, in Milan, the fourth child of Duke Giuseppe Visconti di Modrone. His mother was Clara Erba, heiress to one of the greatest industrial families in Italy. He was brought up, very strictly, in an atmosphere of quite astonishing nobility and richness, two things which were to be part of his works for ever after.

An incredibly precocious child, he was writing and producing

his plays *and* operas in the family theatre where he and his brothers and sisters would perform. Surrounded by immense wealth, love and security, he flourished. But there were hidden cracks in the family. Once so desperately close, it began gradually to pull apart, and when Visconti was a young man he joined the cavalry to become a sergeant in the Savoy Regiment.

He had courage, great strength, dashing good looks, a vast fortune and, very important, a true 'eye' for a horse. He bought his first racehorse in 1929 and continued to race and to breed until the end of the thirties. He once told me that the majority of actors were thoroughbreds and hacks. A cruel description, one filled with his normal arrogance perhaps, but it was none the less accurate, and woe betide the poor hack who fell into his hands! He was not patient with timidity, stupidity, fear, dullness or the least *vapour* of inefficiency. These were inadmissible in his life. The horse which left the horse-box kicking up its heels, nostrils flaring, eyes wide, ears pricked, and which confidently sprang down the ramp would, he swore, lose the race. The horse which came down with care, scenting the air, eyes aware and steady, ears back, would be the one to win. Just like we actors. And he treated us, by and large, in much the same manner as his horses.

Not altogether a bad thing. Unless you fell by the wayside.

It is perhaps difficult for an English reader to comprehend exactly how vast was the area of work, the enormous range, that Visconti covered. He was a master of not only the cinema, but the theatre and the opera *and* the ballet. More, he *understood* them. There was not one facet of the arts in which he did not, or could not, participate, save perhaps for painting. I don't know that I ever heard of him holding a brush in his hands, but he well might have done.

He wrote, composed, directed. He gathered about him many of the greatest players, singers, designers, musicians and dancers of his time. He used them brilliantly and gave some of them (Callas, for example, in *Traviata*) an entirely new existence. Those who loved him stayed close: there were a great many sycophants, but these he knew very well – they amused him and sometimes could be useful. There was no whiff of, say, Gerrards Cross about this man, no chintz, latticed windows, weekly trips to Sainsbury's; there was no Parson's Green either, no stripped pine, coffee in mugs and golf-clubs in the hall. He was, in all respects, larger than life, and so was his work.

Brought up as a prince, in a princely household, that is exactly how he behaved. There was colour, vividness, violence and passion in all he created. There was no dust, no liberalism, no shock-to-shock. His splendour was almost medieval, which was, of course, not always liked by what he called Monsieur Tout-le-Monde. He once said: 'The truth is that these accusations of waste and hedonistic self-indulgence have always come from people who still think it is a luxury to eat in a railway dining-car.'

Just so.

He demanded, and always got, excellence of the highest degree. From a carpenter, electrician, the girl who sewed on the ribbons, his actors, writers, cameramen, the operator of his camera, the boy who 'pulled focus'. All were hand-picked, all were the best; all would have cheerfully died for him. For working for Visconti was a certain sign that you *were* The Best.

There was absolutely no room in his life for 'second best'. He would not tolerate it at any price, even among those in the circle closest to him. And that was close. Very few of us got that near. He was a hellish taskmaster.

Apart from his mother, whom he adored, it would appear the two people who had the most effect on him in his early days were Coco Chanel and Jean Renoir.

Chanel introduced the two men, she intrigued carefully, and very soon Visconti became Renoir's assistant director and costume designer on *A Day in the Country*. His career had commenced. Chanel, naturally enough, fell deeply in love with the handsome aristocrat and sent bunches of red roses every day. 'For *weeks!*' he once said despairingly. A wonderful woman, but not for him, she was one of the favoured few who knew the life in the Erba family villa at Cernobbio where all the most glorious and brilliant gathered. The Noailles, the Beaumonts, Diaghilev, Misia Sert and so on. Chanel was very much a part of this life. Her chic, her simplicity, discipline in design, knowledge in art and everything else were food and drink to the young man. He learned assiduously.

From Jean Renoir he entered a different life. Darker perhaps, closer to real life, a life which at first surprised him and which later he would embrace. Communism and the anti-fascists. He was a bitter anti-fascist, and joined, with Renoir, the tight group of young intellectuals who milled about the fringes of the Experimental Film Centre and a famous Left magazine, *Cinema*. This was a protest against his government and, strangely, against his own heritage. He never changed.

On the death of his father he inherited a villa on the Via Salaria in Rome and moved there for almost the rest of his life. In the villa he held court among his roses in the lovely garden and his paintings and porcelain. During the war it became a safe-house for members of the Resistance movement, and a haven for escaping members of the British and American forces. He was eventually arrested, but after some months in prison he was freed the day before the

Americans liberated Rome. And life, the life he was to make so notable, began.

He directed everything from Shakespeare to Tennessee Williams, from opera to ballet, from films about starving fishermen in Sicily to *The Leopard*. He worked in America, in France, in Italy and in Germany and he lived furiously.

Was he decadent? Not that I ever saw. Homosexual? I never held the lantern, but it was always supposed that he was. Cruel? There were times. And arrogant? Seriously. Kind? Often. Generous? Very. Amusing? I really don't think that he was. I seldom heard his laughter. Only saw a vague smile, a raised eyebrow. Sometimes, and this usually with a good cook, for he was passionate about food, I would hear him give a great bark of laughter, and then speak rapidly in whatever dialect the cook spoke. But I don't think that I have ever known anyone, and certainly not in the cinema-world, who could speak of Klimt and Karajan, Proust and Peanuts, Mozart and Mantovani (he adored the Eurovision Song Contests), Duse *and* Doris Day.

After his stroke I was permitted to see him in the villa at Cernobbio. For ten minutes only.

The drive up was illuminated by rows of figures holding high-burning flambeaux. He was sitting in a wheelchair, wrapped in a tartan rug, small, shrivelled almost, the lion reduced to the size of a crippled whippet. I embraced him, and he took my hand with his good one. I stayed there for two hours while footmen carried great albums filled with photographs of his latest epic, *Ludwig*. He was instantly animated, alert, full of excitement turning the pages. I was the one who wilted under the long car journey from Munich.

When, next day, I had reached home there was a little note written on the square-page of an exercise book. 'Thank you,' it read. 'For coming so far out of your way to see me, now that I am no longer any use to you.'

He had signed it simply 'Papa'.

This was a word which I used, behind his back, to his crew, and had no idea that he knew. He understood that it was used with warmth and affection.

Shortly before he died we spoke on the telephone together about the chances of doing *The Magic Mountain* . . . or, perhaps, the Proust. 'Olivier will be Charlus, you can take Swann, Garbo says that she will play the Queen of Naples, and Signoret, maybe, as Odette . . . we see. Come to Rome next week? When I have got rid of this damned 'flu bug. Telephone me next Monday. Ciao.'

Next Monday was too late.

The Mountain and the Magic had gone.

Daily Telegraph, 24 November 1990

Book of the Year

A bit late, a cruelly neglected book was brought to my attention by the excellent John Sandoe of Blacklands Terrace. In a year of reviewing, P. Y. Betts's *People Who Say Goodbye: Memories of Childhood* (Souvenir) was a read for sheer pleasure and gave me intense delight. It is haunting, unforgettable and one longs for a second-helping. It nudges memory wonderfully, sadly, with great hilarity.

Daily Telegraph, 24 November 1990

This modest little book had been under a great pile at Sandoe's. Johnny de Falbe handed it to me with the words: 'Have a look at this. You might enjoy it.' I did, and obviously a lot of other readers did too: by the end of the year, it had gone into a second printing. A paperback edition was reprinted three or four times.

Sliding Quietly into the Shadows

Eels with Dill Sauce by Countess von Bredow (Peter Owen)

Those glittering emporia of literature which we find now in almost every town are all very well. Glossy, rich, super-stocked. *But.*

There they stand, a million books gleaming on the shelves, very often piped Mozart to assail the browsing customer, and a mass of smiling, eager young people who can find, by pressing buttons, any book you require. *But.* No one will suggest that you might *like* a book: no one will offer you Mrs Gaskell's collected Victorian short stories, no one will say that such and such a book, almost unreviewed but very much worth a look, is at hand. You are therefore in dire danger of missing out on some excellent books which, for one reason or another, have slipped through the nets into oblivion.

I would have missed Mrs Gaskell had I not been guided by a Real Bookseller who also brought to my notice this poorly titled but perfectly glorious book about an eccentric German family of impoverished aristocrats living just outside Berlin in the early thirties.

Eels with Dill Sauce is an unalloyed joy. It has sold over 500,000 copies in Germany alone, gone into the *Guinness Book of Records*, and was the top bestseller in Germany for forty-two weeks. It is subtitled *Memories of an Eccentric Childhood*, and, through the eyes of the youngest daughter, a wise, observant and funny child, the whole family comes alive: so too does the evocation of a time sliding quietly into the shadows.

Ilse, Countess von Bredow, recalls, without a trace of nostalgia or sentimentality, a life now lost to us for good.

Here we have a splendid cast of lunatics: the Count, engrossed in his impoverished lands, cherishing his trees with an all-consuming passion; the Countess, prone at times to giggle, caring for her children. And their friends: crippled Bruno, who lives with his spinster mother in the woods; Otto, his cousin, who teaches everyone how to fish, trap and steal; and *their* 'Grandpa', the most respected man in the area after the Count, for the simple reason that he has a permanent job as a nightwatchman, a well-groomed beard and wears a pinstriped suit to church.

There are hated governesses, an adored cook and the jolliest maid in current literature. Lore is always on the point of getting married, but never quite makes the summit of bliss. Happiness, irreverence and good manners run throughout the book. The memory is jogged so often one sighs at the end with regret.

There is no sadness here, no wistfulness. Although the reader is well aware that the end is very near, that the flight to the West will take place, the family uprooted, dispersed, it never disturbs the funny, happy existence of those final golden summers and snowy winters. All was safe, all secure. It is splendid to have it here in the hand as a reminder.

Daily Telegraph, 29 December 1990

Byron Caught in His Curlers

*Captain Gronow: His Reminiscences of Regency and Victorian Life
1810–60*, edited by Christopher Hibbert (Kyle Cathie)

It is quite possible you are not in the least like me where writing is concerned, in that I am a kind of sleeve-grabber. By that I mean I really do prefer the eyewitness account, however badly written, to the elegance of NW5 biography. There is a terrible immediacy about the former which is totally absent years later when distilled by a writer who, for all the research he or she may have done, never quite hits the elbow of one's emotion. There *are* exceptions of course, but precious few.

This is a modest book, a truthful, beautifully edited put-together-job of some very remarkable reports from the pen of the man Who Was There and saw, and met, and was among the people, battles and events which he describes with such eloquence.

Captain Gronow is not a man of great profundity. He is no politician, and seems to care little for the people who are. Sensibly, in my opinion. But in a strange way he sets down some of the most extraordinary events of his time and, without a mass of clever writing, persuades the reader that what he has seen or heard is exactly as it was. Any man who can claim personal knowledge of Marietta Alboni, Napoleon, Brummell and Waterloo deserves our attention.

These reminiscences were first published in 1867. The sprightly author claimed, with reason, that he had lived through the greater part of one of the most eventful centuries in England's history. And so he did. In the days when he lived in Paris, a French journalist wrote of him thus:

He was small, spare and about fifty years of age – always wore a blue tight-fitting coat closely buttoned, just allowing a white line of waistcoat to be visible – with his hair well arranged, scented, cold and phlegmatic [he] knew the best people in Paris, visited all the diplomats and was evidently intimate with everybody of note in Europe.

But do not be deceived. This little man, who joined the Guards in 1813, was present on the field of Waterloo and wrote this:

There is nothing perhaps in the episodes of a great battle more striking than the debris of a cavalry charge, where men and horses are seen scattered and wounded on the ground in every variety of painful attitude. Many a time the heart sickened at the moaning tones of agony which came from man, and scarcely less intelligent horse, as they lay in fearful agony upon the field of battle.

And this before Miss Nightingale started to busy herself. The flat, unsensational account is, to my mind, more vivid and cruel than the lusher writing of those who only imagined the battle, and were not present. The very simplicity and understatement shocks: '. . . *every variety of painful attitude*' cannot, I think, be sadder-written.

But Gronow did not only observe war and its brutalities. He also noted the food and fashions of the day; he commented on Lord Byron being caught in bed 'in his curlers' and begging that the cat be not let out of the bag – for, said he, 'I am as vain of my curls as a girl of sixteen.' And there you have Byron. Or anyway a very key part of the fellow.

Gronow knew intimately the elegance of fashionable London, attending all the very best balls and suppers. A weekly ticket to the ball at Almacks on a Wednesday was deemed to be 'the seventh heaven of the fashionable world'; and the great hostesses, such as Lady Jersey, Lady Castlereagh, the Princess Esterhazy (whose servants denied Wellington entry to her ball because he was wearing trousers, not breeches) and Madame de Lieven, ruled fashionable society – for not all society *was* fashionable – with rods of iron. And vast purses.

Gronow knew of the Pig Faced Lady of Grosvenor Square, and

a writer who had recently written a famous bestseller, who was bidden to Lady Holland's for supper and sent away because he had no bridge to his nose. 'I conjure you,' she said to the unhappy guest who had brought him to the evening, 'never bring any more of your friends to Holland House who are not blessed with bridges to their noses.'

Of course, all this is trivia – but what excellent trivia it is, and how much more attractive than our own versions of the same put before us in today's glossy magazines, which are altogether grubbier and far less amusing. Have we a Brummell going about? When asked by an envious young beau where he obtained the fine blacking for his exquisite boots, he replied: 'My blacking positively ruins me. I will tell you in confidence: it is made with the finest champagne.' How elegant! Today, footballers and racing drivers shake it up to spray at journalists.

If you don't think it amusing to know that Queen Charlotte took such enormous quantities from her gold snuff-box 'that her nose quivered within and without on the terrace at Windsor'; that a Colonel Disney was disgraced for the sin of 'putting the Queen's gold toilet vase to a use that cannot be named "in ears polite"'; or even that politics of the day have little altered when one reads: '[I] set to work "to bribe every man, woman and child" in the ancient borough of Stafford – gave suppers every night to my supporters, kissed all their wives and children, drank their health in every sort of abominable mixture' – if all this kind of tittle-tattle is of little interest to you, ignore my strong recommendation to buy this diverting book.

You'll miss a lot of fun if you don't.

Daily Telegraph, 23 February 1991

Letters with Flavour to Savour

Beloved and Darling Child: Last Letters between Queen Victoria and Her Eldest Daughter 1886–1901, edited by Agatha Ramm (Alan Sutton)

If you take the glorious jacket from this splendidly edited, and presented, book and spread it wide across your knees, you will surely be amazed. I was.

The painting is by Laurits Tuxen (clearly not a Sunday painter, but no Klee or Léger) and it shows Queen Victoria *and her family* on one presumably imagined day in 1887.

Amid a glitter of gold, candles, ormolu, mirrors and brocaded walls, in full majesty and looking like a plump (fat is too unkind a word) queen ant, sits the Queen, Empress of India, clothed in black. Gathered about her are the family, adorned in great finery – satins, silks and velvets for the ladies, uniforms for the men. Medals bejewel these splendid figures; rubies, diamonds and sapphires adorn their women. The children – a horde of them – are kilted, frilled, ruched and sailor-suited.

I twice started to count the heads of this astonishing family group, and both times I lost my way, but you can reckon on over fifty. Fruitful indeed were those heavy loins.

Fruitful, too, was Victoria's pen. She and Virginia Woolf would seem to be the victors in the letter-writing race. But where Mrs Woolf had the lead over Victoria was in her provoking, and nourishing, intellect. Victoria had practically none; at least, nothing more than that of the usual governess-educated upper-middle-class woman of means with a house in Belgravia and, possibly, The House in Wilts or Norfolk. A respectable, safe, predictable love of all things 'pretty', 'cosy' or 'dear'. A kind of Hush Puppy intellectual.

From these letters to her beloved eldest daughter Vicky, the Empress of Germany and mother of the wretched Willie (who dragged everyone into the First World War with a clanking of medals and a stamp of boots and one arm shorter than the other), it is obvious that she enjoyed watercolours, tableaux vivants, the singing of the de Reszke brothers, Ellen Terry doing her bits of tragedy at command performances in the drawing-room, and Beerbohm Tree doing his. She spelled him, possibly correctly, as 'Bierbaum' – he was of Dutch descent and she was a regular stickler for the facts. But apart from charades and tableaux vivants, she also loved music, had a sweet singing voice and delighted in Gounod's 'pretty opera' and Massenet's 'thrilling tragical opera'.

And why not, indeed? I slide happily between Brahms and the Boston Pops, prefer Austen to either Amis, and enjoy *Oklahoma* more than *Parsifal*. It takes all kinds.

That is the Queen's frivolous side. She was a shrewd lady-of-politics, too: she knew what she liked, what she wanted and what she detested. She handled her huge family with extraordinary tact, even managing to avert political disasters by a sharp reprimand or a metaphorical slap on the wrist. She was Granny to almost all the royal houses in Europe. She was clever, to the point and firm.

These letters, written until a few days before she and Vicky also died, are full of love, encouragement and sense. After it was diagnosed that the Emperor (of Germany) had cancer of the throat, she was adept at smoothing German waters troubled by the Empress's wish that her husband be attended by an English doctor rather than a German. This was a difficult, and dangerous, situation. It was assumed that the English Empress was anti-German, when all the poor creature wanted was a sensible English GP.

Victoria steered that course safely with her advice, as indeed she managed to disarm the frightful Willie with her good manners. She won. *That* battle at least.

Agatha Ramm brings to a close the story of the Queen, derived from her correspondence in the five volumes edited by the late Roger Fulford, the first of which was published in 1964. The last and very moving letters between the Queen and her daughter suddenly bring her closer to us; we recognize this astounding monarch as a creature of human frailties.

Sensibly Dr Ramm has edited out the exceedingly boring bits of family news, common to all letters from mothers to their exiled daughters, and has concentrated on the daily life of the two women, on the political events of the day, and on their reactions to subjects as diverse as the weather in Grasse or the death of Elizabeth of Austria on a lake steamer: 'It is too, too awful . . . she did not see what had happened and so was able to walk on board the steamer but soon fainted and then a stain of blood was discovered on her dress.'

The Queen was aware that high rank made for high risk, but was unafraid. She was equally fearless in arranging marriages: 'Poor George of Russia's death comes rather suddenly . . . I now revert to the idea of the Prince of Hohenlohe Bartenstein . . . It sounds well but the great difficulty and annoyance mixed marriages cause now would make it absolutely necessary to know before.'

She was a wise woman, and her advice might be of benefit in the drawing-rooms of Windsor and Balmoral today. She detested Mr Gladstone, Mossypebble as he was known, but grudgingly gave him praise where due. However, he did not 'enhance England' and fiercely deplored the Boers. A passage in a letter of 1899 has a dreadfully familiar ring:

> I think that all rivals in turn egged on Kruger, to see what we should do and get us into a tight corner, abuse us for being cowardly and weak, unable to fight and afraid of the Boers if we did not make a stand as they now abuse us for our violence, tyranny and rapine . . . We must now hope that the struggle may be short and with as little bloodshed as possible.

I did grow fed up, however, with her constant moaning about her 'sadness', her 'crushing blow' and her 'broken heart'. She obviously loved Albert to distraction and on his death slumped into self-pity and isolation and the black garb of widowhood. It does make one rather impatient.

Yet it has to be remembered, looking at the amazing panorama on the dust-jacket, that she enjoyed a full and pleasurable sex life with her Consort. Although she detested and was acutely embarrassed by the results of this part of married life, she did pioneer the use of what was then euphemistically called 'Twilight Sleep'. She recommended it, with a determination that *all* women should benefit. Perhaps she might come to be chiefly remembered for this generous gesture; but I doubt that many people give her a thought in the labour ward today.

The art of letter-writing has all but gone, and with it the chance to read and then re-read part of one's life. In this book is encapsulated a vividly recorded time, set down for us to enjoy 100 years on.

Would that we were so lucky today; luck today is a bunch of flowers at least, a scribbled postcard at most. The flowers will perish, the postcard will be mislaid, there will be no letter to savour. Sad.

Sunday Telegraph, 17 March 1991

Falling for a Pine Spell

Sketchbook from Southern France by Sara Midda (Sidgwick)
Toujours Provence by Peter Mayle (Hamish Hamilton)

Hot red dust sifting through naked toes, the warmth of a limestone boulder under one's hand in the heat of high noon, the cool of uneven, tiled floors in ancient kitchens, the jagged comfort of the scaly bark of an olive tree, the plush softness of moss at the spring.

And then the scents.

Of olives crushed beneath great stone wheels, the smell of thyme, myrtle and camphor, of lavender, warm bread from the oven, garlic and basil, fresh and green pestled into the 'pistou', of red wine spilled on a scrubbed pine table, candle grease dribbling from guttering candles, warm varnish and the tinder-dry rushes creaking in a chestnut-wood chair. Bay leaves, fennel, sweet-geranium and the drifting scent of night-scented stock and the pungent odour from the spiked heads of nicotiana. Above and through this, the eternal scent of heat-burned pines.

All these, and many more, bring back to me the magic which was the Provence I knew, and all these, and more, are gloriously stored for you among the very simple treasures in *Sketchbook from Southern France*. Here, even if you have never been to Provence, you have an easy-to-read guidebook to undreamed-of loveliness. If you *have* been to Provence, it will evoke such memories of taste, smell and sight that you will be left slightly drunk with sheer pleasure. It is also stuffed full of dotty incidents: like the earthquake which trembled Avignon in 1565, and the date when Picasso started to work in his pottery at Vallauris.

Turn these ravishing little pages and you will discover just where to find stars on a ceiling, what a courgette-ronde is (delicious, I assure you) and exactly how to make geranium cream. Is there a more delectable recipe than this anywhere? 'Scented geranium leaves in *crème-fraîche*, cream cheese and sugar. Cool. Eat with peaches poached in wine.'

Sara Midda has drawn for your eye practically everything you could expect to smell, taste and see during one bountiful year in Provence. She has also discovered the essence of the *colours* of the land and set them to delight in invented designs of wallpapers for which, if they did exist – and they should – you could cheerfully kill.

It is easy just to go to Provence, look at the mountains, sit on some terrace with the London papers, listen to the BBC World Service, drink your beer or tea, and demand steak and chips for your lunch. You need never remove your shoes to feel the red dust, you can wear sunglasses all day against the light, shriek at the sight of a gecko, insist on your tomatoes being spherical and Dutch, wash your lettuce in three rinses of permanganate and eat peanuts with your evening gin and tonic rather than touch a *picholine de Provence*. If all you want from Provence is a mild sun-tan and a cup of tea at four o'clock, I suggest you stay away and go to Bridlington.

Provence is too exciting, too dangerous, daring and 'foreign', and you will use up the room some others may long to occupy. Peter Mayle is one such person, only he stopped *longing* and made his life in Provence a fact.

There is no reason to suppose that his *Toujours Provence* will not be as triumphant as his *A Year in Provence*: it is full of splendidly amusing stories written in a deceptively simple manner. His self-deprecation is engaging, and all his loyal readers who 'laughed until they cried' the first time are bound to do so once again. Here are the funny French, the doleful peasants, the pigs and truffles, the local dog shows, every bit as ghastly as those in our own dear Home Counties; the gargantuan meals consumed, the bottles of drink poured down welcoming throats.

He also deals with the miseries of unwanted and unexpected guests who, quite by surprise, happen to 'find themselves ten minutes away' and descend en masse, disrupting his daily work and life. I could have put him wise to a trick or two had he asked. Don't, repeat don't, have a swimming pool.

The very year that Peter Mayle and his wife moved to Provence and the great adventure of a new life, I was wretchedly forced to leave after the happiest two decades of my entire life. So I know, very well, all that he describes and everything that befalls him. He writes very tellingly of things I loved and well remember, but he does not make everything all geranium cream. He recalls the severity, and the desperation, of the drought in Provence. This short passage, taken at random, is as exact in description as it is possible to be:

> The patch of grass in front of the house abandoned its ambitions to become a lawn and turned the dirty yellow of poor straw. The earth shrank, revealing its knuckles and bones, rocks and roots that had been invisible before.

That's just how it was, and an arrow of remembrance pierces anyone who has ever had the privilege of living in the blinding light of Provence, quite literally known as the 'province of light'. But take heed! Rightly, Mayle reminds the reader it is not as simple as some people think when they try to find a new beginning there. It is tough. Many are defeated, many come away bruised and burned. You have to work very hard indeed, and that means learning the language and realizing, rapidly, that the language is not simple French.

Provençal French is very different. So, too, is Provençal man. The French from 'up north' are as foreign as you yourself. Foreigners are always regarded with grave suspicion. But if you work at it diligently, if you are willing completely to absorb the life and manners, if you are equally willing to be absorbed, 'to lose your identity', and if you are prepared to 'go native', then you might, one day, albeit grudgingly, find that you are *almost* 'accepted' and then you *may* claim the right to say that you 'live' in Provence. But it will take time. And trust.

And remember, as Peter Mayle reminds you, that the winters are as savage as the summers, and that you can break your heart there as easily as you can lose it. But here are two very different books filled with things which will help you to understand, at least in part, this wonderful place.

Daily Telegraph, 27 April 1991

From the Gut of the Land

The Last Enchantments by Robert Liddell (Peter Owen)
The Time of Secrets and *The Time of Love*
by Marcel Pagnol (Deutsch)

My father, born in the last few years of the Victorian age, always considered himself an Edwardian. He spent his whole life imbued with the high standards of Edwardian life and never defaulted. He was able, at twenty, to come to terms with the most appalling world war, and survive it physically if not mentally: for he was never completely free of its dreadful legacy of fear and pain.

He managed, brilliantly and with a great deal of fun, to cope with the amazing changes of the twenties, when I was born, but he never truly discarded the Edwardian standards which he always held so dear and which, to my astonishment, I seem to have inherited. Of course, over the years they have become diluted, but they are still recognizably there, and I am often mocked for having them. However, one stands by them resolutely; they have stood me in very good stead in the past, present – and frankly I don't give a fig for the future.

It is probably because of these standards that I have so enjoyed the three books before me. One English, two French (in splendid translations), and all about a period of time, in differing worlds, in which true standards still applied. If you detect that I am suggesting those standards have sagged like ragged bunting in the rain, you are right. They have. But in these books you will catch glowing images of them all over again – if you knew what they were in the first place. Young people have little way, apart from books, of knowing that the 'day just before yesterday' ever existed. But it did, and it is admirably revived in Robert Liddell's *The Last Enchantments*, about a lightly disguised Oxford trundling towards war.

The writing recalls fragments of Jane Austen in the elegance of its prose and its plotting; there are shades, too, of Ivy Compton-Burnett, and echoes of Dickens and Trollope. First published in 1948, it is, in all degrees, a wonderfully evocative book reminding one of a time when there were scones for tea, of the smell of damp wool drying out before plopping gas-fires in North Oxford lodgings, of Fuller's walnut cake, and children who wore liberty bodices and indulged in nothing more harmful than skipping; of a place where it was essential to have a servant (one could manage without a lover, not a servant).

A different world? Very different, and Liddell writes with grace and elegance about this forgotten time; his clear, civilized mind shines sparklingly through every deceptively simple line, prodding one with the dry humour of a writer who spikes his wit with danger. His doting, fingerless, chittering, chattering, tragic Mrs Foyle is an extraordinary creature who remains long in the mind, as one of the oddest, and saddest, creatures in modern writing.

The excellent Marcel Pagnol is known here mainly for the filmed versions of *Jean de Florette* and *Manon des Sources*. *The Time of Secrets* (translated by Rita Barisse) and *The Time of Love* (translated by Eileen Ellenbogen) continue the childhood memoirs he began in *My Father's Glory* and *My Mother's Castle*; they, too, are set in his beloved Provence, an almost inexhaustible source for all his works. This is the true Provence, the land in which he was born and in which, a few years ago, he died. His overwhelming love for the place burns on every page. This is not the suburban Provence of the swimming-pool-gin-and-tonic brigade; it is stuff from the very gut of the land.

Pagnol's Provence has no motorways, no estates of tacky little Paris-Rustic houses, no swarms of sweating tourists, red of neck from over-exposure to the burning sun, no camera-freaks lugging rucksacks through the lavender in floppy shorts and dirty trainers; there are no fat property-developers converting the crumbling barns, or ripping out the orchards for patios and swimming-pools or setting up barbecues as if they had never left Pinner or Bexleyheath for a kinder climate.

Pagnol is, I suppose, to the French what H. E. Bates is now to the British, although I do not think the British 'love' a writer as much as the French can. Nothing very much happens in these two books. They are about growing up in a lost world. His works evoke the simplicity-that-was of family life in the country, its virtues, its trivia, its minor tragedies, its great, if utterly simple, joys. They are about daily existence in a land which burns under the brilliant southern light. He brings us the heavy and comforting odours of camphor, pine-resin, lavender, red dust, drying hay, and the delicious mystery of the scents in the fat *marmite* simmering quietly on an iron stove in red-tiled kitchens. If these things give you pleasure, you will find them in abundance here.

There is no violence in these gentle books, no rape, no murder, no cannibalism, no randy plumbers in Putney, no robbery, no child abuse. It is out of time, old-fashioned. Comforting, healing stuff, far away from the frenetic world we now inhabit. You cannot fail to be lulled into complete surrender and calmness by the delicate simplicity of the world in which the child, Marcel Pagnol, lives and which as an adult he recaptures with such glowing remembrance. Never can a reader have been made so aware of senses past. Unless my Edwardian slip is showing very badly indeed.

Daily Telegraph, 20 July 1991

How Could Such Hatred Exist?

In the Shadow of Death: Living outside the Gates of Mauthausen
by Gordon J. Horwitz (I. B. Tauris)
Voices from the Third Reich: An Oral History by Johannes Steinhoff,
Peter Pechel and Dennis Showalter (Grafton)
Łódź Ghetto: Inside a Community under Siege,
edited by Alan Adelson and Robert Lapides (Penguin)
Surviving the Holocaust: The Kovno Ghetto Diary by Avraham
Tory. Edited by Martin Gilbert.
Translated by Jerzy Michalowicz (Pimlico)

The last time I wrote about the Holocaust, I received so much 'hate mail' that I was, I confess, greatly taken aback. Even though I had grown used to reading rubbish about myself in the tabloids for many years, I had managed, after a while, to come to terms with the business. Coming to terms with mail addressed *directly* to one is quite another matter. I had never before been called a 'Dirty Jew Lover' nor a 'Lying Bastard' nor a 'Filthy Communist Jew'. But then I reaped the sour harvest. No letter ever bore a signature, or an address; some writers simply mailed me back my own article, clipped from this newspaper, heavily underlined here and there in red and green ink.

The fact that I had been a witness to Belsen, had fought through Normandy, France, Holland and Belgium and ended up in the ruins of the just-conquered Berlin seemed to make no impression. I was still branded a liar, and what I had seen in Belsen had never occurred. It might be interesting to consider that, in spite of the scrawled obscenities, these letters all came from apparently educated people and were reasonably well written.

How, I wondered, could such hatred still exist? Most especially in this land of mine, on this treasured soil, never occupied since the Normans? The land which had given the world the terms 'fair play' and 'tolerance'?

After reading these four fascinating books, 1,665 pages, I was left bruised with wonder and an intense sadness. This had all happened well within my lifetime. What had the Jews done that they deserved so much loathing; that they had to be 'exterminated like vermin'? Why so much mistrust, fear and dislike? It is no good using Christ's death as a convenient excuse for the enormity of more than six million people deliberately being destroyed in a period which lasted just less than a decade.

One fact sticks out of all the books like a snagged fingernail. No one ever poses the question which raced through my mind all the time: 'Why?' The death and destruction is accepted simply as fact. The mindless cruelty shocks deeply; the methodical killings, the listed deaths, the book-keeping for obliteration, the loathing: all these things numb the mind. But why the Jews? No one can give me an answer, and these dreadful (that is, terrifying) books do not help me to come to terms with the attempted slaughter of a whole race.

Gordon J. Horwitz's *In the Shadow of Death* describes vividly the construction of Mauthausen, the most vicious and hideous and probably least well known of the camps for the Jews' annihilation, in a quarry three miles from a pleasant little village and a few yards from two thriving farms, set in the gentle, rolling hills of southern Austria. Everyone saw it being built, everyone knew it was there; no one it seems, dared ask why. Local people worked for it as carpenters, telephonists, secretaries, typists, plumbers and all the rest.

People knew. They heard the sounds, saw the smoke from the furnaces, smelled it as the winds carried across the woods and fields, leaving greasy deposits of soot on the hay in the meadows and on the washing on the line. No one raised a finger, no one questioned, even though latterly they watched the shuffling lines of people being marched through their streets, staring, terrified, lost. Fear ruled; fear won. It is as obscene to imagine a killing-camp set down in the fields around Cuckfield and everyone pretending it was not there.

In *Voices from the Third Reich*, an oral history of the war by survivors of the Reich's collapse, fear is the predominant feeling. There *were* 'good' people in Germany, people as appalled as those of us who knew what took place in that decade, but the great majority were ruled by terror for themselves or for their children. The Nazis had absolute power and froze any protests, or any questions, by the severest punishments. People did cry out in horror, they did protest, they did hide their friends, and they paid the most terrible price if found out. It is easy to understand, from this book, how a people could ensnare themselves trying to move towards a better life after the disasters of the Armistice in 1919.

It is important that we are reminded of the past, so we may prepare for the future. If you are young, say thirty-five and under, I recommend this book. It is salutary to discover just how similar 'ordinary' people are, wherever they happen to live. If you are older, and feel you know all about it, let me assure you that you do not.

How, you may well ask, could all the good Germans be trapped by fear? Easy. It could happen here. The Nazis appealed to, and collected, all the yobbos and lager-louts of their day and gave them boots, badges and imposing caps to wear, which gave them a towering superiority joined to the simple fact that they were 'recognized by the State'. The bureaucrats and yobbos made a hideous fraternity.

Control, power; with permission. Not here? You think? But we have them all ready-made: the Union-Jack-underpants fraternity who wreck Spanish bars, Channel ferries, railway carriages, football stadiums. Drunk with beer and rage, mindless, stuffed with false National Pride, they rampage everywhere. And who stops them? Who dares interfere with a rape? Or a street mugging? We dare not. *You can die that way.* So, too, in the Germany of 1934–45.

Both *Lódź Ghetto* and the Kovno Ghetto diary, *Surviving the Holocaust*, are incredibly detailed journals of exactly where, how, and when the unbelievable became fact. The courage is amazing, the sadness overwhelming. To write about Hell may sound simple. To write about it and make it totally plausible and undramatic is

staggering. Not all the witnesses in the Lódź Ghetto survived. Their writings have, and have been remarkably edited.

In January 1940 it was announced that the Jewish quarter of Lódź was 'a region of epidemic danger', the signal for the ghetto to become the final prison for the city's Jewry. The area was evacuated and the Jews herded into the crumbling houses and little streets. Jews who lived in the city, normally, were forced to leave their houses and flats within fifteen minutes. Those who did not were shot.

And there they existed without sanitation, and in condemned wooden buildings or rat-ridden slum houses, until they were finally pushed into the cattle-trucks and taken away to be burned or gassed. A 'king' was appointed, a tall, cultured man, white-haired, powerful, compassionate, who was known as Chairman Rumkowski.

He managed to bring order into chaos, and by cooperating as far as possible with the Germans, by *supplying* people for the transports, he managed to save a great majority. There was a semblance of normal life eventually, and under terrible pressures the Jews struggled on in some blind belief that they would survive.

Eventually Rumkowski himself was forced to behave like Herod. Believing that each deportation which he made for the Nazis would be the last, and that somehow, finally, the ghetto would survive the war, he bargained and fought. And lost. 'That part that can be saved is much larger than the part that must be given away,' was his despairing, and final, appeal. He went himself, with his family, to Auschwitz as a voluntary deportee in order to accompany his brother.

There are differing accounts of what happened to him. In one he was beaten to death on his arrival, by Jews from the ghetto; in another, he and his family were taken on an apparently friendly 'tour' of the camp and were burned to death 'without being gassed'; another version is that he was separated from 'those who could work' and put to death in the normal way.

He is generally considered to have been 'deceitful and misinformed', and responsible for unimaginable deaths. But was he? If he had not persuaded so *many* to go as volunteers to the camps, would 'so many people have boarded the trains'? An enigma.

Those who survived have written in this book, and those who did not left diaries and letters; it is mainly from them, and from the photographs (some in colour), that this dreadful story has been made available to an uncaring world. The ghetto at Kovno, in Lithuania, follows much the same pattern. But the supreme courage burns through the writing of this personal diary, hidden and retrieved many years later.

Today the Croats hate the Serbs, the Arabs hate the Jews, the Iraqis hate the Kurds . . . nothing changes. Is all the suffering of the past for nothing?

The other day a gigantic mass grave was unearthed in the Ukrainian pine woods. Poles murdered by Russians. I found my first mass grave just outside Hanover in 1945 when my tent peg slid into the soil-covered slime. It was like walking over a mossy custard trifle. We forced local villagers to witness the unspeakable filth: the old people bit their lips, a few wept; the young women (there were no young men), usually with a child in hand or one on the hip, just spat.

Housing estates now cover many of the camp sites, and the week before last planning permission was finally refused for the building of a glittering supermarket on the site of Ravensbrück. Water under the bridge. Why light candles in the windows? Who cares now? The red-and-green-ink brigade will tell me that it never happened, the rest of us seem to have forgotten.

Daily Telegraph, 10 August 1991

No Answer to the Sorrow and the Pity

A personal view

Something very strange happened to me during the past three weeks. Unnerving, unexpected, but very strengthening indeed.

I was asked to review, in the normal course of my duties on this newspaper, four books. One was on the ghetto at Lódź, one on the building of the camp at Mauthausen, another on the ghetto in Kovno and a fourth on the eye-witness accounts of the war from citizens of the Third Reich.

At first, I demurred at the thought of this mammoth and frankly depressing task. I felt there was no good reason I should have to plough through pages of misery and distress.

I was, however, prevailed upon to do the job – I think perhaps because I had been a witness to the unthinkable and unspeakable when I was a part of the British Army which, one April afternoon in 1945, reached the gates at Bergen-Belsen.

For that reason I accepted. I worked my way through more than 1,000 pages, and then wondered where on earth to start. Who now would care? It was all so long ago. And time heals; even grief.

But then I remembered that it had taken *me* a great many years to forget that afternoon in the pine forest and heath. When I did try to speak of it a few years ago I failed, choked on distress, and unmanned myself. But I had been there and I had seen.

Who now, apart from the surviving witnesses like myself, would give a fig? Who would even bother to answer the question I posed in my review three weeks ago: *Why?*

To date nearly 200 people have tried to assist me: the letters now fill a box-file, and I did my best to reply to every one.

Except for the dozen or so examples of hate mail which arrived,

219

as I had known they would, unsigned and with no return address – abusive, ugly, worrying. Hate still exists very strongly.

But for the rest the warmth and kindness, the anxiety to try to answer my simple question, were incredible.

I must make it clear that these letters came from all over Britain. Some from Europe; one or two, even, from Australia. A nerve had been touched. It was, as it turns out, not quite as simple as I had thought.

These letters were not only from people of my age or from people who, like me, had been witnesses themselves; they came from a much younger generation, too, who wanted to know and, more importantly, wanted their children to know.

The letters written to me were forwarded, including the hate-mail and the glossy – and well-produced – pamphlets and booklets explaining the details of the 'Jewish conspiracy against the Gentile'. There was also the photographic, colour brochure which sets out to prove conclusively that no Jews were ever gassed at Auschwitz. That is entirely false Jewish rubbish, according to the brochure. The gas chambers were merely there to fumigate the 'clothing of the Jews'.

So now we know. The hatred still exists. And even in the kindest letters there lurks a sad feeling of worry and anxiety. A Jew is not to be trusted. I am counselled to read my Old Testament. To read the Psalms. To understand that the Jews were responsible for the crucifixion of Christ.

That feeling is ever-present: but, equally, there is a feeling of distress that this hatred still exists among otherwise rational, normal, decent people who have tried to come to terms with their own doubts. Some younger writers had actually been to Dachau, Belsen, even to Auschwitz and Treblinka. Some deliberately, as a sort of pilgrimage, some just by chance, suddenly on a country lane finding themselves signposted to a familiar and dreadful name where, beyond the lush meadows, the bird song and the tree-dappled shadow, they came across horror beyond comprehension.

One reader wrote: '. . . although saddened and sickened by Treblinka and Auschwitz . . . I now feel reassured that other people, like yourself . . . continue to ask the same *unanswerable* questions and are having problems coming to terms with those events of fifty years ago. Most importantly, the questions are *still being asked.'*

Some people have pointed out, wrongly, that the Jews were not a race but a religion. They are a race; they wandered into history, it is thought, from India, a nomadic tribe. And as a race, a tribe, what you will, they, with millions of other outcasts, such as communists, socialists, gipsies and homosexuals, were deliberately marked down by the Nazis for total eradication.

I still ask: *Why?* And from the overwhelming response to my original question it is clear that many others do.

Some have gently chided me, some have sadly agreed with me: there is no answer to the simple question of why more than six million people, not only Jews, were systematically, methodically, determinedly and expertly put to death in a very few years. Surely it goes beyond simple 'hate'?

Man's inhumanity to man is vile and still, to me at any rate, incomprehensible. But these letters have given me great heart, and my gratitude to their writers is limitless.

Daily Telegraph, 5 September 1991

This was by no means the end of it. I was asked to speak to senior pupils at a number of public schools: it was always the history master who invited me, never the headmaster. I went to Tonbridge and gave a talk to the sixth-formers. I had never spoken before to anyone in detail about the subject. I found it so upsetting that afterwards I was forced to decline my host's invitation to sherry in the senior common room and fled instantly back to London. I couldn't go through that again. However, in 1992 the Board of Deputies of British Jews prevailed on me to address a meeting on a Sunday in May at the Adelphi Theatre, where the Polish-Jewish Ex-Servicemen's Association was commemorating the Warsaw uprising. I was the only goy in the whole house. Craven with fear at saying the wrong thing, I tried not to be influenced by the hate-mail I had received. When we had parked the car, even the policeman was bloody. 'What are you doing with this lot?' he asked.

I realized I must stop this meddling, so I pulled in my horns and went back to the typewriter.

Upon My Tisket!

Swearing: A Social History of Foul Language, Oaths and Profanity in English by Geoffrey Hughes (Blackwell)

A quick look at the index of this erudite and splendidly researched book lifted my heart: surely I had found the ideal Christmas gift for that ephemeral creature, the Man Who Has Everything. This, I thought smugly, will keep him glued to its pages for days. He will snigger and whistle and boast from Club Dining Room to Club Bar and eventually become the Club Bore, thanks to these heavily detailed pages on the art and the derivation of – and indeed the reasons for – swearing.

But I was wrong. This is no lightweight piece of amusing froth. It is a very serious work indeed, by Geoffrey Hughes, a Professor of History of the English Language from Witwatersrand University, and it has as much fun going for it as an open grave. But it is quite fascinating.

If the word 'bum' causes you to wince with distaste, do not read the Professor's book. For 'bum' is as pure as spring-water in comparison with some, almost all, of the heartier words it requires you to consider.

Swearing, many will say, is reprehensible, unnecessary and vulgar, but others will have it differently. 'Swearing', a scholar has said, 'is as necessary to a human as hissing is to a cat.' And with this I cannot disagree. A long stint in the armed forces dented a great deal of my prudish armour as a young man. I rapidly learned to survive by my oaths – the pepper and salt, paprika and chilli, of barrack-room intellect. But in genteel life swearing is deplored; and for many years those of higher birth and breeding have bidden their young to wash out their mouths with soap and water at the unthinking fall of an oath. Ladies and Gentlemen simply *don't*, we are assured.

Geoffrey Hughes says the worst expletives he ever heard in his own decent bourgeois background were uttered by his betters and elders and they usually amounted to nothing much stronger than 'bloody fool' or 'bastard!' It was only during his national service that he came across the unprintable 'four-letter words'. He makes up for that lost time in his scholarly book.

We dive straight into derivations – Old English, Anglo-Saxon, Middle English – and are left in little doubt about what the words mean, where they originated and how they were used. Sometimes, naturally, one is desperate for a translator. Not all of us can cope with Chaucer, for example, without a crib: '*Thow mortherere of the heysoge on the braunche/That brought the forth, thow rewtheless glotoun!/ Lyve thow soleyn wormes corrupcioun!*' In fact no real swearword is concealed in this diatribe from a merlin against a cuckoo. But there is a good deal of stuff, later, which is as hard to understand and far more bawdy. Chaucer did call a spade, so to speak, a spade.

So the Man Who Has Everything might not be exactly over-whelmed to find this book in his Christmas stocking. He would, on the other hand – and if he had the patience to batter his way through the dense prose (pretty humourless and as dry as a ship's biscuit) – be modestly amused to discover that the simple word 'Drat!', used often in my early days by a deeply respectable matron, actually means 'Curse!', loud and clear; that 'By Golly!' derives from the negro slaves in America, who adapted 'By God!'; and that 'bludger' is quite the worst word one can use to an Australian.

You will discover a great deal within these prosaic covers: from Chaucer right up to, naturally enough, Kenneth Tynan. You will learn all about Expansionism and Xenophobia, both of which have provided an abundance of swearwords, and if you didn't know what a euphemism was, you certainly will know a few when you close the book. You may even find yourself startled to discover that a silly little song of some years ago, 'A Tisket, A Tasket, a little yellow basket . . .', is *very* suspect. Basket is a euphemism for 'bastard'. The phrase 'little yellow basket' refers, regrettably, to a particular race.

Such a lot of interest here: perhaps, after all, it *might* be an idea for Christmas? The index alone is worth the cover price. Nothing whatsoever is omitted; there are enough words to render unconscious for days the two per cent of the population who apparently grow faint at the uttering of the word 'damn' on television or radio. All in alphabetical order too.

Out of all the splendid, alarming, raunchy and disgusting words listed by the excellent professor, only about a dozen are *not* euphemisms. One has to be extremely prudent: it is fair to say that we really do not know what we are talking about even when we use a very modest word like 'drat'. But this book will go a lot of the way to making things perfectly clear.

I wonder, idly, what you have made in the past of the show title, *Oh! Calcutta!* You might be surprised to find out. But don't say I didn't warn you that thumbing through these pages may burn your fingers and dry your mouth. Upon my oath!

Daily Telegraph, 31 August 1991

A Companionable Lizard

Me: Stories of My Life by Katharine Hepburn (Viking)

Hand on heart, I confess there were moments during the reading of this rather curious book when I felt, quite distinctly, that I was drowning in syrup. Suffocating in a surfeit of sweetness. However, I struggled on, as indeed I strongly advise you to do, and found I could breathe. It is wise, when sliding deeper and deeper into a fat tin of Abram Lyle's best Golden, to remember the label, with the weary (or dead?) lion on its side below a swarm of bees, and the admonishing reminder: 'Out of the Strong Came Forth Sweetness.'

It will help you survive this ruthless onslaught of kindness and overwhelming good nature. For Miss Hepburn *is* strong, amazingly so, and from her emanates a natural sweetness. It will get to you in the end. If she prefers to offer a portrait of herself as a sort of Bambi-in-the-Woods, wide-eyed, tear on cheek, among the flowers, ignore it. She is far closer to a brontosaurus, or any other type of dinosaur (from the Latin, 'terrible lizard').

By this I mean absolutely no disrespect to an enchanting, altogether astonishing, maddening woman. I merely point out that she is about as shy as a charging bull. Hardly, in fact, strokeable. Strong, determined, stubborn, tough, but under it all, like the brontosaurus itself, harmless. Unless, of course, you happen to be another brontosaurus . . .

Although one longs for a merciful editor to hack away at the plethora of 'Thrilling!'s, 'Oh! My golly's and 'Wow!'s and the almost constant protests of 'I've been so lucky!', you will swallow them easily. At the very least you will feel at the end of this book that Miss Hepburn has shared a private compartment with you on a pretty long train journey. She is telling you all she feels you can reasonably be expected to know about herself, with a scatter here and there of little things which she feels you might only have guessed at.

All this is done with extreme good nature, bravado and utter relentlessness. She will have you trapped, a finger hooked in your buttonhole, and you will not be able to budge. You probably won't want to anyway.

I said this was a curious book, and so it is. I wonder, did she actually, word of honour, *write* it herself? If so, her punctuation is as disgraceful as my own. She uses dashes where, in ignorance, I use dots. Maddening. Or did she actually dictate it all? Speak it to some machine or some loyal minion (lots of them around Miss Hepburn) who dutifully typed it all down? Whatever she and her editors and minions have done, it is very well put together, and one could be quite convinced that, apart from all her wondrous gifts, she is also a nifty writer.

The book has great style; it is economical; the intense ego never becomes in the least objectionable, as it does in many other film-star books; and there is elegance in the phrasing as well as gracefulness in the manner in which she never hurts anyone. (However, it is irritating occasionally when you *know* something of the facts recounted.) If the pronoun 'I' is heavily used, that is only right and proper in a book called, simply, *Me*.

And even that title is not in capital letters, although it would appear from the start of her life that she was all capital letters anyway. Born to patrician parents, Father a doctor, Mother a suffragette and more besides, she had siblings in quantity, was swamped with loving and plenty. A perfect example of an East Coast family of moderately comfortable means: never too rich, never too poor. Educated, educatable, together, sharing, loving intensely. A splendid way to begin; very useful for an actress. All this, *plus* the comforting chink and clink of pennies in the pocket, gives enormous courage and stability, even arrogance. You can turn down anything you like, without too much fear.

Thus her childhood was spent in the comfort and safety of a loving, rumble-tumble family. There was History, English, French, motorcars, golf clubs, tennis courts; and her father had the local police chief as a patient. Useful for a learner-driver, a tom-boy, a determined young woman. Nannies, governesses and so on were followed by the elegance of Bryn Mawr, which she disliked and which did not seem to like her much either. But there she stood, educated, secure and sure of herself. Not bad for a budding actress. Better than being scooped up in some drug store on Sunset, or working at a gas station.

With a patrician background, a firm education, this striding young woman was also blessed with amazing beauty. A beauty manifested very early on, according to photographers, which would serve her without fail all her life. The astounding bones which gave her the determined, but beautiful, jawline, the high cheeks, the brow, the wide-set eyes. With a singular voice and a flaming head of hair, she hit the theatre. You cannot have better equipment than that to assault the capricious, cruel profession. And assault it she did; absurdly easily, it seems.

She never intended to fail and, for a time, she did not; but, naturally enough, she did. Failure was modified, hardly the wrist-slashing kind; slapping rather. None the less, to an arrogant creature it was daunting; making her sit back and reassess, then carry on again. Never one to fall with failure, she simply tripped. She learned hard.

It seems to me that she absorbed very easily. She read a script like a sheet of music, she saw Great Acting in simplicity. Here is her description of one of the greatest actresses in the American theatre, Laurette Taylor, in *The Glass Menagerie*:

> . . . she seemed to me to sort of sketch and be the inside of the part, the outside of the part: just indicate dialling the phone, indicate anything the audience had in its immediate experience, suggest it, let them get it, then get on with it, effortless, easy, then suffuse, illuminate the character. *One could never see the wheels go round.*

The italics are mine.

That is perfect acting, the kind that many critics detest. It is disliked because they prefer a watch to have a glass back so that

227

they *can* see the wheels go round. That was not for Miss Taylor, nor for Miss Hepburn, and not for, perhaps, the greatest *film*-actor of all, Spencer Tracy. Of them she writes:

> A few strokes here – there. No agony of preparation – like the Method – no constipation. They were born able to show you . . . make you watch. It WAS real life. That's what tore them apart.

And that is how it is. Accurate, on-the-nose reporting.

She married, a loving, kind, dullish fellow whom she loved – but to whom she did not stay married – all her life. She stuck it out in Hollywood, quietly hating it, but sensibly knowing that the work was there.

She had four idyllic years with Howard Hughes whom she both loved and admired greatly, but finally broke with him and led a solitary life until the arrival of Leland Hayward, a different fellow in every respect, but passionately loved, as indeed were all her men. Actually she is never unpassionate about *anything*: acting, love, making soup or purchasing a Maserati.

Finally, with Spencer Tracy, the passion reached a pitch of sheer, devoted, uncompromising, selfless love for almost thirty years. For this incredible man she sublimated the strident, arrogant, ambitious, flamboyant creature that had for some years made her box-office poison, gained her a fistful of Oscars, packed out legitimate theatres from New York to London and made her a triumphant, blinding Star.

She retired, more or less, into a small house at the bottom of George Cukor's garden on Cordell Drive. With the love of her life. Between them Cukor, Tracy and Hepburn brought to world screens some of the most elegant, funny and glorious films that had ever been seen: *The Philadelphia Story*, *Adam's Rib*, *Born Yesterday*, among others.

She has an odd way of liking quite unlikeable people, from Louis B. Mayer to the cold David Lean with whom she worked on *Summertime*, giving the only performance with true heart in a Lean film since the somewhat irritating *Brief Encounter*: not only true in heart but (amazing in a Lean film) heartbreakingly funny (an astonishing feat to pull off with a brilliant 'Technical-Director').

Less-gifted directors have said that Miss Hepburn is 'undirectable', for which one has to thank God, having seen the effects of their work on others. She always went to work and did it *her* way when the going got bumpy; and you cannot fault her work on *Summertime* or the enchantment, delight and love she offers in *The African Queen*. After Cukor, whom she adored and who was her greatest friend in California, she was her own best director.

Tracy never married her; a Roman Catholic, he would not divorce his wife, who always thought Miss Hepburn was 'merely a rumour'. He died, making a cup of tea in the kitchen when she was not, at that precise moment, with him. She heard him shuffle about, clink a pot, stumble and fall. His life had ended. She got back into the saddle again and rode on. Brave, indomitable, tough. The most courageous, beautiful, fearless 'terrible lizard' of her time.

Oh! My golly! How lucky WE have been to have her! Thrilling!

Daily Telegraph, 28 September 1991

Slack-Jaw'd at the Nodding Daffodils

The World of Minack: A Place for Solitude by Derek Tangye
(Michael Joseph)

Having lived abroad for more than two decades, I find I am greatly out of touch with many things in the UK. It has its complications. I did, with yearly regularity when my parents were alive, return to see them, have my annual check-up, buy a few tins of tongue or a brand of tea I preferred, and go to Hatchards for a stack of books to keep me occupied through the long, sometimes harsh, Provence winters.

Somehow or other, however, I missed out on Derek Tangye and all his works; and *The World of Minack* sat me down slack-jaw'd with admiration and surprise.

Mr Tangye, long before clever Peter Mayle discovered a sort-of-Provence for the urban-lost, opened up Cornwall and, in consequence, has caused enormous happiness and joy to the baby-bunny lovers and all those who think, as the subtitle of this present volume suggests, that they are seeking 'A Place for Solitude'.

His book is a compilation of 'favourite passages, many of them chosen by readers, from sixteen of the Minack Chronicles'. Sixteen, you may whisper to yourself; well, that's a lot of books on the one subject. I had no idea so many volumes could be, and indeed have been, mined from so thin a seam.

A cottage on the Cornish coast, a sea view, all swamped with daffodils and potato fields. I did not know, as now I do, that hundreds of worshipping readers make pilgrimages there, that these slender books sell in trillions and that so much bounty had been denied me for so long. I admire them, certainly, but I close the covers in baffled silence.

Mr Tangye has tapped an amazing 'nerve'. He writes for all those

who have never been able to manage, for one reason or another, the lemming-urge to get up and run away from the dull, mediocre, noisy, agonizing pressures of city life. The desire just to clear off to that 'magic dream cottage', or to accept the 'I MUST have that' gut-reaction to a place suddenly seen round a bend in a country lane or buried deep in a (usually damp and always dark) bluebell wood.

It is, one is always assured, a return to our roots. Once we get to our dream, instead of fighting British Rail and its mostly sullen and ill-spoken servants, we can wrestle joyously with the climate, the beasts of the field, the elements generally.

This is exactly what Mr Tangye and his extremely pretty wife did years ago. They wrenched themselves out of the rat-race (it is always called that by the rats who get trapped in it) and started their lives anew on a wind-swept point of land sticking into the sea. And they discovered they had tapped a continually running spring of nostalgia and longing, which would slake the thirst of the thousands of readers lost, for one reason or another, in the monotony of Hendon Central. It is persuasive stuff. Consider this:

When disgruntled people in the cities march to meetings on May Day holding high their banners of protest, the white flowers of the blackthorn lie in drifts in Minack woods and along the shallow valley which slopes towards the sea.

Pretty good, if all you have is a view over someone else's roof, and they are chucking beer cans at each other on the street below.

Escape to the sound of howling wind in the chimney, the crackle and sigh of logs in the hearth, the womb-like feeling of snugness and safety, the touch of good earth under the fingernails and a good stew, of local produce you have nurtured yourself. Satisfaction! An escape to what-will-never-be. Dreamland. Most people would absolutely hate it if they actually had it; they have lost the habit of that life, lost the way on the road.

There are sad bits, too, in Mr Tangye's story, which is right and proper for a 'good read'. A loving assistant on the farm dies suddenly, taking everyone by shocked surprise. 'A year ago she was celebrating her prize for bunched violets. She was so pleased with that win,' they are told, and the lady was 'unconscious even when she fell off her bicycle'.

But mostly it is a happy saga; you will hear the gulls, smell the salt spray, see the nodding daffodils and, very probably, 'laugh and cry' all the way through. You could not want more. Nor do you, so it seems; the amazing sales have quite proved that. And now the World of Minack, owing to all your efforts and love, has become part of English heritage.

Daily Telegraph, 23 November 1991

Book of the Year

A towering, magisterial, epic hurricane of a book has roared into the fat-end of the year and sent the dust, the candy-wrappings and the dead leaves of the seasons swirling into oblivion and the Colefax and Fowlers of chic Lit. London scattering back to their wallpapers and tapestries. John Osborne's *Almost a Gentleman: An Autobiography, Vol. II 1955–1966* (Faber) is what a book should be like, how a book should be written, and shows how words can explode with muscular magic. It is a complete triumph.

Daily Telegraph, 23 November 1991

Precious Little Compassion

They Tied a Label on My Coat by Hilda Hollingsworth (Virago)
A Time for Love by Shirley Anne Field (Bantam Press)

In the late summer of 1939 I was eighteen and awaiting my call-up papers. This slack period, for me, was taken up by being sent off with a pretty girl named Cissie in her red MG sports car stuffed with gas-masks into which we forced elderly and resisting 'cottagers' who lived beyond the village confines: 'Dad 'ere 'as 'ad 'is beard nor what he were twenty an' 'e ain't about to let you chop it orf now!'

We were not, I fear, very successful all the way from Chailey to Piltdown, which was the geographical limit of our endeavours.

We were suffused with pride in 'doing our bit for the war', and when the gas-mask caper ended we set to, along with our willing hands, to 'make good' a couple of aged barns in which to shelter, provisionally, the hordes expected to descend upon our timid village. This was the time not of the cuckoo, turtle or swallow, but of the Evacuee – a new word in our lexicon and one which struck terror into anxious hearts. It also bore the full weight of scorn, loathing, curiosity and dread. There was precious little compassion flying around.

At this time Hilda Hollingsworth and her sisters Roberta and Pat were being readied to leave their homes in the East End of London for ever. They were destined to be a part of this new group, the Evacuees. Dressed in their best, a paper carrier-bag of personal possessions (change of knickers and vest, one clean dress) in their hands, a gas-mask slung around their necks, a label tied to their coats, they were marched off, with thousands of others, to an unknown destination.

No one, it seemed, knew exactly where they were going, not

even their parents. All they knew was that it was to a Safe Area far from the expected destruction by high explosives and instant gassing. Unfortunately, Hilda and her siblings did not reach our immaculate barns or our pretty, kindly, anxious Lace-Up-Shoes-Middle-Class village. They passed us by: we got an upgraded lot from Croydon and Cricklewood. Nice enough, to be sure, but not East Enders.

Hilda and her sisters were sent straight on to an astonished Kent, which rather considered itself to be Front Line. But they were welcomed and treated kindly and almost started to enjoy it all, until Kent in fact became a Danger Area and they were moved about the country like a grubby pack of cards in a bar-room poker game. Hilda, because of her incredible courage, resilience and strength, held what remained of her family firmly together, with love, sense and a blinding belief in belonging. She was ten years old.

Eventually, after two comparatively pleasant 'postings', they were sent off again out of harm's way to a mean, bigoted, dank, suspicious, On-The-Knees-Twice-A-Day-At-Chapel mining village in the dead heart of Wales. And dead it was. After the rumble-tumble of the East End, the gregariousness and warmth, any sense of happiness swiftly drained away and childhood came to a terrifying end. The acute distress experienced here was quite unique. The cruelty, even viciousness, of the people among whom they had to live was extraordinary and utterly 'foreign', as indeed *they* appeared to be to the people in the village.

These children had never had to deal with slyness, deceit and a form of godliness and piousness which actually included their being sexually abused by an apparently kindly 'Uncle'. Laughter was forbidden, even playing outside was frowned upon; servitude was to be their lot. They were trapped, these once lusty, laughing East Enders, all spirit, or almost all, snuffed out, until someone would come to their rescue. But although Hilda wrote desperate notes to her distant mother on the inside of old cigarette packets which she had scavenged, they went unanswered.

The appalling thing is that the parents of these evacuated kids, by which I suppose I mean the Mothers (Dad was usually at war, at sea, in the desert, or dead, or a prisoner), quite often dumped their children deliberately, and then cheerfully, wantonly, lipsticked and nylon-stockinged their way off with some Yank.

With their children out of sight and out of mind, husbands elsewhere or dead, they risked a new chance at life. Shirley Anne Field tells in her autobiography, *A Time for Love*, how she lost *her* mother for thirty years. This lady surfaced in Georgia with a different husband and a slew of new children. The call from the West had proved too strong to resist, and poor Shirley Anne, and her brother Guy, had to cope with a half-forgotten Mum, as adults. 'I've never had a mother,' her brother said. 'So I don't know how I feel.' Reasonable?

But Hilda Hollingsworth was lucky: at the very end of the war *her* mother found her and her sisters in their desolation and misery. The children saw her, by chance, one day in the village:

> 'Coo'ee . . . ! Coo'ee . . . !' The call raced towards us; it sounded strange but yet familiar . . . wonderingly I stood up. Words formed inside my head. IS it? Can it really be? . . . A pink chiffon scarf floated in a soft floppy bow under a face that was smiling showing slightly crooked teeth between bright red lips.
>
> It was Mum.

This, after years of uncertainty, misery and despair, mental cruelty and physical abuse. Relief in reading of the 'rescue' is overwhelming. But Hilda tells this sorry story with an amazing generosity of spirit. She brims with 'reasonableness'. Everyone was, after all, strange. The Welsh were isolated by language, geography and culture, religion and, to be fair, guilt. The East Enders were alien, noisy, free, uninhibited, and who would want a dirty bed-wetting child from the slums? An English child at that! An Evacuee; even if the money paid out by the Government did come in handy. Why mess up the neat little houses hiding behind their lace curtains? There was plenty of coal, sheep on the hills, potatoes a-plenty, and God was in His Heaven.

It was a tragic, blundering intrusion into everyone's life.

Hilda Hollingsworth's excellent, disturbing, but passionately lived book is wonderfully evocative of its time, funny and sad, amazing in its courage. It is the kind of book which suddenly makes one realize why the British deem Dunkirk to have been a victory. This is a book written from the courage of the soul. The writer is now married, a mother, and all is well after those punishing years; there seems to be no shred of bitterness. However, I do not suppose she will hurry across the Severn Bridge for some time to come.

Daily Telegraph, 11 January 1992

The Danger of a Nation Flexing Confident Muscle

The Germans: Who are They Now?
by Alan Watson (Thames/Methuen)
Tomorrow Belongs to Me by Peter Millar (Bloomsbury)

You know perfectly well that they always get the best places by the pool, the best deck-chairs on the cruise, and often push ahead of you in the queue for the ski-lift. Frightfully irritating; we British simply do not behave like that. We are (apart from that small group who attend football matches abroad) far too modest, polite, reticent and – shall I say it? – far too British And Proud Of It ever to behave with such vulgar displays of selfishness. We do not grab, shove and push ahead. That is simply not our way.

A pity that the Germans do. They are presently ahead of us not only in the queue for the ski-lifts and the towels at the Tenerife pool-side. We have been taken unawares again. I wonder why? The largest ethnic nation in the whole of Europe has quietly, implacably, moved centre-stage and will not be budged. In a very short time Germany will once again dominate Europe completely: I am quite glad to know that it is fairly unlikely I shall be around to see the results.

If this sounds like 'Dismal Desmond', then I must agree and regret, but let me turn your attention to a couple of books which will open indifferent eyes to a few unattractive truths about our present situation. And we really should know something, now that the Channel Tunnel is a fact and about to provide us with an umbilical cord to Mother Europe; we *cannot* ignore Mama. We did nothing to stop this idiotic scheme; all we have ahead is a mutilated chunk of Kent and a mass of apprehensive, squabbling people whose lives are in danger of the New Railway. It does not exist yet. It probably never will. For the moment, we can get from Paris, Berlin,

Amsterdam, even Rome on the fastest trains ever, until we reach Dover. Then we take the bus or British Rail and wobble along to London. Eventually.

Both of these books are extremely well written, concise, fully researched. One is a sort of documentary, the other an historical appraisal. Both should be read.

Alan Watson's *The Germans: Who are They Now?* is less easy for the beginner. It is an almost complete history of the German people from the start to the present, with disquieting hints of the future. It shows a race whose determination to survive, and win, is daunting, whose passionate belief in their country overwhelms by its very intensity, and it demonstrates how amazingly this once utterly destroyed country has roared back into full action, puffed with pride, sleeves rolled up, passionate with self-belief, leaving behind for ever, it would seem, the total destruction which was its lot only forty-five years or so ago.

Mr Watson ends his book on a rather hopeful note – one of rebirth, renewal, awareness. There are 'new voices' in Germany today, and of them he says:

> . . . they are . . . the voices of a pluralistic nation and a demo-cratic state . . . cautious voices, informed and, to an extent, tortured by the past, but they are not the voices of arrogance, ignorance or hate.

Can one be reassured by that generalization? What does 'to an extent' actually mean? Arrogance? Ignorance? Hate? Mr Watson is a learned historian, he sets down his facts clearly and precisely, he knows his Germany well. But I wish that a little seed of doubt did not weigh so heavily in my metaphorical pocket; that it did not rub at the thin fabric of my belief. I feel that in the near future my little seed will have fallen on to fruitful ground and flourished once again as a tree of terror.

I crossed the Rhine on my twenty-fourth birthday in March 1945 to find a ruined, blazing landscape of craters and dead cows. I reached what had been Berlin early in May. A landscape of hell. Nothing higher than 10 foot, apart from blind façades here and there; no human life apart from three shadows slaughtering a horse at the entrance to the Zoo, no sound except sparrows, the stench of death a pungent scent. It clung to one for weeks. Dust, rubble, shrapnel-riddled trams, splintered trees and gently smouldering tanks in the Tiergarten. Death was abroad. This was *certainly* defeat, wasn't it? No. Not really. Only provisionally.

I was there again in 1952, to work. The rubble was immaculate, the trams were running, there were glamorous shops all along Kurfürstendam housed in Quonsett or Nissen huts but with immensely chic fronts and windows crammed with gloss and riches. Hotels and restaurants, night clubs, neon flashing, music, paintings, libraries, traffic racing. The city was alive again, breathing. The occupants were jolly, laughing, working and playing hard. They were reaching already for the towels, the deck-chairs, the place in the queue. They were flexing confident muscle. We merely admired, exclaimed approvingly, ordered another Pils. Unaware.

In 1972 I was there again, to work. The Wall had been built, the city severed, East and West. I worked and lived for three months in the shadow of that Wall which sundered not only the city but the entire nation from top to bottom. In the East it was dark, no lights glimmered; in the West they blazed, life was bursting. Thrusting. On the sleek gold doors of my hotel elevator someone had scored, deeply at eye level, a row of swastikas: a reminder?

Peter Millar's *Tomorrow Belongs to Me* is a racy, chatty book about the ordinary people who were trapped behind that Wall on the East side. He has dealt with a group who managed to survive in and around a tatty bar in a run-down sector. Possibly these eyewitness accounts, excellently set down, will be an easier, less political read for the beginner. When you finish, you will be forced to realize how appallingly similar we are to each other. We have the same courage, and strength, the same pride, theirs even stronger from surviving a hideous war. The 'woolly' over the print dress, the socks with sandals, tight perms, baggy suits and Doc Martens, the same interests from pigeons to vegetable marrows, the same lavatorial jokes – it makes one wonder why we have spent so much time fighting each other; we are far nearer to each other than to the French, Spanish, Italians or even the Poles. And yet, and yet, of course we are different.

The Germans are diligent, industrious, clever, good and religious, caring, resilient and inventive. So are we, but as a nation we are lazy, hidebound, suspicious, and self-regarding, to this day. Why? We both endured the first, terrible, modern war, but they suffered total, humiliating defeat, while we did not. They were brought down, cut up, occupied. And they emerge as the victors. Can anyone say why?

Watching the Wall tumble down that winter night troubled me greatly. Part of me was filled with admiration, joy that tyranny and totalitarianism were being overturned, delight that the young had finally erupted, that families so cruelly divided would be once again together, that Russia would feel the savage wind of change. All that, plus a secret dread at the political idea of a unified Germany once more. These would be New Germans with some lessons learned, survivors of the engulfing fire, young without a trace of guilt. Why, indeed, should they have guilt after so long?

This new-forged nation could be the most frightening in Europe. Alan Watson writes of 'new voices' in a 'pluralistic nation and a democratic state . . .' Is it? How long will it stay like that? Have they learned from that bitter past? Have *we*? Only the old are left to remember; the young have always been headstrong. One fears for this impoverished, rather smug, island of ours which I so cherish but which I fear is unaware of the extreme dangers it will have to face once again.

The Germans are building a fantastic cruise liner for P&O because no one in the United Kingdom would, or could, accept the tender. Why? And why does almost every young German speak at least two languages apart from their own when our politicians cannot even speak diplomatic French? Why don't our new carriages fit the tunnels? Why are the coal mines closing because coal from abroad is cheaper? Why will all the fast trains in Europe stop at Calais? Why does Christmas here last a fortnight?

Perhaps we should flood that wretched tunnel, secure ourselves behind Dame Vera's white cliffs and call out the Home Guard again.

We will need them unless we start to reach out and grab the towels, deck-chairs and the places in the queue for ourselves. We could, of course, be too late. If you read both, or either, of these two excellent books you might close them with an uncomfortable feeling of trouble ahead. See what you think.

Daily Telegraph, 1 February 1992

Burned Deep into the Soul

Hell's Foundations: A Town, Its Myth and Gallipoli
by Geoffrey Moorhouse (Hodder)

Bury, in Lancashire, is a modest town. A town hall, market square, parish church, a drill hall and a mayor. The normal trappings of provincial life. It lies some five miles north of Manchester. When I knew it, in 1941, I was a newly commissioned, very nervous officer billeted up the road in a cotton-mill-owner's abandoned mansion on a hillside in a suburb called Ramsbottom (locally known as Tupsarse because it was at the 'end of everything').

From the terrace of the house, grimed with soot and wind, one looked down into a grey, fogged landscape of endless slate-roofed 'back-to-backers' and soaring mills throbbing with trundling looms, glittering with acres of lighted windows (dark in the black-out after 3.30 in the afternoon), and huge chimneys trailing and belching smoke endlessly into the curdled air, which loitered out over the spoiled valleys until, eventually, it was dispersed across the distant moors. Not a very attractive vista. I have known better views from happier terraces. It was sad, cobbled, drab, poor.

However, Bury was near at hand. The centre of our lives at that time. It had a cinema, bars, a theatre even; holystoned door-steps, lace curtains, kindness and incredible warmth for a 'soldier'. For Bury was an Army Town; not like Aldershot or Pirbright: just a modest place which had, at one point in its life, slowly bled to death from the loss of its young men in the First World War. It suffered so brutally from war and killing that even after a second time around, in '39, after the havoc of Korea, the cut and thrust of Malaysia and Aden, the carnage of the Falklands and the bizarre, media-encouraged sand-deaths in the Gulf – even after all that, the terrible word 'Gallipoli' is burned deep into the very fibre of every soul who was born in Bury, or who had family there.

Bury lost a large number of its youth in the Dardanelles. It was the home-town to the Lancashire Fusiliers, who, because of muddles, bickering, ill-planning and ignorance, lost 13,642 men in the Great War − 1,816 of them in the scrub and shale of Gallipoli. It is little compensation to know that no fewer than six earned themselves the VC; myth has it that they were all won before breakfast. The death toll and the casualties were far too shocking to be absorbed by Crosses for Valour. Even six at once. The young Fusiliers had been patriotically offered up for the politicians' errors; they had even been bullied by the militant women brandishing their white feathers, and they went cheering, singing, promising to come home victoriously to the grime and love of their Lancashire womb.

Today Bury, as I well know, is a very different place. The mills are all but gone, the chimneys felled; the air is clean, the town is green with trees and wide spaces; it is proper, neat, contained; cobbles, clogs and polluted drizzle from the thundering cotton-mills have long since been abolished. You might think all is serene and calm, which on the surface it is. But the wounds made in those distant days of 1914−18 are too deep to be stitched and re-skinned by the arrogance of today. The pain still lurks because the town itself is, frankly, too small for agony to be forgotten; far too many families were affected by the slaughter in Gallipoli.

In this elegant, compassionate, deeply researched book, the tremendously caring Geoffrey Moorhouse sets before us the facts and figures, the jingoism, pride, pain, as well as the hideous smugness, the cock-ups, the arrogance and the disasters made by 'those who know better'. And who seldom, if ever, have to 'go'. The myths are here as well, for anything as brave as this, as unutterably sad and devastating, *has* to breed myth. Both good and bad. Legends, too, play a part. Finally it all becomes a kind of folk drama: Moorhouse gives us the truth word by word. Not all of it is palatable.

I suppose the most damaging and erroneous of the myths is the belief, and disdain, held in Australia and New Zealand that the Mother Country sent weedy wrecks to fight alongside hefty, bronzed, open-air Gods of Nature, or, even worse, sat about 'drinking tea'. The valiant Colonials, on the other hand, shed their blood, bitterly but willingly, to keep Mother England secure: all those miles away. Nonsense, of course. But it has stuck.

It is worth looking carefully at the lettering cut deep into stone in Canberra's vast war memorial: Australia, 8,709; New Zealand, 2,701; India, 7,597; France, 9,874; Britain, 21,255. Turkey, the enemy, lost rather more than anyone with a grand slam of 86,692. However much we bicker, shout and protest, however much we all shake knowing heads, the body-counts are never in doubt. The Great War and those more recent conflicts were put together and 'paid-for' on behalf of politicians who could not make up their minds or bring the problems to the debating-table; who preferred the shouting and smearing, the innuendo and hate for their opponents' parties, to the welfare and the good of their people.

Geoffrey Moorhouse uses Bury as his pivot: he explores it fact by fact, family by family; this little town in the moors bore a hideous amount of the slaughter in the Dardanelles, no matter what your Australian neighbour may tell you as he leans on the bar and his legend. Mr Moorhouse is a Fabergé journalist on the one hand, and a brilliant and caring historian on the other. He has written here a spinningly glorious book. You will not be dumb with military history, exhausted by facts and figures, wearied by the detail of long-forgotten battles. There is plenty of strategy here, but more heart and pain than you could possibly have room for.

I know now, although I think I knew at the time, why one was so cared for by the ordinary people of Bury in 1941. It is an Army Town and we were its children, destined, if unlucky, to go the way that nearly 2,000 of its children did years before and would do again. While we were among them, they would see to it that we were cherished. And we were, until embarkation.

Daily Telegraph, 4 April 1992

Father to Society's Little Grey Mice

The Man Who wasn't Maigret: A Portrait of Georges Simenon
by Patrick Marnham (Bloomsbury)

In my copy of *Larousse* (1977), Simenon merits a slim five lines. In Patrick Marnham's excellent, detailed biography he gets a whacking 300-plus pages, which he deserves if only because he was, in his lifetime, the world's bestselling writer – quite apart from being vastly rich, ferociously active sexually, gifted with a talent some would call genius, casual in his affairs, and known best in the English-speaking world as the creator of the rather tedious detective Maigret.

To put M. Maigret on television here, even though it has frequently been a success, has always seemed to me to be quite mad – like putting Miss Marple into a harem. Maigret is essentially a Frenchman, or a Belgian: Continental anyway. The cases he has to solve bear little resemblance to any British problems. The mastery of Simenon, however, was the incredible manner in which he explored, dissected and displayed his '*petites gens*'. They are the guts of his works, not merely in the Maigret stuff, but in the novels which, to my mind, are far more compelling and extraordinary.

Born in Liège in 1903 into a poor family, half-Flemish, half-Walloon, Simenon was forced to leave school at fifteen to help support his enormous family on the sudden serious illness of his father. He became a journalist by chance, simply because he happened to wander into an office – and the writing began.

In a lengthy lifetime he wrote about 400 volumes. World sales amounted to 500 million in more than fifty languages (exceeding Shakespeare and Jules Verne); fifty-five films were made of his books, and no fewer than 280 TV films: they are being hurled on to the screens to this day. That is a pretty good mark-up for a poor boy with little, if any, education, and a deliberately limited vocabulary of only 2,000 words. This, he insisted, was so that his 'little people' would be able to read his works. And they did, in their millions.

He had a fuller vocabulary for his personal and private life; just as well, since his sexual demands were voracious (three or four women in a day was not unusual) and his charms cannot possibly have been only in his looks, for he was a stocky little chap, with solid peasant bones and the face of a kind chemist.

His brilliance as a writer, his undoubted charm, drew towards him (quite apart from sexual partners) the cream of the literary world of his time. It ranged all along the line from Anouilh, Cocteau and Colette, to Pagnol, Miller and Thornton Wilder, with all stations in between. His novels, and I must join in the praise here, were compared with those of Balzac and Dickens. His extraordinary insight and full understanding of the *bête humaine*, of the terrible dark corners which seem to lurk within the brightest, most ordinary, lace-windowed, clean and neat existence, are never for one second misplaced, patronizing or false.

He knows the world of which he writes as intimately and thoroughly, and as depressingly, as Van Gogh knew his peasants: the potato-gatherers and eaters, the men and women of the Flanders mud, the wooden-sabot people. Simenon set his people down on paper in print rather than paint, but with the same vibrant passion.

You will see exactly what I mean in two examples I take at random. Both essentially different in place and locale, but both brilliantly evoking – dissecting, even – his *petites gens*. Try *La Veuve Couderc (Ticket of Leave)* or *La Neige était sale (The Stain on the Snow)*. These are two of his most perfect novels: I leave his Maigret to others. I simply do not care for detective fiction; neither Simenon's dark sonnets to the bars and cafés of his *quartiers*, nor Agatha Christie's terrible Tweed-Pearls-and-Purdy Froths.

The novels are as richly textured as his life, which was a pretty flamboyant tapestry of booze, women and, from time to time, children, for if his women satisfied his incredible lust they also became pregnant now and again. He spent most of his life in a *ménage à trois*, but it all *seems* to have worked satisfactorily. At least for him. His women all had exceptional patience and were devoted to him. Until . . .

His first wife, Tigy, took a maid called Boule, a simple fisherman's daughter who rapidly became Simenon's mistress and stayed on for years sharing bed, board and Master. It all appeared to be quite acceptable, and Tigy bore him a son in 1939. Life was rich! Simenon had an heir!

He also had a war. Which caught them all unawares, as indeed it did many Frenchmen (we must now count Simenon as French) at the time. The disastrous defeat of June 1940 threw them into black despair, fear and disbelief. It is impossible for anyone who is not French, or who has not lived closely in that country for a number of years, to comprehend exactly how devastating the Occupation was.

Life was fraught with incredible dangers and terrors, not only for the unhappy Jews, the Communists, the Undesirables wherever and whoever they were, but even for Simenon's adored *petites gens*, the little grey mice of society, who only wanted to keep out of trouble and survive silently. But during the four dreadful years of Occupation a new and vicious word quietly slipped into his sparse vocabulary of 2,000 words: collaborator. A word which, even today, strikes fear into the heart and wrenches at the conscience of men and women in France.

Simenon and his *ménage*, however, managed to survive this period by shifting from place to place and keeping quiet. Accused at one time by the Vichy French of being a Jew – wrongly as it happens – and threatened with immediate deportation, he fled to a tiny village miles away from the cruel world, but not far from Oradour-sur-Glane, a town which was torched by the Germans along with its entire population. He moved on again.

Friends began to disappear, were hauled off on the trains for deportation; others collaborated willingly, and Simenon managed to stick to the resolve that many writers, painters, actors and the rest had forged just before the Fall: to carry on, as far as possible, in a normal manner and keep the culture of their country alive in the face of the greatest disaster it had known in modern times.

Simenon remained true to the resolve, writing, as he always did, in a blazing fury. When the war ended he prudently gathered his 'family' together and managed to get himself – he was always good at having useful friends – to America. Tigy finally put her foot down and Boule remained behind. The family was for once intact, for a short time. Within a few weeks Simenon had met a 24-year-old French-Canadian girl, Denise, started an affair, and would eventually take her as his second wife. For the time being America was home: five fruitful years produced no fewer than fourteen novels and thirteen Maigrets.

Simenon always called himself 'an instinctive' worker rather than an intellectual. When he wrote he did so as one possessed, cutting off the outside world. When the 'mechanism' started, the 'music' just ran and ran. He always insisted that he dared not interfere with the 'mechanism', could not, nor would, ever alter or introduce something 'new'. It was a gift which he had received and he was the only person who could use it properly.

In 1973 he announced his retirement. The gift was exhausted, or perhaps had exhausted him. He began to dictate a series of highly unreliable, but naturally entertaining 'memoirs' which he continued until he died at eighty-six in 1989. His children heard the news on the radio after his cremation; and by the time the press and the family had reached his last home in Lausanne, his ashes had already been scattered beneath a giant cedar tree, as he had requested, by the faithful companion he had taken, Teresa.

A giant, a genius, a glorious storyteller had slipped quietly away, leaving more splendours and riches than any Egyptian king. Glories which were, and always would be, eternally available to his *petites gens*, the people who gave them life, and made his fortune.

Daily Telegraph, 18 April 1992

Strike Me Pink!

London Observed: Stories and Sketches
by Doris Lessing (HarperCollins)

This is the first time in four years of contributing to the *Daily Telegraph* that I have had to bring to the typewriter the book I am reviewing – for the simple reason that I do not remember a single thing I have read, including the titles of the stories. They do not hold or entertain me; they merely make me skip with irritation. I do not comprehend how a writer of such intensity and renown could produce so limp a lettuce.

The title is hugely provocative. *London Observed*. London! *My* London? It does not remotely *touch* London. It could happily transfer to *Bombay Observed*, *Athens Observed*, *Darlington Observed*. It is correct in only one word: *Observed*. This higgledy-piggledy slew of characters is indeed 'observed'. None is at any level *understood*.

It appears that Doris Lessing has merely pressed her face to the thick glass of an aquarium and worthily recorded the fish she has seen. They dart, drift, skim, turn, move elegantly, roughly, shoot for a fight: all this she has observed, written down, as well as the bright colours, the streaks of light, the ripples of bone and flesh beneath jewelled scales. But she describes these splendours in sepia. Her prose has no colour. I longed for brilliance, for a bit of vulgar passion.

Naturally, the stories are very capably handled. Neat, tidy, set down as motions. In one, a girl of O-level age has a baby on a rough blanket in a back-street shed. A slavering dog is sniffing about. We are awash with sanitary towels, blood and water and filth, but at no time with tears, or anxiety, or sympathy. I, frankly, did not give a tinker's gob for the wretched child or its teenage mother. Nor did I believe one syllable of the dainty dialogue. Who *are* these people?

Later, we have a story about a journey by Underground from St John's Wood to Trafalgar Square. A kind of defence of the Tube. The varied life passes before one from stop to stop. It is, I gather, impressive that at the height of the rush-hour we are likely to see that 'half the carriage' actually reads! In the morning:

> people betray their allegiances: the *Times*, the *Independent*, the *Guardian*, the *Telegraph*, the *Mail*. The bad papers some of us are ashamed of don't seem much in evidence . . .

Well, strike me pink! There is more. Someone was actually reading *The Iliad*. And across the aisle 'a woman read *Moby-Dick*', and, as if that were not enough joy, in this ordinary carriage a girl with 'a new baby asleep on her chest' held up a copy of *Wuthering Heights*. This clearly pleases Mrs Lessing. The unlikeliness, plus the innate snobbery, amaze me.

There is a common fault with novelists: they cannot write speakable dialogue. Dialogue written to be spoken aloud reads gloriously on the page. But there is an idiotic legend that it does not; that you have to 'write' dialogue for the eye only, and this Mrs Lessing does. And how! There seems to be very little prose here. This is the opening paragraph of 'The Pit':

> A final sprig of flowering cherry among white lilac and yellow jonquils, in a fat white jug . . . she stuck this in judiciously, filling in a pattern that needed just so much attention. Shouting 'Spring!' the jug sat on a small table in the middle of the room.

Well, there you go. A noisy, not to say energetic, fat white jug. I cannot help feeling, with the greatest humility, that perhaps an editor would have been useful here. I mean, jugs do not 'shout'. The word 'in' is scattered about like rice at a wedding.

I only hope Mrs Lessing never sets foot in her kitchen to take kindly notes for, say, 'Observing the Settings of a Strawberry Jelly'. That would indeed be worrying.

Daily Telegraph, 23 May 1992

Return of the Dreaded V-3s

Vita and Harold: The Letters of Vita Sackville-West and Harold Nicolson, edited by Nigel Nicolson (Weidenfeld)

It is rather like being under shell-fire. To begin with, a sudden thundering roar, explosions, flashes; then a rattling and clattering. Sudden silence. A calm. A distant rumble. Stillness.

Just when you think it is safe to stick your head above the parapet to get a gulp of air, bang! crash! wallop! and once more one is cowed by salvoes of the dreaded V-3s. Vita, Violet and Virginia. We have been shrapnelled with their infidelities, passionate excesses, intellectual indulgences. Now these wanton, and frankly rather tedious, creatures are upon us again.

I had hoped that all had been said about them and about the strange marriage at Sissinghurst. Nigel Nicolson thinks otherwise. He has already published his father's diaries and letters, as well as a plump volume of Virginia Woolf's diaries. His moving, if contentious, *Portrait of a Marriage* was the basis of a fairly dreadful television dramatization. Newspapers have chattered about the union for years. Now we have the letters between his parents from 1910 until 1962.

Less knowledgeable writers than Mr Nicolson have had a hand in turning the hay of this harvest and filled their barns. But, alas!, here we have another 400 pages and at first sight there is nothing much that we do not already know: accounts (Harold's) of Churchill, the Royals, writers, politicians, nuggets of scandal. And *yet*: reading slowly, carefully, it appears that this amazing marriage was a bit out of kilter. The play was ill cast. Vita should have been 'Papa' and Harold should have played 'Mama'. Why does an elderly gentleman – he writes the *Spectator*'s 'Long Life' column – see fit to rake through the cold ashes of his parents' love and expose their very private thoughts to all and sundry for, as Vita would have said, 'the delectation of the common herd'?

A cloud of despair descends as one starts to read. It is all familiar. Meeting in 1910. Innocence and sweetness. Love gradually dawning. Families considering. A fairly vain girl. A very vain, curly-haired 'cherub' with a pipe. The wedding. The sumptuous background of the Sackville Family and Knole. Her money. Not his. Soon the slow canter towards Violet Trefusis. Forbidden love and lesbian passion. The escape and the chase. The Road to Arras, husbands, poor, damp Harold; helpless, useless Denys. The final capture. Racked with jealousy and rage, Harold wrote in 1919:

> . . . Damn! Damn! Damn! Violet. How I *loathe* her . . . if you arrive with her I shan't meet you . . . I feel I should lose my head and spit in her face.

Nothing a little stronger? More forceful? One can only be grateful there was no tabloid press in that time. They would all have been done for; but the 'scandal' was suppressed, until another stole upon the scene.

Enter the heron-elegant, fastidious, sexually repressed, sad Virginia Woolf. More hopeless passion; the carousel spins again. Tough on Harold, but he, it appears, was much to blame. That fact emerges clearly from this collection. Harold was, frankly, the villain of the piece. He was undoubtedly a brilliant diplomat, a clever politician, a quite dedicated gardener, but as sure as hell-fire he was a selfish, spineless husband.

Consider this. At no time did he, apparently, ever try to help his wife to come to terms with her homosexuality which, as she makes perfectly clear, distressed her every bit as much as it obsessed her. The cries for help, in her early letters, were ignored by her husband, or – and this seems hardly possible, but must be considered – were blithely misunderstood. At any rate they made no impression. He was quietly, happily, pursuing his sexual adventures: not always with 'members of his Club' either. Rough trade was fun. But, in 1941, when her affairs with Violet and Virginia, and one or two others along the line, had cooled a little, Vita wrote:

. . . I was thinking. 'How queer. I suppose Hadji [her private name for him] and I have been about as unfaithful to one another as one well could be from the conventional point of view, even worse than unfaithful if you add in homosexuality, and yet I swear that no two people could love one another more than we do after all these years.' It *is* queer, isn't it? It does destroy all orthodox ideas of marriage?

It does, I suppose, and the fact is that they did adore each other passionately. Intense love, without carnality, was something they both understood very well. That love was probably kept intact by constant separation: he on diplomatic missions for years at a time, she with friends in 'lovely places' or, more important, Sissinghurst. Of course it is possible to enjoy a full and long-lasting love without sex, and it is often far more profound than the orthodox kind. This they knew, and explored and stretched it to the limits, and beyond. One is impressed and moved.

However, there is a fearful coyness in many of his letters, a sort of 'What a naughty boy I am', a thumb-sucking cuteness, a heavy use of baby-talk, which I find unattractive. (I keep in mind that these are private letters.) When she needed a masculine toughness to match her own, his softness, his cool detachment were what she actually got; and it jars.

He considered the hideous bombing of Guernica to have been merely 'really horrible', and even his reporting of Churchill's greatest speeches to the House in the 1940s sound, here, as interesting and rousing as bead-stringing. However, he loved his wife. He was eager, boyish, sharing her love and passion for the houses and gardens which they created together, and he behaved with circumspection in his affairs; but he was, as he confesses, at all times woefully in need of care and protection. As far as she was capable, Vita afforded him that. Contentment, you may think, was finally assured. However, in a 1960 letter, just two years before she died, she wrote:

I think it [the Trefusis affair] was partly your fault, Hadji. You were older than me, and far better informed. I was very young, and very innocent. I knew nothing about homosexuality . . .

You should have . . . told me about yourself, and have warned me that the same sort of thing was likely to happen to myself. It would have saved us a lot of trouble and misunderstanding. But I simply didn't know.

There it is. A cry, which jogs the heart, which came too late and which went unanswered. Help was never forthcoming; never even considered. A sign of what? Monumental selfishness? Helplessness? Ignorance? Perhaps all these things. However; the love, amazingly, stood firm for this mismatched couple. They invented, as it were, a private love together until the day they died. Their letters are a glorious example of 'Civilized Behaviour'.

Daily Telegraph, 6 June 1992

A Sprig Enfolded in Tendrils of Love

A House in Flanders by Michael Jenkins (Souvenir)
Memories by Lucy M. Boston (Colt Books)

Nostalgia, they say, is not what it used to be. Perhaps rightly so: who can possibly look back on the past thirty years with any true degree of longing or nostalgia? In a country which is now *paddling* into moral decline rather than merely being apprehensive of such a thing; when elegance, truth, dignity, kindness and discretion have become words to deride rather than to cherish, and when the whole sorry fabric of what we believed was safe, secure and perfectly sound now tilts as sickeningly as the tower of Pisa, how then can we possibly look back with nostalgia over the years which have brought us to this lamentable state?

But there was a time, just a little before the hectic, hysterical, 'Swinging Sixties' (which started the tilt in our once upright status), when all those sneered-at and reviled words still applied and we were leaner, kinder and better fitted for life. Have you, I wonder, ever cupped an evening moth, released it into the dusk and discovered to your delight that you had trapped a hummingbird? Well, if that fortunate error has not yet been yours to rectify you may do so now by reading Michael Jenkins's *A House in Flanders*.

Here, in slender format and under a not very enticing cover, you will find a whole spectrum of colours and lights, of delights and elegances, of wistfulness and love. You will even come across glory, in a sense, as well as sweet grief. This is a *radiant* book and one I beg you not to overlook. You will pick it up again and again for sheer delight.

There is not much of a story here, really: an English youth of fourteen, some time in the early fifties, is despatched to France to live for a long summer with 'the French Side' of his family. A clutch of ageing 'Aunts', an 'Uncle' and various relations, living in a great old house on the Franco-Belgian border, welcome this unknown English sprig and enfold him in tendrils of love and affection. The 'Aunts' happen to own a number of small farms in the district, and the daily life, the coming-and-going in the great house, the scents and lights, the ease and gentle peace engulf both the hero and the reader.

The house has stood for centuries fair and square and solid in a part of Europe which has been the site of battle upon battle. Wars have ravaged the fields and woods repeatedly, banners have been unfurled across its plough-lands, cannons trundled down its lanes; but somehow the house, its land and its owners, battered, starved, occupied, bullet-pocked, shelled to mud and splinter, have stayed firm. The only reminder of its last brutal occupation is a swastika cut into a terrace stone.

There is, in the eloquent descriptions of the great Flanders plain, in the sharp, clear, understanding portraits of the people, in all the almost melancholy sweetness of this high summer of ripening corn and under candled chestnut trees, a sense of Colette and Alain-Fournier. Reasonable, one might suppose, since it is a book set in the heart of the French countryside. But Sir Michael is an Englishman – indeed he is our Ambassador to The Hague – and he sees all about him with the eye of a fresh and delighted witness to the intensity of beauty.

It may be a slender 'story' with not a great deal of 'intellectual chattering' and absolutely no pretensions. This is perfect, simple prose at its best. You will not reach for your Fowler or the OED, but you will be transported back to a time which, although so recent, is nevertheless lost irrevocably to us today.

If Michael Jenkins drifts gently downstream in a quiet punt to nostalgia, then Lucy M. Boston takes us down the same river in a bucketing motor-launch. *Memories* is a reprint of her two books of childhood and early life, *Perverse and Foolish* and *Memory in a House*. It reminds us that, apart from being the writer of twelve books for children, she was also a poet, a gardener, a musician; she painted, made patchwork quilts, rebuilt a derelict old house, was 'wayward',

'undiplomatic', 'fearless', 'incapable of emollience' and hurled herself about in a world where 'glumness was a sin'. All a bit exhausting.
But you may very well enjoy the early years of nursery and rather
peevish parents, not to mention a fearfully tiresome husband, soon
got rid of. Nostalgia in a different guise indeed. Romantic, perverse
and, to be honest, slightly irritating.

Daily Telegraph, 27 June 1992

Strength of a Collared Cheetah

Lee Miller's War: Photographer and Correspondent with the Allies in Europe, 1944–45, edited by Antony Penrose (Condé Nast)

American, upper-middle-class, elegant, witty, educated, warm, tough, sexual (not just 'pretty' or 'beautiful'), Lee Miller was a writer, photographer and *Vogue* model. In Paris, in the twenties, she was the centre of a glittering circle led by the Surrealists: she was a 'muse' to Man Ray, friend to Max Ernst, Picasso and Cocteau, and wife to Roland Penrose, with whom she moved to England to become part of another glowing circle. She was never at any time in her life 'somewhere around'. She was 'there', a fully formed 'woman' with the sensuality, strength and subtlety of a collared cheetah. Restless when war broke out, enraged by the violence of the Blitz, desperate for an outlet to her anger and energy, she got *Vogue* to send her on a 'job' to photograph an evacuation hospital in Normandy. She did not return until the war was over. From the siege of Saint-Malo, to the hideous finish in a rubbled Berlin and, in a final act of defiant victory, a bath in Hitler's bathtub, she was always present. When the war finished, so did she. Left in the vacuum of peace, she had no function. Like so many of us she found it impossible to adjust.

This is a deeply moving and fascinating book, compiled by her son Antony Penrose from a mass of her old articles and photographs. They were written, and taken, for British *Vogue* in the heat of battles or in their weary aftermaths. It seems only America can breed this particular kind of woman: there was certainly no equivalent in our armies. She was an extraordinary witness to a brutal and gigantic killing, yet she remained feminine always.

The task that Penrose set himself was daunting: to reassemble scraps of yellowing papers into a whole, and to edit not only the photographs themselves, but *details* from a negative, so that a look of joy, of grief, of agony, explodes timelessly on to the page. With the disaster of Bosnia and Serbia now upon us, it is all hideously contemporary.

Lee Miller's stubbornness, her skill, observation and compassion, her simple, yet passionate use of words which she sent to her admirable editor, Audrey Withers, constantly astonish and hold one. Remember, these items were stuck between advertisements for lipsticks and face creams. They still hit between the eyes. From photographing gilded creatures in chiffon and taffeta it seems to have been a simple thing for Miller to move to truckloads of huddled dead at Dachau, a mayor's family sprawled in suicide in his parlour in Leipzig, or the first explosion of a napalm bomb on Saint-Malo. She was in it up to the hilt.

Not all was grief and destruction. Joy was there too, in the extraordinary liberation of Paris. I was there that amazing weekend in August 1945, and she has caught it exactly. A gaudy butterfly of joyous hysteria, precisely pinned down for all time:

Paris has gone mad. The long, graceful, dignified avenues were crowded with flags and filled with screaming, cheering, pretty people. Girls, bicycles, kisses and wine, and round the corner sniping, a bursting grenade and a burning tank. The bullet holes in the windows were like jewels, the barbed wire in the boulevards a new decoration . . .

And so it was. Exactly. She was able to find 'lost' friends from that glittering circle, denied her by four desperate years. Here again was Picasso, chattering, laughing, shocked only by Dalí's collaborationist behaviour in Spain; here were Aragon, Dora Maar, Eluard, secure, damaged but alive; above all, Colette, still in her cluttered room in the Palais Royal, fit, gruff, amused, curious for news, dazzling with vibrant life even though confined to her couch.

Perhaps for Lee Miller, certainly for me as the reader, Colette perfectly symbolizes the ultimate triumph of the Liberation and the now certain ending of the war, and victory. Miller caught the image in the form of an ageing French woman of letters, alone, eyes hooded in private thought, holding fast to her pen. Caught it as surely and as clearly as she had fixed the deaths, the brutalities, the destruction and the supreme image of victory.

Daily Telegraph, 25 July 1992

Chewing Over Table Manners

Rituals of Dinner by Margaret Visser (Viking)

Margaret Visser has written a fascinating book on a fairly ordinary – or so I thought – subject. She starts 6,000 years ago, when we were chomping our way delightedly through the bones of our neighbours; cracked skulls and sucked marrow-bones testify to that.

The early Spanish conquerors had a fearful time when they became caught up with the Aztecs, who ate their enemies with gusto: 'The flesh was cooked with peppers and tomatoes, served up upon bowls of maize . . .' The thighs were the particularly delicious joints. Montezuma was offered one from each corpse. Waste not, want not. I know that in South-East Asia, during the War, the Japanese served crisp little appetizers with the drinks in the Officers' Mess. Cubes of American pilots' buttocks. So what is new?

But, all that aside, this is a study of the ritual of eating, of how and why we eat. It considers not only the etiquette of the table – pretty useless in this day of Deep-Frozen and Take-Away – but also why we sit at one, why the rules were made. It is full of very exciting little 'did you know?'s

I mean, did you know that the phrase 'licking into shape' was coined because mother bears, seen at a distance cleaning their newborn cubs with their tongues, were thought to be, literally, licking them into the shape of a bear?

Did you know that paintings of *The Last Supper*, with everyone sitting on stools at a long table, are absolutely wrong for the period? Jews normally sat on the floor around trays of food: a banquet, which the Last Supper probably was, was taken lying down in the Roman fashion. That would have made a very different composition.

If this sort of stuff amuses you, you are in for a treat. Mrs Visser has done her research quite brilliantly. She describes exuberantly the gigantic feasts of the Romans, the Chinese and our own Edwardians. Manners, naturally, like our appetites, have altered. We no longer wipe our greasy fingers in the hair of the waiter (slave) who attends us. We may be tempted, but napkins are now provided. Their use is explored here too. One leaves them on the table at the end. Never on the chair or seat. That implies you will not return to the table.

'A man,' it is said, 'may pass muster by dressing well . . . sustain himself tolerably in conversation, but if he is not perfectly *au fait*, dinner will betray him.' Think on that the next time you spoon cold baked beans from a tin over the sink.

Mrs Visser writes with the greatest elegance about the annoying human problems which can beset us at table, from 'snot' to 'vomiting' and even to 'farting'. She scorns nothing.

It is impossible not to be charmed by a writer who can say of Erasmus that 'he firmly condemns people who, in the name of courtesy, demand that involuntary misdemeanours of the body should be stifled'. Her book is chock-a-block with such delights.

Daily Telegraph, 5 September 1992

Soggy, Breathy, Chubby

Sin: A Novel by Josephine Hart (Chatto)

One person emerges with honour from this soggy, breathy, chubby little book, heavy with fey undertones. The designer has managed to arrange thirty chapters into 160 pages, set it in Bembo and given it a glossy little *Harpers & Queen* cover. It measures 7½ins, by 5 ins, by ½in thick (minus the cardboard covers) and is yours for £11.95. It is as plump as a bookie's wallet stuffed with IOUs.

Amateur Night in Dixie. The script is strictly a 'John and Marcia' deal. Each character calls the others by name at every exchange. Married for thirty years, rolling about in a bed, just sitting by the fire. It makes no difference: it is 'John and Marcia' every time. They talk 'laughingly', they 'smile back' at each other; one waits for one of them to 'dimple'. They do not. Thank goodness. But their eyes 'beat' people down.

The story? There is one, of a sort. Imagine Mrs Danvers with a saintly cousin Elizabeth whom she hates and longs to destroy. We are never absolutely sure why. Mrs Danvers is called 'Ruth' and she is dark (natch), the saintly cousin is blond. Of course, Ruth is voluptuous, with eyebrows which 'wing themselves across her brow'. Elizabeth paints skies eternally and smiles 'gently' at everyone in sight. They have adolescent sons, one with asthma. The family house is called Lexington, it has a lake. We get that info on page 17, so watch out, they *swim*! Plot thickens.

No chapter will stretch you: Chapter One has thirty lines, Chapter 22 is composed of school reports, so the author is saved the business of describing the adolescents. You even get a facsimile signature of the Headmaster. I do not know why. The narrator is not very good at describing anyone but herself with her wing-like eyebrows; very good at clothes – flowing skirts and silken shifts, etc. Oblique on sex: 'As the nakedness moved towards me I remembered the choreography.' Wow. This is her pallid husband in the marriage bed. Not a hairy stoker in the boiler-room. She has a habit of anguished despair: 'Silently, I screamed around the room.' Can one? Or, nibbling away at sex again: 'I went to the bathroom to prepare for my husband's return.' Golly. What *were* they about to do? Anyway, Ruth is out to get Elizabeth with 'A small silver hammer of exquisite design'. Why not any old hammer?

Very recently a highly considered writer packed three quarters of her entire life, plus lovers, husband and son, into a detailed description of high tea in Edinburgh. The details we must await until 'next time'. It seems to be a fashion to write less for more. However *Sin* has the grace to finish thus:

> These questions long engage me. Do you have answers? Please. Please answer me, as I leave you now.
> As I leave you.
> As I leave.

Well, dear, you won't quite do, frankly. This is utter tosh. Sorry.

Daily Telegraph, 19 September 1992

Book of the Year

Miranda Seymour's magnificent biography, *Ottoline Morrell: Life on the Grand Scale* (Hodder), carefully, and with affection, unravels the tangled skeins of lies, rumours, gossip and sneers which have been woven into a cruel tapestry by the chirruping, bantering, buns-and-cocoa set of Bloomsbury, to reveal in exquisite detail a generous, loving, funny eccentric, and an amazingly brilliant woman. You have not read a better biography for years.

Daily Telegraph, 25 November 1992

No Marx Masses for Him

Sacheverell Sitwell: Splendours and Miseries
by Sarah Bradford (Sinclair-Stevenson)

The first time I saw John Singer Sargent's family portrait of the Sitwells in the drawing-room at the family seat, Renishaw (1900), I was stunned. The facts that I was, at the time, a callow youth and that Sargent even then was considered to be a mere theatrical painter not remotely in the class of Gainsborough, Rubens, Reynolds, or even Vigée-Lebrun, fit only to paint the most glittering portraits of the rich and famous, did not trouble me at all. I was enraptured by the splendour and magnificence of this group who for me epitomized the grace, elegance, serenity, grandeur and power of Edwardian Society.

They still do to this day, even though I now know the painting to be a complete fantasy, and, after this immensely detailed and diligently researched book, a distorted vision.

No one on the canvas is exactly what he or she seems to be. The tall, benign father (dressed, rather oddly, for shooting), a protective arm on his scarlet-gowned daughter, was known in the family as 'Ginger'; feared, disliked, arrogant and parsimonious, he was, to my mind anyway, halfway to madness. The slender, elegant Lady Ida, apparently dressed for an evening gala but wearing an afternoon hat, was equally dotty; so well bred that she was 'brought up to be professionally helpless', she eventually went to jail for problems with money and loans. She quite liked whisky, too.

The two tumbling children on the floor, with their golden curls, frilly skirts, sailor suits and pug dog, became brilliant men of letters, Osbert and Sacheverell. The slender, adoring, scarlet-clad daughter was Edith. And there you have the holy trinity of poets.

An ancient family, this, who fortuitously had discovered 'minerals' beneath their Derbyshire acres. They were rich, but haunted always by the spectre of poverty. Like most very rich people.

The painting is simple, clear, uncluttered. Five elegant figures, a fine commode, a fragment of tapestry. The story is told; one needs no more. However, Sarah Bradford has to go deeper than the canvas to get at the full text. *Sacheverell Sitwell* is an excellent work, living up fully to its subtitle, *Splendours and Miseries*, but it is a colossal clutter of names, places and events, so that it reads like a cross between the *A-to-K Directory* and 'Jennifer's Diary'. But what is the biographer to do, dealing, as she has to here, with a brilliant family of aristocrats, poseurs, aesthetes and, often enough, dilett-antes, and a family who knew everyone of note in the Arts and Society, were extensively travelled, and had seen everywhere from Bond Street to Budapest? They were copious letter-writers, kept detailed diaries, lived full and complicated lives with utter abandon.

From the group Mrs Bradford chooses 'Sachie', the youngest, the cleverest and certainly best-looking. To find him, both writer and reader have to rummage about in this gigantic bran-tub, and Bradford has succeeded pretty well, isolating him, almost, in his glittering apparel. However, he appears to me a rather tiresome creature, spoiled, arrogant, vain and quite unaware of 'ordinary life'. He raced through his own, constantly falling in and out of love with almost anything and anyone who was aesthetic and beautiful or precious. Not for him Mr Marx's masses. He, and his life, were too rarefied and above the mainstream of ordinariness.

For example, wars rather irritated him. When he was caught up in them at all. In 1917 he wrote '. . . if I am meddled & muddled much more . . . I shall really become a maniac . . . one is only 20 or 25 once – and one does not forgive these years being spoilt . . .' Quite so. However, he did not have long to wait until he and his siblings would startle and amaze London Society with their literary brilliance.

The trio were wildly famous very soon. Sachie's poetry was known worldwide, Osbert wrote beautifully, Edith made the best of the very little beauty she had by turning herself adroitly into a figure of (some said absurd, others admirable) eccentricity, and they were firmly established for the rest of their lives. No mean achievement.

Sachie married a banker's daughter from Canada; they managed to live together, and love each other, until their deaths. Osbert married well, but finally raced off to Italy with a male love, and Edith discovered the delights of alcohol: in 1961 Sachie found out that her daily tally was 'a double-brandy for breakfast – about 1 bottle of brandy in all every day; 2 bottles of wine, and several martinis!!!'

Sachie survived well into old age. It is almost impossible to pull him from the bran-tub unencumbered, so deeply was he smothered in the flour of his siblings and disastrous parents. However, Sarah Bradford has dusted him down for us and made us aware that so splendid and civilized a figure could never remotely exist in the Ratner Republic which certain sections of the press today advocate for our future. We will find no Sitwells in that world to embellish our lives with beautiful writing, poetry and grace. Fortunately, we can still read their works to add a little lustre to the shabby-dog days we now inhabit.

This is a real plum-pudding of a book. Stuffed full of delicious fruits, nuts and silver-trinkets; it is pretty rich, and by the finish one does rather long for the soothing of the sorbet. But, taken in moderate slices, it will do you no harm at all.

Daily Telegraph, 12 June 1993

Move off My Runway

Deconstructing Madonna, edited by Fran Lloyd (Batsford)
I Dream of Madonna: Women's Dreams of the Goddess of Pop
by Kay Turner (Thames and Hudson)

At the beginning of the sixties I overheard a very young actor cry: 'God! There is a movement afoot to take Dirk Bogarde seriously!' If you care to substitute the name 'Madonna' for mine you might, perhaps, experience the same degree of amazement and amusement that I did. Taking seriously this coarse, vulgar, over-hyped exponent of a sub-art seems to me pretty wild, but then, as I write for the *Daily Telegraph*, I would think that, wouldn't I? I have clapped eyes only once on Madonna and recoiled in fastidious shock.

Here are two silly little books about the woman which might, possibly, give you an idea of her importance today – for a very limited period, I would venture – to the Youth Culture with which we are presently burdened and on which, or from which, some are, in different ways, getting very rich indeed.

Vulgarity, ugliness, blatancy, greed and overt sexuality, mostly of the perverted kind, are the present-day norm. So it seems fitting that Batsford, of all respectable people, should attempt a slender book called *Deconstructing Madonna*. The second word is, of course, in larger print on the jacket, to attract the reader who will be shattered by the contents. Far too erudite and, if it was not all so potty, 'grown up'.

Why in the name of Heaven anyone should remotely want to deconstruct the woman fills me with alarm. From all accounts, she is doing a pretty good job of it by herself. But try this little extract for size. See if it will fit the theory that some people, somewhere, sometimes, are taking this quirky phenomenon seriously. Here we

271

are, from 'Madonna as Trickster'; a run-up on Jung and Freud, then:

> In simple terms, it can be described as a certain kind of symbol found in the dreams, myths, and beliefs of large numbers of people. It both arises from and stimulates what Jungians call the collective or transpersonal unconscious. It springs from that level of the psyche that derives from shared human nature, somewhat like the body which, notwithstanding its identifiable uniqueness to each individual, possesses generic features in common with enormous numbers of other people.

What they will make of that on Purley Way or in Carshalton Beeches?

I don't really know what it is that troubles me about Madonna, or why I let it. I suppose it is because the sheer ugliness of the whole 'Madonna concept' seems to be so degrading; I mean, it is a far cry from Jessie Matthews, and that is as it should be, evolution and all that, but *should* it be so vile? So coarse, so cruel, blatant and violent? Is it, as they will try to argue, that Madonna is used as a female symbol of revolt and 'I Can Do That As Well As A Fella'? A kind of: 'Move off my runway – I'm in charge'? Maybe.

Her fans certainly seem mostly female, the males are all around the middle years and leer about in plastic macs. The young are far too timid – they gaze in awe – I have seen them; they snigger and clench their hands in their trouser pockets. But the girls go one better, and in the second little volume submitted for my bleary consideration, they actually write it all down in copious detail. The perfect fantasy book. This is called *I Dream of Madonna* and, by golly, they do:

> I was in bed, naked perhaps, and mad at Madonna – why, I have no idea. I was pouting when she came into the room. It was her body alright and she was talking excitedly about her performance. Something about how she had to get into a certain position so she could sing her best. Arching back into

the pose, her nipples grew erect. Next thing you know, she and I were rolling around, and I have a very vivid memory of staring into her genitals. (Pamela, aged 29. 26 September 1992.)

And there are plenty more such goodies where that came from.

The little book will fit neatly into your pocket. I don't mind that you may be tempted to carry such crap about with you, but I *do* mind that you don't *know* that it is crap. The book announces that it is printed in Slovenia. Ah, well . . . But perhaps Madonna has had an amazing effect on female liberation? I do not honestly know. Perhaps women do feel relieved and exultant and equal because of her audacity and overt masculinity? It is quite possible.

The fact that she deliberately, and to splendid effect, downgrades the males in her 'act' may have a tremendously liberating effect on a thousand-thousand crushed women. It is possible. Heaven knows, we have come a long way from Louisa M. Alcott and her tedious *Little Women*, but this all seems to be a desperately powerful swing in the wrong direction. There danger lies.

I do not think it is too extreme to suggest that the ugliness, cruelty, brutality and absolute viciousness which performers of this kind offer a young and gullible public can, and often do, lead to subliminal degradation of the human spirit, so that one will discover repercussions in hideous acts of wanton violence, such as that which we have been forced now to witness in the untidy death of a small child on a railway line.

Unleash brutality and, like the dogs of war, we will pay most dreadfully and brutally. Think about it carefully.

Daily Telegraph, 20 November 1993

About a year later a most surprising letter reached me from America. Signed by a secretary. Purporting to come from Madonna and her photographer, Steven Meisel, who wanted me to cooperate with them on a forthcoming book called simply Sex. *I had a vision of myself stark naked, with a belt, boots, biker's cap, plus rhinestone collar at my throat, and lashed to a tree*

273

in some public street. I declined. Perhaps that is not what they had in mind? I might have made a fortune: the book sold extremely well. I can't think how Madonna got the idea, if she did, because at the time I was already over seventy. Maybe she'd seen a rerun of The Night Porter?

Book of the Year

Alan Clark's *Diaries* (Weidenfeld) were my most joyous reading experience of the year – rich, ruthless, audacious, gloriously self-regarding. I read them with a caught breath of admiration. Clark is a writer of simple, beautiful prose who calls the spade the spade and the bloody fool exactly and precisely that. Hell, I would think, to live with; a glory to be led by. He is a brisk, bracing wind blowing clear, instead of the sneaky little draughts for which we seem to have settled. My second choice would be the first half of Richard Eyre's autobiography, *Utopia and Other Places* (Blooms-bury). If he ever decides to rewrite the second, stuck-together part, he will have a magical book on offer.

Daily Telegraph, 27 November 1993

Our City of Little Splendours

The Faber Book of London, edited by A. N. Wilson (Faber)

A thousand years ago, when I was a child, two phrases became stuck in my mind. Probably because both were burned into plywood calendars which hung in the nursery.

One was 'A Garden Is A Lovesome Thing: God Wot', which confused me and took me years to understand; the other was 'When A Man Is Tired Of London He Is Tired Of Life', which did not at all confuse me because I refuted it absolutely. I loathed London, and lived very happily in Sussex. In no possible way could I be thought to be tired of life. Utter nonsense! I still cannot admit to adoring London, even after all these years, and, now that I am forced to live in it, I find it quite hard to come to terms with the place. But here on my lap is a perfectly splendid anthology, edited by the indefatigable A. N. Wilson, which points out, most plausibly, why I might be persuaded to revel in this ugly city.

First of all, define for me, please, London. Is it the hideous sprawl which cancers from Cockfosters down to Chessington? From Mill Hill to Orpington? It must be, for they – sad, lost little villages – are all part of Greater London. Some even have London postcodes.

When Dr Johnson made that epic remark in 1777, London consisted of a titchy compound; you could walk it in an hour or two. The City was its centre, then there were the seat of government, the King's house, the languid, if busy, loop of the River Thames under Whitehall . . . St James's, Piccadilly, Pall Mall . . . But it was a close-knit place, fringed with unspeakable slums and squalor. Knightsbridge was a crossroads, Chelsea a busy riverside village. They grew vegetables around Kensington, there were potters up in the wilds of Notting Hill, and St Paul's towered above the pencil-slim spires of the City churches.

However, the London in this excellent, and diverse, anthology, must be addressed as the London we know today. As a giant, if unlovable, city, it fairly teems with little splendours (as well as important ones) which Mr Wilson has Hoovered up for our delight. As he points out in his brisk introduction, there is no logic to it. It is a sprawling collection of villages, many of which have harboured some of the most exciting people, and events, of all time. In these carefully culled pieces we can again read what those people wrote, hear what they said, be privy, albeit by proxy, to those astonishing events.

Savour the story of George II, 'mugged' as he walked in Kensington Gardens. No harm done, great good manners abounded; the King handed over his valuables, including a seal which he cherished, eliciting a promise from the 'mugger' to return it next day, on condition he remained silent for twenty-four hours. He got his seal. Which, alas, is not what would have happened today. A comforting story, very English; there are many more like it.

Mr Wilson offers us his personal choice of elegant pieces which give a graphic overall picture of a throbbing, ever-changing, metropolis. Items from, and about, everyone you ever heard of and many, I wager, that slipped your mind, if you ever knew them.

Evelyn Waugh takes his son for a big treat to London: the Hyde Park Hotel, the dome of St Paul's, Harrods and a whole pound note, but the boy still finds it 'a bit dull'. An elderly (unknown) gentleman searches Trafalgar Square for the purse he lost in Dover Street because the light in the square is so much better. To my mind, in a dotty way, this is as moving as the agonizing description of Lady Jane Grey on her way to the scaffold, or Thomas More's head stuck on a spike on London bridge.

The book is a splendid hodge-podge. History is scattered about with the present. Queen Caroline blunders sadly around, locked outside the Abbey; Joe Orton defaces books in his local library; Mrs Pankhurst chucks bricks at windows in the Haymarket and Piccadilly; Samuel Pepys has his first sight of the Great Plague in Drury Lane. At one time, you might have seen the Dukes of Northumberland and Gloucester, the Duchess of Devonshire,

Garrick, Sir Joshua Reynolds and many others dancing to 'a band of two hundred and forty instruments' under the stairs in the Ranelagh Gardens.

All London, even the bits not quite fit to be seen, are contained in this delightful collection. If you are tired of London, this book could easily help you to change your mind.

Daily Telegraph, 8 January 1994

I am Right, You are Wrong!

Roald Dahl: A Biography by Jeremy Treglown (Faber)

I find it incomprehensible that a respected writer like Jeremy Treglown should attempt to write the 'unauthorized' biography of a man he never met but so clearly dislikes. Why bother for Heaven's sake? This is an unsatisfactory book about a gloriously complex man.

Writing about the recently dead brings the most fearful problems. So many people alive knew the subject and are still around to holler 'Whoa! It wasn't *quite* like that!' I have already undergone this irritation with David Caute's excellent biography of Joseph Losey, but Caute (who also disliked his subject) flayed him, dissected him and laid him on the slab. This is right and correct for a good, *authorized* biography. No suppositions, no holds barred, everyone questioned, friends and enemies.

Here we have an unauthorized effort stuffed with opinions from enemies, disgruntled publishers and sulking American editors (an unlikeable breed anyway), plus a surprising amount of people who slipped along for a little ungenerous chat. Dahl is not dissected here, not examined, has no dimensions. Surface facts for a surface book. It will probably please the 'average reader' who may demand no more.

The Dahl I knew, both as neighbour and, years later, when I was an actor playing him in a film about a particularly distressing period of his life, ain't the man in this book. He was more complex, infuriating, gentle, charming and funny. I recall with satisfaction Hilary Spurling's terrific biography of just such a difficult man – Paul Scott. A detailed, compassionate understanding of the subject. So too with Miranda Seymour and her life of Ottoline Morrell; a besmirched reputation restored to its proper position in the Bloomsbury world. But Treglown only disparages his subject: there is an almost visible sneer beneath his perfect, correct prose; less an in-depth biography of a brilliant, difficult genius than an elegant bit of reportage.

Dahl was born to a middle-class Norwegian couple in Cardiff. He grew up in a tightly knit family until the death of his father when he was four, which left his mother alone with two stepchildren and four children of her own. Roald was her only son, adored and cosseted. Hardly a healthy situation, and it obviously had immense bearing on his character. Mama was the dominant force in his life: Nordic, tough, brave, brilliant, a walking *Larousse*, a fiery matriarch. Her effect on her son was ineradicable.

'*I am right, you are wrong!*' was his leitmotif. Bloody irritating it could be. Sometimes it *was* advisable to approach him with a tiger-whip plus a sense of humour. Not always easy, but it could be done. The humour was essential. Dahl knew exactly who he was, without the slightest shadow of a doubt. His authority about himself was absolute and served him throughout his life. This authority was easy to cope with unless one was married to him. But, remember, he did marry and stayed married for two long periods: ladies of all kinds loved him deeply.

Bully, braggart, racist, plagiarist, misogynist, liar – all this, and more, is slung at him by Treglown. Well, maybe. I don't honestly know. I do know that there were many other qualities not always offered up to a stranger for inspection. A form of protection, privacy?

Dahl was, I suppose, a bully. I must concede that. I recall a couple of disastrous supper parties at my house where he reduced the American guests of honour to sobbing misery by studied rudeness and sarcasm. He was finally forbidden the house. He didn't mind, and we occasionally met in the local butcher's, or in antique shops across the Home Counties. Affable, warm, never really close (he did not care for the cinema), we had no common bonds, apart from gardening, paintings and animals.

Later, when I was asked to portray him in the film, about the harshest part of his life, I felt no compunction in accepting. I was certain I knew him well enough, but telephoned him for his permission. He was furious about the film, but helpless to stop it:

'We are in Public Domain. You *weren't* the first choice, you know?' I said I knew, but had I his permission? He said I was better casting 'than the other sod', and sent me a mass of details about the clothes he wore, the actions taken and the words said during the desperate time when his first wife, Patricia Neal, suffered an appalling stroke whilst working on a film in Hollywood.

In a deep coma for weeks, she was never expected to recover. He brought her through. By bullying. Two years later she was back at work. *'I am right, you are wrong!'* had paid off. Easy to 'knock' a man if you don't know him; if you never saw the courage, determination, and the love. He could be tender, cruel, funny, wondrously conceited, but then so would I be with millions of children worldwide in thrall and full of glee at my every word.

When he saw the film we had made, he sent me a copy of *Danny the Champion of the World*, and in his scrawly handwriting suggested that I could do whatever I wished with it as a film. His inscription gave me enormous joy.

He really *wasn't* such a shit, you know.

Daily Telegraph, 19 March 1994

In The Patricia Neal Story, *Dahl's stricken wife was played by Glenda Jackson. We worked together under brutally unhappy conditions in Hollywood, but managed together to survive. She gave a staggering performance. The film was originally intended for the cinema, but it was eventually cut up and shown on television with slots for commercials. Critics who saw previews were hysterical in their praise and we both felt certain it would win the Emmy. However, it failed catastrophically because the whole of the Mid-West, the heart of America, switched channels to watch a rival programme, complaining that our film was too depressing and hospital-bound.*

I dedicated to Glenda what I thought would be my final volume of autobiography, Backcloth *(1986). The bond of friendship between us, forged in the destructive shambles of the film's production, is one which even her appointment in 1997 as Transport Minister has failed to weaken.*

All Rage, All Tenderness, All Wit

Damn You, England: Collected Prose by John Osborne (Faber)

A torrential, wet, summer Sunday in the country. Two drenched figures squelching up the drive. Unexpected, unknown. Announced by my disapproving houseman as 'A John *Osburn* and friend . . .' They had walked from the Green Line bus stop. All of half a mile. He stooped, sodden in a raincoat; she (Mary Ure) in high heels, blonde hair streaming, dark roots gleaming in baby-pink scalp.

Dried, provided with fresh clothing, taking tea by a blazing log fire, they gave me a limp, wet, rolled manuscript. Would I please read it? Immediately? They had to take it back to London. Up in my bedroom, vaguely irritated, I peeled apart transparent pages of blue carbon typescript: 'The action throughout takes place . . .'

I read *Look Back in Anger* to the last sodden sheet. Lay supine, weak, and mentally exhausted. Emotionally shattered. A *real* play! And *what* a play!

I had never read such words, heard such anger, groped about in such despair, been flattened by such bitter fury, rage and truth. After years of prim, tepid film-scripts, mostly written by maiden aunts of both genders, I now held in my hands a piece of blistering honesty. I was mouth-dry with excitement. Would it make a film, Osborne asked? Could I 'get it to someone at Rank?' Well, easy enough. At the time I was Golden Boy, but the typewritten reply to my urgent request begged me to remember that 'The Cinema is a visual medium. This is all talk, much of it unacceptable or incomprehensible.' So there you go. And there it went.

I lost the film, but gained a cherished friend whose fury and kicking against the smugness and narrowness of the average Englishman of the time matched my own frustrations and anger with my bosses, and many of my producers. In time I managed to sublimate much of my anger. Osborne never has.

In this hugely enjoyable collection of his prose, his scouring fury blazes anew, delighting, or shocking, depending on the way you feel. This is an assembly of pellucid, elegant, vibrant English you would be foolish to ignore. Much was written in the decades when I lived abroad, so a lot is new-minted for my delight. His sly, but sharp, stiletto-cuts at people are so good and so perfectly judged, so deadly, that one hugs oneself with glee to find that one is not – yet! – a victim. Here you will find all rage, all tenderness, all wit, plus seething explosive invective. It is a roller-coaster ride of swooping ups and downs. You could choke to death with fury, or with relish at his glorious audacity.

Try this one, on Bernard Shaw: 'He writes like a Pakistani who has learned English when he was twelve years old in order to become a chartered accountant.' Right on target! I have wrestled myself into the ground trying to make sense of Mr Shaw. Osborne's is a cruel remark. Of *course* it is! It is meant to be. Accuracy, culled from experience, often is. But if he swipes at one hallowed British figure he can revere another, Max Miller, a genius:

> I loved him because he embodied the kind of theatre I admire most. His method was danger . . . 'Mary from the Dairy' was an overture to the danger that *he might go too far*!

Alas! We no longer have a Max Miller to enthral, delight and outrage us. Now comedians slide from a 21-inch screen and cannot 'hold' a house.

It seems to me that Osborne's spleen, his rage, his brutal bayonet-thrust with words, his utter impatience with timidity and fools have got him into such a situation with his critics that almost anything he writes or says will be used against him. He, frankly, terrifies them. Beneath their scorn (and a lot of that gets chucked about) lie deep unease and fear. Fear that they are swimming in a pack which they dare not leave as individuals because they really do not quite know how to swim. They can survive only in shoals, and he is the cruising shark above, snapping and spitting acid into the little wounds of their mediocrity. After all, if they wrote as he does, would they still be stuck, filling two or three columns for the minorities?

Osborne's writing is as chilli to their muesli. He blazes against the crushing, ill-led uniformity and idle disarray of Britain today. Against the defensive lying of our politicians, the sexual bizarreness of our drab society. Against our apparent pleasure in self-loathing, self-denigration, in our backward-looking, and longing, for the chrysalis of the nineteenth century from which we still, unlike most of the rest of Europe, seem reluctant to emerge.

His title here is, I think, misleading. Osborne does not 'damn' *England*. Only the amorphous mass who live in it, defeated, sullen, resentful, sneering, bigoted. He actually *loves* England. He still lives here, in his 'blue remembered hills'. All he tries to do is to alert us to our terrible apathy and casualness, our dangerous inward regard. However, we shall all read him differently. Rummage about in his bran-tub . . . it is stuffed with glorious bits and pieces, all most elegantly wrapped. Just be careful of the sharp pieces.

You could get cut.

Daily Telegraph, 16 April 1994

Top Brass Outwitted by Army Wife

To War with Whitaker: The Wartime Diaries of the Countess of Ranfurly 1939–1945 (Heinemann)

If you buy one more book this year, do make it *To War with Whitaker*. I assure you that you will not be let down, nor demand your money back, and that you will discover a veritable feast of mixed delights, with a few bits and pieces of sadness scattered about like candied peel to add bite. It is a sort of mélange of *The Perils of Pauline, What Katy Did*, 'Jennifer's Diary' and the collected movement orders of the entire Middle East and Mediterranean Forces from 1940 to 1945.

That is as simple as I can make it. There is no literature here, no abstruse words, no Latin quotes, nothing to upset the squeamish. You will merely be reading the personal diary of a very young woman who was exceedingly brave and so much in love with her husband that when he went off to war she went along with him. And his valet Whitaker. (Her husband also took along his mother's favourite hunter, but you had better read that for yourself.) Such things were possible in those days.

The canvas is vast, from Palestine to Paris, and the cast-list too long to itemize, ranging from Orde Wingate to Queen Wilhelmina. Sometimes it is so manifestly absurd that you rub your eyes as you laugh, and have to put it all down to the glory of English eccentricity, now a commodity in short supply, alas.

Whitaker, the valet, springs from the pages imbued with such love, such sense, and with such a wondrous English attitude to all things foreign that when he arrives with a piano from Tobruk you are not in the least surprised.

Shakespeare may have had a pattern for him, but I cannot recall any other writer who discovered such a paragon. A yeoman-

follower, brave, funny, wise, loyal and trusting. A lost breed today
– unless the next war turns one up. Which is doubtful.

In outline, here is the story. The two young Ranfurlys, just
married, in their early twenties, were up in Scotland shooting
things on the moors when Hitler invaded Poland. Their lives, like
everyone's, were changed for ever. The Earl of Ranfurly joined
his regiment on the day of the first anniversary of his wedding and
was sent off, with Whitaker (plus borrowed horse), to the Yeomanry
in North Africa.

His wife, Hermione, determined not to be left behind, slipped
secretly out of London to the Middle East as an 'illegal' Army wife.
By dint of her wiles and wit, bloody-mindedness, ability to type
perfectly, and speak French, she managed to hang on against vigor-
ous opposition until the end. Being well born, and indeed well
connected, was not exactly a handicap. I doubt whether she would
have been such a wild success if she had been the daughter of a
dentist from Herne Hill.

Perfectly self-assured, filled with an irresistible awareness of herself, a glowing self-confidence, she just went at every disaster until
it was mastered, and disarmed everyone she met, except for one
disagreeable brigadier who had her deported when he found her
working for the Red Crescent in Palestine.

She jumped ship (it was torpedoed later) in Cape Town, returned
to Cairo and worked with SOE until she became distressed and
alarmed by certain 'errors' there which forced her to 'spy on the
spy'. A difficult, exhausting task. General Alexander admitted that
he was honoured to be the only general who had not been 'outman-
oeuvred' by this pretty, brave, tenacious young woman.

Her husband was taken prisoner, sent to Italy, and it was three
years before they were to see each other again. But she stayed on,
determined to be as close to him as possible. Terrified of flying,
she nevertheless flew constantly, kept the files, was private secretary
to the C-in-C of the area, wrote letters for the wounded, did the
political *placements* at the big world leaders' meetings.

Eventually General Wavell, C-in-C of the Middle East, granted
her the chance to stay 'officially' in the area. His wife had, after all,

trailed after *him*: all the way to Russia. There was a brave similarity. But in among the official works as his private secretary she found another duty:

> . . . put on your gayest frock, paint your face . . . Then at the hospital, the smell of rotting flesh meets you in the long, dark corridors, and you begin thinking again. You owe them so much and there is nothing you can do except try not to talk of things they will never do again. Today when I took down letters in shorthand for those that cannot write I sat with my back to them so they should not see my eyes . . . They all wrote of victory; not one of them mentioned the price.

To War with Whitaker is perhaps a little bit Claridge's and caviar, rather than Kilburn and kippers, but what is wrong with that, in the face of such compassion, guts and bravery?

Daily Telegraph, 10 September 1994

I was alerted to this book, months before it came out, by my literary agent, Pat Kavanagh, who told me I should grab it for review as soon as I could, because I would find it wholly enchanting. I did. It went swiftly into a second hardback edition, then a third, and a fourth. A handsome paperback was reprinted seven times.

Book of the Year

Impeccably researched, incredibly moving, exciting, often bitterly sad, Lynn H. Nicholas's *The Rape of Europa* (Macmillan) is beautifully and engagingly written, even when recording the appalling rapacity of the Nazis and Soviets as they, in Churchill's words, dragged the 'red hot rake' of looting and destruction through Europe's greatest art treasures. This account of the people who fought to retrieve and save a vast majority of the treasures for our future makes exhilarating and humbling reading.

Daily Telegraph, 26 November 1994

Book of the Year

In Gillian Tindall's *Célestine: Voices from a French Village* (Sinclair-Stevenson) a bundle of old letters found in a cupboard of a holiday home in France reveals an entire way of life, a whole village lost in time. Yesterday is made as clear and vibrant as today. Heartliftingly simple, quite beautifully told. Martin Gilbert's brilliantly researched, plainly stated *First World War* (Weidenfeld) is a throat-catching book, which you will find hard to set aside.

Daily Telegraph, 25 November 1995

Book of the Year

You could call Beryl Bainbridge a miniaturist. In *Every Man for Himself* (Duckworth) her prose and her exactness of detail make a slender novel shine like the Koh-i-Noor. She has done the unbelievable by making the weary tale of the *Titanic* brand new, terrifying and extremely distressing. This is a beauty of a book. The same may be said of Alec Guinness's *My Name Escapes Me: The Diary of a Retiring Actor* (Viking). His simplicity and directness at once disguise and embellish everything around him and, as in his theatrical work, he manages to conceal a great art with extreme economy. His way with words is a lesson to many an erudite writer – note especially the very last lines. The book is an enchantment and one hopes he survives long enough to write more with which to delight us.

Daily Telegraph, 30 November 1996

Book of the Year

Claire Tomalin's *Jane Austen: A Life* (Viking) is a perfect biography: detailed, witty, warm and a great comfort to read. Mrs Tomalin involves us so deeply that Austen's final illness and death come almost as a personal tragedy to the reader. *Cold Mountain* (Sceptre) is a quite brilliant novel – Charles Frazier's first – set during the American Civil War. A familiar plot is remarkably handled and wincingly painful.

Daily Telegraph, 22 November 1997

INDEX

Figures in italics refer to text illustrations.